SPENSER'S *AMORETTI*:
A CRITICAL STUDY

For Elizabeth

SPENSER'S *AMORETTI:* A CRITICAL STUDY

Donna Gibbs

Scolar Press

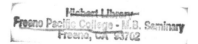

Published by
SCOLAR PRESS
Gower Publishing Company Limited
Gower House
Croft Road
Aldershot
Hants GU11 3HR
England

Gower Publishing Company
Old Post Road
Brookfield
Vermont 05036
USA

British Library Cataloguing in Publication Data

Gibbs, Donna
    Spenser's Amoretti: a critical study.
    1. Poetry in English. Spenser, Edmund, 1552–1599:
    critical studies
    I. Title   II. Spenser, Edmund, 1552–1599. Amoretti
    821'.3

    ISBN 0–85967–777–X

Printed in Great Britain by
Billing & Sons Ltd, Worcester

Contents

Preface

This book offers a substantial revision of previous critical accounts of Spenser's sonnet sequence, the *Amoretti*, with regard to several aspects of its form and meaning, including the structure of the sequence; the treatment of the lover and mistress personae; the relation of the author to his lover persona; and the relation of the sequence to Neo-Platonism. Critical commentary on the *Amoretti* has tended in the past to undervalue Spenser's achievement in the sonnet form and treat his sonnets as an inertly imitative and unimaginative example of the Elizabethan sonneteering fashion. The principal concerns in this study are to demonstrate and explore the witty and playful qualities of Spenser's artistry in the sequence and his lively and imaginative manipulation of poetic conventions. Spenser's work is examined in relation to the sonnet tradition as a whole, and mutually illuminating comparisons are made with many other Elizabethan sonneteers, including Sidney and Shakespeare.

It is argued in this study that Spenser's sequence does not deal with the poet's transformation from a lower to a higher state of spiritual perfection, or with his being educated in love in any progressive way. An analysis of the organization of the sequence suggests that it is the development of the courtship, rather than any gradual education of the lover in the elevated ideals of love, which is the significant structural principle. The progress of the courtship is not straightforward in any sense. But there is an underlying pattern of development in the sequence which is evident in the gradually increasing confidence and more personal address of the lover to the mistress, and which culminates in their acceptance of each other and their subsequent betrothal.

The mistress of the *Amoretti* has frequently been viewed as a static, Petrarchan figure, and as akin to the 'donna angelicata' of the Platonists. Whilst it is readily acknowledged that there are traces of this ideal character in Spenser's presentation of the mistress figure, it is also true that Spenser's Elizabeth is presented as a figure of distinctive personality. She is found, for the most part, to be a spirited character who engages in lively quarrels with her suitor; who acts wilfully on occasion; and who expresses doubts and fears about their union. She is examined in this study in relation to mistress figures in other sonnet sequences and is, in this comparison, found to be of unusally independent spirit and character.

The complex relations between Spenser as creator of the sequence, and the persona of the lover, his fictional creation, are another subject of discussion in this book. The recognition that it is possible to differentiate between Spenser and his lover persona opens up the possibility of perceiving the ironic relation of 'creator' to 'creature'. This allows the exploration of a range of often complicated and witty techniques which are a mark of Spenser's style in the *Amoretti*. The lover persona's emotional and intellectual responses to love, and the moral and religious struggles in which he engages throughout the courtship are also fully explored.

The view that Spenser was profoundly influenced by Platonism, or by medieval and Renaissance developments of Platonic ideas, and that in the *Amoretti*, as in many of his works, he expresses faith in the value of such ideas, has been particularly influential in shaping attitudes to the sequence. It is argued here that although Platonic ideas are clearly present, the sequence as a whole cannot be regarded as an extended exposition, or poetic celebration, of Platonic ideas of love, as it has often been in previous critical accounts. The analysis of the ways in which Spenser employs Platonic ideas in the sonnets indicates that, where they do occur, they are often treated playfully and are generally to be found wanting as a solution to the problems of love in which the persona is involved.

The edition used for quotation from the *Amoretti* is vol. 8 of *The Works of Edmund Spenser*, A Variorum edition, 9 vols., eds. E. Greenlaw, C. G. Osgood, F. M. Padelford, and R. Heffner, 1947; reprinted by The Johns Hopkins Press, Baltimore, 1966, (referred to as *Works*, vol. 8, throughout the text). Other references to the

Variorum edition are indicated by the short title *Works* and the relevant volume number.

Editions of sonnet sequences and poems used throughout the book for quotation are indicated with an asterisk in the section on primary sources in the Bibliography.

References to sonnets, and their line numbers, are indicated in roman and arabic numerals respectively, immediately after quotations and references.

'U' and 'v' spellings in early texts have been modernized throughout.

Acknowledgements

Throughout the preparation of this book, I have received help and guidance from many people. My main debt of gratitude is to Professor Elizabeth Liggins, who has been an unfailing source of inspiration, and a rigorous and skilful critic of my work. Other staff members of the School of English and Linguistics at Macquarie University, in particular Dr Tony Cousins and Dr Lyndy Abraham, have also been generous with their advice and counsel, and I express my thanks to them. Brian Last of Scolar Press has made many valuable suggestions and comments. Responsibility for shortcomings and imperfections remains with me.

I would like to acknowledge the cooperation and kind assistance of staff at the following libraries: the British Library; the Senate House Library at the University of London; the library of the University of North Carolina at Chapel Hill; the Biblioteca Nazionale Marciana, Venice; the Australian National University Library; the state libraries of Victoria and New South Wales; the Fisher Library at the University of Sydney; and Macquarie University Library.

I owe a great debt of gratitude to my husband, Tony, as well as to other members of my family and friends.

Donna Gibbs

Chronology

Date	Spenser	Other sonneteers
1552 (?)	Born in London.	
1563		*Ecloges, epytaphes and sonettes,* Barnabe Googe
1569	Spenser's translations from the French included in *A Theatre, Wherein Be Represented as Wel the Miseries and Calamities that Follow the Voluptuous Worldlings,* ed. Jan van der Noodt.	
1569–76	Student of Pembroke College, Cambridge. Graduates B.A. 1573, M.A. 1576.	
1576	Moves to Lancashire. Is thought to have fallen in love with unknown woman – the 'Rosalind' of *The Shepheardes Calendar*	
1577–8	Returns to London. Meets Philip Sidney, Robert Dudley, Earl of Leicester	

Date	Spenser	Other sonneteers
	and Edward Dyer. May have visited Ireland. Appointed secretary to Bishop Young of Rochester.	
1579	Publication of *The Shepheardes Calendar*. Begins writing *The Faerie Queene*. Is thought to have married Machabyas Chylde. (The date of her death is unknown.) Two children, Sylvanus and Katherine, born of his first marriage.	
1580	Appointed private secretary by Arthur, Lord Grey of Wilton, and goes to Ireland.	
1581	Leases abbey and manor of Enniscorthy.	
1582	Granted the lease of New Abbey, County Kildare.	*The Hecatompathia*, Thomas Watson.
1583	Appointed commissioner of musters in County Kildare.	
1587–8 (?)	Takes up residence at Kilcolman, County Cork.	
1589	Succeeds Lodovick Bryskett as clerk of council of Munster. Returns to London and the court of Elizabeth with Sir Walter Raleigh.	

Date	Spenser	Other sonneteers
1590	Publication of *The Faerie Queene*, books I–III. Visits Ireland.	*The Tarantula of Love*, William Fowler.
1591	Publication of *Complaints* (includes *The Ruines of Time, The Teares of the Muses, Virgil's Gnat, Mother Hubberd's Tale, Ruines of Rome, Muiopotmos, Visions of the Worlds Vanitie, The Visions of Bellay* and *Visions of Petrarch*). Publication of *Daphnaida*. Granted pension of £50 by Queen Elizabeth. Returns to Ireland.	*Astrophil and Stella*, Sir Philip Sidney.
1592		*Delia*, Samuel Daniel.
1593		*Parthenophil and Parthenophe*, Barnabe Barnes. *Licia*, Giles Fletcher. *Phillis*, Thomas Lodge.
1594	Marries Elizabeth Boyle. A boy, Peregrine, is born of this marriage. Resigns clerkship of Munster.	*Zepheria*, Anon. *Diana*, Henry Constable. *Ideas Mirrour*, Michael Drayton. *Sonnets to the Fairest Coelia*, William Percy.
1595	Publication of *Colin Clouts Come Home Againe, Astrophel, Amoretti* and *Epithalamion*.	
1595–6 (?)	Returns to London for approximately a year.	

Date	Spenser	Other sonneteers
1596	Publication of *Fowre Hymnes*, and *The Faerie Queene*, books IV–VI, with a second edition of books I–III and *Prothalamion*.	*Fidessa*, Bartholomew Griffin. *Diella*, R[ichard] L[inche]. *Chloris*, William Smith.
1597		*Laura*, Robert Tofte.
1598	Kilcolman sacked. Spenser escapes to Cork. Carries despatches to London. *View of the Present State of Ireland* entered in the Stationers' Register.	
1599	Dies in London, 13 January. Buried in Westminster Abbey near Chaucer.	
1609	Publication of the 1609 edition of *The Faerie Queene*.	*Sonnets*, William Shakespeare. (Thought to have been composed between 1593 and 1600.)
1633	Posthumous publication of *View of the Present State of Ireland*.	

Introduction

> As to that which *Spencer* [*sic*] calleth his *Amorelli* [*sic*], I am not of their Opinion, who call them his; for they are so childish, that it were not well to give them so honourable a Father.
>
> (*The Works of William Drummond of Hawthornden*. Edinburgh, 1711)

Spenser's *Amoretti*, a collection of 89 sonnets published in a small octavo voulme in 1595, has generally been regarded as a gentle, lyrical sequence of poems remarkable mainly for their gracefulness and 'dainty devices'[1]. It is true that grace and delicacy are important qualities of the poetry of the *Amoretti*, but critics who find these qualities exclusively, or in excess, usually damn the sequence with faint praise, or positively condemn it. The presence of qualities such as wit and irony, complex argument and intellecual playfulness, has, until recently, been largely ignored in critical accounts of the *Amoretti*. On their publication, William Ponsonbie referred to Spenser's 'sweete conceited Sonets', a description similar to the one Mere gave Shakespeare's 'sugred Sonnets'.[2] Shakespeare's sonnets have long since freed themselves from this reputation, but Spenser's sonnets have never fully done so.

During the seventeenth and eighteenth centuries, critical commentary on Spenser's works was almost entirely confined to *The Shepheardes Calendar* and *The Faerie Queene*, and the sonnets were largely left out of account.[3] A few sentences are devoted to the sonnets in John Hughes's introduction to his edition of Spenser's *Works* in 1715: 'An Essay on Allegorical Poetry'. Prefacing his remarks on the *Amoretti* with the comment that the sonnet was by

1

then 'a Species of Poetry so entirely disus'd, that it seems to be scarce known amongst us at this time', he nevertheless conceded that most of Spenser's sonnets had qualities of 'Tenderness, Simplicity and Correctness'. For an eighteenth-century critic, this is no mean praise. But the force of Hughes's compliment in relation to the *Amoretti* is rather undermined by the fact that he chooses sonnet XV of *Astrophil and Stella* ('You that do search for every purling spring') as an illustration of the qualities he admires in Spenser's sequence.[4]

In the nineteenth-century, critical commentary on the *Amoretti* continued to be little more than incidental remarks in discussion of Spenser's work as a whole. Critics praised the sonnets for being 'always tender and chivalrous',[5] or for their 'intricacy',[6] but did not fail to complain about their artificiality,[7] and their 'frigid conceits'.[8] The sequence was frequently condemned for lacking the boldness and vigour of Shakespeare's and Sidney sequences.[9]

The beginning of the twentieth century saw the publication of a new collection of Elizabethan sonnet sequences, edited by Sidney Lee and published in two volumes. Whilst Lee had some praise for the *Amoretti*, the sequence came in for further damaging criticism. He found the sequence for the most part unimaginative and imitative in its use of image and convention, and that most sonnets illustrated 'the fashionable vein of artifice':

> But despite all his metrical versatility and his genuine poetic force, the greater part of Spenser's sonneteering efforts abound, like those of his contemporaries, in strained conceits, which are often silently borrowed from foreign literature without radical change of diction.[10]

Critics of the first half of the century continued to treat the *Amoretti* as generally inferior to the major Elizabethan sonnet sequences. Legouis judged that 'except in their general purity and maidenliness', Spenser's sonnets were equalled or even surpassed by those of his great contemporaries'.[11] Renwick had some admiration for the sequence, but concluded that Spenser 'never wrote one outstanding sonnet to rank with Drayton's masterpiece or Sidney's best', and that he was without Shakespeare's compression or Ronsard's solidity.[12] Yeats dismissed the sequence as 'many intolerable, artifical sonnets'.[13]

T. S. Eliot's critical essays of the 1920s, in which he celebrated the kind of poetry that Donne and the other Metaphysicals wrote, as part of his own revolt against Victorian and Georgian models, established certain criteria of poetic value which influenced critical writing about Renaissance poetry at least until the middle years of the twentieth century. The combination of analytical intelligence, erudition and sensuous immediacy which Eliot admired in Chapman and Donne, and the 'tough reasonableness beneath the slight lyric grace' which he found in Marvell,[14] became standards of excellence against which the work of many other poets, from Spenser to Tennyson, was to be judged and found wanting. F. R. Leavis, who regarded Spenser as the early model for the 'mellifulous' line of poets, which Eliot had condemned, added his persuasive voice to this line of critical thought. In his description of Milton's *Lycidas* he argued that

> The consummate art of *Lycidas*, personal as it is, exhibits a use of language in the spirit of Spenser – incantatory, remote from speech. Certain feelings are expressed, but there is no pressure behind the words; what predominates in the handling of them is not the tension of something precise to be defined and fixed, but a concern for mellifluousness – for liquid sequences and a pleasing opening and closing of the vowels.[15]

Leavis does not specify which poems he had in mind in this reference to 'a use of language in the spirit of Spenser'. But the terms in which he described Spenser's language no doubt contributed to a fairly widespread devaluation of Spenser's works in the middle years of this century.[16]

Critical commentary during the 1950s tended to be very much in tune with Leavis's general description of the Spenserian 'use of language'. J. W. Lever, probably the most influential of the critics of Spenser's *Amoretti* at this time, acknowledged the beauty and delicacy of the sonnets, but found much to condemn. He described the sequence as 'structurally defective' and thought it should have been reorganized into two separate sequences, with two mistress personae, in order to avoid the problem of a mistress with irreconcilable differences in her nature. Further 'retrogressive' tendencies, in his opinion, were that

> imagery [had] lost the complex values of personification and conceit; the scope of metaphor was restricted; and similes, though sometimes of remarkable beauty, forfeited a wide range of sensuous appeal. Finally we

may add the archaisms of diction, and the merely decorative or sonorous effects of verse-form.[17].

Even C. S. Lewis, a champion of *The Faerie Queene* during the 1950s, had only qualified praise for the *Amoretti*:

> Spenser was not one of the great sonneteers. Yet his *Amoretti* do not quite fall into the class of works which are negligible because all they can do for us is better done elsewhere. More brilliant and certainly more passionate love poetry is easy to find; but nowhere else exactly this devout, quiet, harmonious pattern.[18]

The revaluation of Spenser which began in the 1960s was characterized by a range of approaches to his work, including numerological, structural, allegorical, iconographical and rhetorical studies, as well as studies which concentrated on close textual analysis to demonstrate that qualities of wit and playfulness are present in Spenser's poetry.[19] Most critical analysis during the 1960s was directed towards *The Faerie Queene*, but some sympathetic and favourable attention was also paid to the minor poems.

In the case of the *Amoretti* this trend continued during the 1970s and '80s. Some of the approaches taken by critics to *The Amoretti* in this, more recent, period reflect new critical attitudes to *The Faerie Queene*, and most represent a reaction against the old, 'maidenly' view of the sonnets. The search for an explanation of the *Amoretti* in terms of its various structures, for example, is one preoccupation of recent times. Since Kent Hieatt's publication, in 1960, of *Short Time's Endless Monument* in which Hieatt described the calendrical structure of *Epithalamion*,[20] scholars such as Alastair Fowler,[21] Alexander Dunlop[22] and Carol V. Kaske[23] have isolated various kinds of numerical patterning in the sequence. This criticism[24] usually assumes a relationship between numerical organisation and thematic intention. Dunlop, for example, sees the calendrical symbolism of the *Amoretti* as having 'not only a temporal correspondence but also a causal relationship to the central theme'. The key to this integral meaning in the *Amoretti* is, he says, 'the identification of love with Christ, revealed in the calender symbolism of the sequence and in the arrangement of dominant themes'.[25]

There have also been some studies of the *Amoretti* as a sequence demanding allegorical intrepretation. In part, this has been prompted by reaction against autobiographical criticism, but it owes something to the resurgence of interest in the allegorical aspects of *The Faerie Queene*.[26] Critics who follow this line include Robert Kellogg, who argues that the 'fictional poet-lover-worshipper's *actual* or *typical* experience' is close to ideal experience: 'The technique of the *Amoretti* with their wealth of Petrarchan conceits, is in many ways analogous to that of *The Faerie Queene*, "a continued Allegory, or darke conceit"'.[27] Peter Cummings expands on Kellogg's view, and claims that the sequence is 'an objective correlative for the exclusive experience of Man and Woman'.[28] The calendrical and allegorical approaches described here have encouraged an interest in the sequential meaning of the *Amoretti*, and as such are a valuable corrective to the view that the sequence is only remarkable for its poetic devices.

The *Amoretti*, along with Spenser's other poetic writings, have long been thought to provide evidence of a strong interest in, and direct acquaintance with, Platonic and Neo-Platonic ideas.[29] In 1960 Robert Ellrodt expressed reservations about the degree of Platonic influence which had been claimed for some of Spenser's poetry. The *Amoretti*, he suggested, fell somewhere between 'the soft haze of Platonism in *The Faerie Queene* and the hard glare of the Neo-Platonic theory of love in the hymns'.[30] Other critics who take up the question of Neo-Platonic influence, as well as the more important question as to how Spenser uses Neo-Platonism in the *Amoretti*, include Veselin Kostic in *Spenser's Sources in Italian Poetry: A Study in Comparative Literature*, and Jon A. Quitslund in 'Spenser's *Amoretti* VIII and Platonic Commentaries on Petrarch'.[31]

A significant turning point in the direction of criticism of the *Amoretti* occurred with the publication of Louis Martz's 'The *Amoretti*: "Most Goodly Temperature"'. Martz stressed the importance of parody, wit and humour as part of the tone of the sequence. He used the terms tentatively – 'good-humoured, yes, even humorous, in our sense of the word'; 'close to mock-heroic'; 'It would be too much to call it parody' – but in paying attention to such qualities, he opened the way for exploration of hitherto neglected qualities of the *Amoretti*.[32]

Since the appearance of Martz's article there has been some progress in the direction in which he pointed. McNeir[33] and Dunlop,[34] for example, discuss and analyse the dramatic qualities of the sequence. Elizabeth Bieman[35] pays attention to the language of the sequence, which she finds more 'playful and intimate' than has been previously allowed.

The critical accounts of Spenser's sonnets since the 1960s have gone some way towards supplying a necessary revision of the commonly held view of the *Amoretti* as a sequence which is only to be admired, if at all, for its grace and delicacy. But these accounts do not analyse, with sufficient precision or in enough detail, the nature of the dramatic qualities of the sequence, the manner in which the two principal personae and their developing interaction are presented in the sequence, and the relation of the *Amoretti* as a whole to Neo-Platonism and to the Elizabethan sonnet tradition. This study provides a complete reappraisal of Spenser's achievement in the *Amoretti*. It aims to show that qualities of wit and irony are more pervasive in the sequence than has been previously recognized, and that they are combined with a finely attuned sense of the complex psychology of human love.

NOTES: Introduction

1. B. E. C. Davis, *Edmund Spenser: A Critical Study*, Russell and Russell Inc., New York, 1962, p. 167. Davis has taken this phrase from the title of Gascoigne's miscellany *The Paradyse of Dainty Devices* (1576).
2. William Ponsonbie, 'To the Right Worshipfull Sir Robert Needham Knight', *Works*, vol. 8, p. 193.
   'As the soule of *Euphorbus* was thought to live in *Pythagoras*: so the sweete wittie soule of *Ovid* lives in mellifluous and hony-tongued *Shakespeare*, witnes his *Venus and Adonis*, his *Lucrece*, his sugred Sonnets. . .'. Francis Meres, *Palladis Tamia: Wits Treasury*, ed. Arthur Freeman, Garland Publishing, Inc., New York, 1973, p. 281.
3. The *Critical Heritage* volume on Spenser, which includes a comprehensive collection of Spenser criticism until 1715, has only three references to the *Amoretti* (See R. M. Cummings (ed.), *Spenser: The Critical Heritage*, Routledge and Kegan Paul, London, 1971). Jewel Wurtsbaugh's *Two Centuries of Spenserian Scholarship* does not include any critical comment about the *Amoretti*. The only references to the poems are to publication dates or matters of autobiographical interest. (See Jewel Wurtsbaugh, *Two Centuries of Spenserian Scholarship: 1609–1805*, The Johns Hopkins Press, Baltimore, 1936.)
4. R. M. Cummings, op cit., p. 276.
5. Francis L. Palgrave, 'Essays on the Minor Poems of Spenser', in *Complete Works*, ed. A. Grosart, 9 vols., The Spenser Society, London, vol. 4. p. lxxxvii.

6. William Minto, *Characteristics of English Poets*, Blackwood, Edinburgh, 1874, p. 169.
7. J. R. Lowell, for example, refers to Spenser's 'somewhat artificial *amoretti* [*sic*]'. See J. R. Lowell, 'Spenser' in *The Prince of Poets: Essays on Edmund Spenser*, ed. John R. Elliott, Jr, New York University Press, New York, 1968, p. 31.
8. Minto, op. cit., p. 169.
9. See, for example, R. W. Church, *Spenser*, Macmillan and Co., London,. 1883, p. 168:

   There is no want in them of grace and sweetness. But they want the power and fire, as well as the perplexing mystery, of those of the greater master.

   See also G. Saintsbury, *A History of English Prosody From the Twelfth Century to the Present Day*, 3 Vols., Macmillan and Co. Ltd., 1906, Vol. 1, p. 361:

   They are of course inferior in passion and intensity to Shakespeare's and to Drayton's enigmatic masterpiece; in variety and in charm to Sidney's.

10. Sidney Lee (ed) *Elizabethan Sonnets.*, 2 Vols, Archibald, Constable and Co. Ltd., Westminster, 1904, Vol. 1, pp. xciii–iv.
11. Emile Legouis, *Spenser*, J.M. Dent and Sons Ltd., London 1926, p. 86.
12. W.L. Renwick (ed.), *Daphnaïda and Other Poems*, The Scholartis Press, London, 1929, pp. 195–96.
13. *Poems of Spenser*, Selected with an Introduction by W.B. Yeats, T.C. and E.C. Jack, Edinburgh (undated), p.xx.
14. See T.S. Eliot's essays 'The Metaphysical Poets' and 'Andrew Marvell' in *Selected Prose of T.S. Eliot,* Faber and Faber, London, 1975, pp. 59–67; p. 162.
15. F.R. Leavis, *Revaluation: Tradition and Development in English Poetry*, 1936, rpt. Penguin Books, Harmondsworth Middlesex, England, 1967, p. 53.
16. A reaction against this occured in the sixties and seventies when the use of word-play and the intricacies of language in *The Faerie Queene* became the focus of considerable interest. The scholarship of Paul Alpers, A.C. Hamilton and others has helped to dispel the notion of *The Faerie Queene* as a work lacking in wit and playfulness. See, for example, Paul J. Alpers, *The Poetry of The Faerie Queene*, Princeton University Press, New Jersey, 1967, and A.C. Hamilton, 'Our New Poet: Spenser, "Well of English Undefyld"', *Essential Articles: For the Study of Edmund Spenser*, ed. A.C. Hamilton, Archon Books, Hamden, Connecticut, 1972.

17. J.W. Lever, *The Elizabethan Love Sonnet*, 2nd edn., 1966; rpt., Methuen, London, 1974, pp. 98–99, 136–37.
18. C.S. Lewis, *English Literature in the Sixteenth Century Excluding Drama*, Clarendon Press, Oxford 1954, p. 373.
19. James Brown gives a comprehensive account of the range of Spenser criticism in the sixties and seventies in 'The Critics' Poet: Spenser in the 'Seventies', *AUMLA*, 43, 1975. Harry Berger also mentions some of these approaches, though he warns that good commentators do not take 'rigorous stands' within these positions. See Harry Berger Jr. (ed.), *Spenser: A Collection of Critical Essays*, Prentice-Hall Inc., Englewood Cliffs, New Jersey, 1968, p. 1.
20. A. Kent Hieatt, *Short Time's Endless Monument*, Columbia University Press, New York 1969. See also A. Kent Hieatt, 'A Numerical Key to Spenser's *Amoretti* and Guyon in the House of Mammon', *Yearbook of English Studies*, 3, 1973.
21. A. Fowler, *Triumphal Forms. Structural Patterns in Elizabethan Poetry*, Cambridge University Press, Cambridge, 1970; A. Fowler (ed.), *Silent Poetry*, Routledge and Kegan Paul, London, 1970.
22. A. Dunlop, 'The Unity of Spenser's *Amoretti*' in A. Fowler (ed.), *Silent Poetry, ibid.*; 'Calendar Symbolism in the *Amoretti*' in *Notes and Queries*, 16, 1969.
23. Carol V. Kaske, 'Spenser's *Amoretti* and *Epithalamion* of 1959: Structure, Genre and Numerology', *English Literary Renaissance*, Vol. 8, Autumn 1978, No. 3.
24. Other critics who have followed this line of thought include James Brown who places emphasis on lunar, numerical and calendrical patterns (See James Brown, '"Lyke Phoebe: Lunar Numerical and Calendrical Patterns in Spenser's *Amoretti*', *Gypsy Scholar*, 1, 1973), and William C. Johnson, who argues that Spenser's use of the calendrical structure of the Christian year as set forth in *The Book of Common Prayer* has not been given enough attention. (See William C. Johnson, 'Spenser's *Amoretti* and the Art of Liturgy' in Studies in English Literature, 14, Winter 1974. His doctoral dissertation 'Vow'd to Eternity: A Study of Spenser's *Amoretti*' discusses Spenser's fascination with 'micro-macrocosmic parallels expressed in the multi-faceted calendar schemes which ultimately unify the whole series.')
25. A. Dunlop, 'The Unity of Spenser's *Amoretti*', op. cit., p. 159, and p. 166.
26. See, for example, John Erskine Hankins, *Source and Meaning in Spenser's Allegory: A Study of 'The Faerie Queene'*, Clarendon Press, Oxford, 1971, and Frank Kermode, *Shakespeare, Spenser, Donne: Renaissance Essays*, Routledge and Kegan Paul, London 1971.
27. Robert Kellogg, 'Thought's Astonishment and the Dark Conceits of Spenser's *Amoretti*', in John R. Elliott, Jr (ed.), *The Prince of Poets*, op. cit., p. 145.

28. Peter Cummings, 'Spenser's *Amoretti* as an Allegory of Love', *Texas Studies in Literature and Language*, 12, Summer 1970, p. 165.
29. A typical statement of this position is Davies's comment, 'Of all the English poets, Spenser is the most learnedly and dedicatedly Platonist'. See S. Davies, *Renaissance Views of Man*, Manchester University Press, Manchester, 1979, p. 33. Other critics who hold similar views are discussed below, pp. 141–42.
30. Robert Ellrodt, *Neoplatonism in the Poetry of Edmund Spenser*, Librairie E. Droz, Geneva, 1960; rpt. Folcroft Library Editions, 1978.
31. Veselin Kostic, *Spenser's Sources in Italian Poetry: A Study in Comparative Literature*, Faculté de Philologie de l'Université de Belgrade Monographies, Belgrade, 1969; and Jon A. Quitslund, 'Spenser's *Amoretti* VIII and Platonic Commentaries on Petrarch', *Journal of the Warburg and Courtauld Institutes*, 36, 1973.
32. Louis L. Martz, 'The *Amoretti*: "Most Goodly Temperature"', *Form and Convention in the Poetry of Edmund Spenser*, ed. William Nelson, Columbia University Press, New York, 1961, pp. 126, 128, 129.
33. Waldo F. McNeir, 'An Apology for Spenser's *Amoretti*' in *Essential Articles for the Study of Edmund Spenser*, ed. A.C. Hamilton, op. cit., p. 525.
34. Alexander Dunlop, 'The Drama of *Amoretti*', *Proceedings from a Special Session at the Thirteenth Conference on Medieval Studies in Kalamazoo*, Michigan, 1978, p. 274.
35. Elizabeth Bieman, '"Sometimes I mask in myrth lyke to a Comedy": Spenser's *Amoretti*', *Spenser Studies: A Renaissance Poetry Annual*, A.M.S. Press, Inc., New York, vol. 4, 1984, p. 132.

1. Structure in the *Amoretti*

Spenser's sonnet cycle creates the fiction of a developing relation between a middle-aged poet and a beautiful, virtuous lady, Elizabeth. The persona of the lover perceives the relationship in different ways at different times. Within the pattern of his fluctuating moods of disappointment, hope, near despair, anger and good-humoured playfulness, there is an underlying pattern of development. This is suggested in a number of different ways, relating both to the external chronology and to changes in the psychological temper of the relationship between the two personae.

Among Elizabethan sonnet cycles, the *Amoretti* contains an unusually large number of fictional events; and whilst the narrative thread remains slight, the events do provide some evidence of progress in the courtship. The events include the wearing of a laurel leaf by the mistress (XXVIII), her decking her hair in a net of gold (XXXVII), her smiling at the lover (XXXIX, XL), her sending him home in a storm (XLVI), her burning his letter (XLVIII), a kiss (LXIIII), his watching her embroidering (LXXI), his walking on the strand with her and writing her name in the sand (LXXV), her absence (LXXVIII, LXXXVII, LXXXVIII, and LXXXIX) and his anger at the venomous tongue that disturbs their peace (LXXXVI).

The passing of time is marked by various calendrical events such as the New Year (IIII and LXII), Spring (XIX and LXX), Lent (XXII) and Easter (LXVIII). The inclusion of pairs of sonnets occasioned by the same calendrical events at different periods of the

10

courtship provides a number of focal points for analysis of the
development of the relationship.[1]

The poems of Petrarch's *Canzoniere*, begun in the early 1330s and
written and revised until the last years of his life, were an important
model for Spenser's sequence, as they were for all Elizabethan sonnet
sequences.[2] The unifying principle of both the *Amoretti* and the
Canzoniere lies in the mind or personality describing the experiences
of loving, rather than in the events of an unfolding narrative. A thin
narrative thread, an episodic rather than a sequential pattern of
events, a random swinging between moods of confidence and
despair, and the inclusion of relatively extraneous matters are
features the sequences have in common.[3]

There are, however, important differences. Petrarch's passion for
Laura remains unrequited, whilst the love affair of the *Amoretti*
moves towards resolution and consummation. It is not a straight-
forward or direct progression. There are places where there is no
progress at all; there are slides backwards, digressions and circular
movements; but by the end of the sequence, progress in the
courtship has been made. This is not true of the *Canzoniere*, or
indeed of most Elizabethan sonnet sequences.

In the *Canzoniere* there is no particular order or pattern in the
presentation of the experiences which the lover describes himself as
enduring. The echoes of the sighs that feed his heart ('il suono / di
quei sospiri ond'io nudriva 'l core', sonnet 1) are described as they
are recalled. There are a few small details to mark the courtship,
which culminate in the hint that Laura has allowed her admirer to
touch her ungloved hand (CXCIX). There are occasional references
to the time at which a sonnet is being written (CCXI, CCCXXXVI),
there are moments of premonition about Laura's death (CCXLVI,
CCXLVIII, CCXLIX, CCL, CCLIIII) and there is the actual event
of Laura's death, but there is no significant change or development in
the relationship between lover and mistress.

The *Canzoniere* contains groups of sonnets that sustain a particular
mood (misery, self-pity, elation), or preoccupation (the solace of
nature), as does Spenser's sequence, but in the *Canzoniere* many of
these groups could be moved about without seriously affecting its
structure. Although Laura's death means that Petrarch is no longer
able to worship her living form, he yearns for her as he did in sonnets
I–CCLXIII – the division called *In vita di madonna Laura*. Petrarch's
longing for something which is unobtainable is the theme which

unites the two sections, and it would be possible to transpose many of the sonnets between the two divisions, *In vita di madonna Laura* and *In morte di madonna Laura*.

Overall, Spenser's cycle displays a much firmer pattern of sequential order. The patterns underlying the apparently random recalling of events, and the changes of mood, would be seriously disturbed if sonnets were to be transposed in the *Amoretti*. Although there is no systematic or readily predictable pattern in the development of the relationship between the lovers, the delicate stages in its progress are discernible in such things as the lover's method of address, his gathering confidence, and the increasingly reciprocal nature of the relationship.

One of the more significant patterns in the sequence is the broad movement from sonnets of praise at the opening to sonnets of blame or complaint in a longish middle section, followed by sonnets of praise in the last third of the sequence. The sequence opens with the lover singing his mistress's praises and continues in this vein until sonnet IX. The only divergence from this path is in II, in which the lover expresses anxiety about his 'unquiet thought'; in IIII, which is mainly devoted to a celebration of the New Year; and the aggressively defensive note about the mistress's pride in some lines of V and VI. The quality of the lover's praise is primarily that of someone who sees the object of his worship as unobtainable. His mistress is an 'Angel' of sovereign beauty (III) who dazzles the eye and mind; and she is seen to have qualities similar to those of her Maker (VIII, IX).

At sonnet X the aggressive note that the lover took pains to repress earlier in the sequence is released in a powerful outburst against the mistress's pride. The lover is uncharacteristically vindictive in his desire to see his mistress reduced to his level:

> Unrighteous Lord of love what law is this,
>   That me thou makest thus tormented be?
>   the whiles she lordeth in licentious blisse
>   of her freewill, scorning both thee and me.
> See how the Tyrannesse doth ioy to see
>   the huge massacres which her eyes do make:
>   and humbled harts bring captives unto thee,
>   that thou of them mayst mightie vengeance take.
> But her proud hart doe thou a little shake
>   And that high look, with which she doth comptroll
>   all this worlds pride bow to a baser make,

and al her faults in thy black booke enroll.
That I may laugh at her in equall sort,
   as she doth laugh at me and makes my pain her sport.
                                                (X)

From this point on until LVIII, most of the sonnets have some form of blame or complaint as their theme[4]; and the longest runs of unbroken complaint are found in this section of the sequence.[5]

After sonnet LVIII there is very little complaint, and scarcely any criticism of the mistress, though criticism is directed at the venomous tongue which stirs up 'coles of yre' in the mistress (LXXXVI). The last third of the sequence is made up predominantly of sonnets of praise.[6] The mistress continues to be perceived as the lover's 'soverayne saynt' (LXI) and as worthy of his absolute worship, though at this stage he also meets her on more equal terms.

Some critics find the melancholy mood of the last four sonnets of the *Amoretti* out of character both with the happier mood that prevails in the last third of the sequence and with the spirit of the Anacreontics and the *Epithalamion* which follow in the same volume. The Anacreontics, light-hearted, amatory poems[7], are playful in tone, and the *Epithalamion*, a nuptial hymn in which the praises of the bride are sung, is a poem of joyous celebration. The differences in mood between the last four sonnets and the Anacreontics and *Epithalamion* caused Lever to suggest that the sequence ought to end at LXXXV, since 'Nothing more is needed to complete the tale of successful courtship, to which the marriage ode bound up in the same volume would provide a fitting finale'[8].

The mood of discord in the final sonnets can be explained by positing a causal link between the venomous tongue in sonnet LXXXVI and the separation of the lovers[9]. Yet Spenser does not imply any connection between the slander and the mistress's absence, and the angry and contemptuous tone of LXXXVI seems quite unrelated to the sonnets which surround it or to the poems which follow the *Amoretti*. The lover looks forward to the return of his mistress at the end of the sequence, and although he expresses sadness at her absence, there is no reference to concern about her feelings of anger or displeasure which would mar their reunion. A pattern of sudden swings of emotion (usually from praise to blame, or hope to despair) has been established early in the sequence, so that the jarring note of LXXXVI, although not part of such familiar antitheses, and unexpected in view of the more even pattern of the last third of the sequence, is not entirely without precedent.

It is true, as Kaske argues, that the end of the sequence provides a prelude to the Anacreontics and *Epithalamion*, rather than an ending. She suggests that this stage corresponds to the length of the engagement period, and so lasts for 20 sonnets:

> When the *Amoretti* works up through the triumphant 60's to its major climax in the Easter sonnet and then returns to complaint, albeit about lesser grievances, in the remaining twenty sonnets, I propose that it serves structurally to carry the reader on towards the *Epithalamion* and emotionally to express the somewhat anti-climactic character of the engagement period itself.[10]

But in characterising this whole group of sonnets (LXIX to LXXXIX) as anticlimactic, Kaske fails to take account of the variety of moods that the sonnets contain, and the fact that the dominant note is one of joy and celebration, not of complaint. The proud and triumphant celebration of the winning of the mistress (LXIX), the happy meditation and playful exchange enjoyed while watching the mistress embroidering (LXXI), the good-humoured exchanges of LXXV, and the wonder the lover feels for his mistress's beauty in LXXXI all make it impossible to accept the view that the sequence 'returns to complaint'.

The betrothal sonnets do clearly form a prelude to the triumphant celebration of *Epithalamion*. But they can also be seen as providing in themselves a climactic resolution of the frequently troubled earlier relationship between lover and mistress. The lover's sense of assurance about his possession of the mistress is not unmixed with feelings of anxiety and melancholy. Such negative feelings, however, are expressed within the bounds of the knowledge that the contract between the two is 'fyrmely tyde'.

Spenser's lover is left pining at the end of the sequence, but he is not wasting away from lovesickness, as is the case with the lover in many other Elizabethan sequences. It is not because his mistress has failed to respond to him, but because she *has* responded to him that he is left mourning her absence and awaiting the return of 'her owne joyous sight'. The lover's pensiveness and sadness at his mistress's absence provide a natural close which matches the mood of conventional sonnet endings in some respects, and provides a pause in relation to the poems which follow.

The teasing, humorous Anacreontics represent a movement away from concentration on the serious business of courtship, to a light-hearted account of Cupid's delights and woes. When Cupid is stung by the bee towards the end of these poems, the 'sting', which wins for Cupid Venus's laughing sympathy, and which is presumably symbolic of the sting of love which the lover also experiences, is viewed with comic detachment. Venus's curative treatment and loving attention makes the pain of the sting fade into insignificance:

> Who would not oft be stung as this,
> to be so bath'd in Venus blis?

The verbal echo in these lines of the term 'blis', which has occurred throughout the sequence but which particularly recalls the lover's being 'bath'd in bliss' in LXXII, emphasizes the parallels in the two sets of experience. The humour of the remark is, however, underlined by the contrast in the two sets of circumstances, and by its relation to the broader context of the lover's frequent complaints about the pain of love. The momentary excursion into conviviality and light-hearted humour in these poems marks an interval before the culmination of the marriage song, *Epithalamion*.

It is not surprising in a sonnet sequence which is distinguished from other sequences by its anticipation of a happy ending that the emphasis should be on the developing courtship and that this should be used as an important organisational principle. If the organisational framework is viewed from this perspective, then the acceptance by the mistress of her lover becomes its climax, dividing the sequence into those sonnets which build towards her acceptance (I–LXVII) and those which deal with the betrothal period which follows it (LXVIII–LXXXIX). This creates a pattern not unlike the division of the Italian sequences into two parts with the first much longer than the second, though, of course, it does not follow that Spenser was simply imitating the Italian model.

Neely notes that the primary structuring device in the major English and Italian sequences is a division into two unequal parts. The first part, she claims, 'sets forth the static relationship of the adoring/lamenting poet lover to be an immovable beloved', whilst 'in the second, shorter part there is alteration – in the beloved, the poet, the relationship'.

In the case of the *Amoretti*, she finds 'the poet-lover's humility, awe and tenderness', up to about sonnet LXII, to be 'quintessentially Petrarchan', and the second part to deal with the 'reciprocal, sexual relationship – a courtship towards marriage'[11]. Whilst agreeing with Neely that a division of this kind is sometimes present in the English sequences, it is necessary to point out that characterization of the first long movement of the _Amoretti_ as the one that deals with the static Petrarchan relation does not take into account the way in which Petrarchan ideas are dealt with in the sequence. Petrarchan ideas are an important part of the framework in the first section, as indeed they are in the whole, but they do not circumscribe or become identical with the lover's experience in any way. They sometimes find an echo in the lover's attitudes, though there are often times when the spirit of his attitude is not Petrarchan.[12] Throughout the sequence Petrarchan ideas are only one of a number of systems of thought that are drawn upon in the expression of the lover's dilemmas and aspirations. The attitudes and behaviour of the lover in the first long section are neither as static nor as long-suffering as that of the lover in the corresponding section of the _Canzoniere_.

Certainly a change such as Neely describes as taking place in the _Amoretti_ does occur. But it is necessary to define the nature of this change and to locate the point at which the change occurs. Most critical accounts suggest that the change in the relationship between lover and mistress depends on change in the lover. Those who find some version of the Neo-Platonic ladder in the sequence, for example, tend to relate the lover's success in courtship with his having learned to love in the 'right' way. Casady sees the _Amoretti_ as 'a study of the lover who in his struggle to attain spiritual love succeeds now and again in raising himself up to rung three or four, only to be drawn back each time to a lower rung by physical love'.[13] For Casady, change in the lover is not a straight-forward progression, but involves movements backwards and forwards, as he strives to attain a more spiritual love that is worthy of the mistress. Ricks, on the other hand, claims that progress in the courtship cannot be made until after LXI, because until that point the lover loved his mistress 'for the wrong reasons and in the wrong way'.[14] Ricks places the lover's development in a broader Christian framework, as does Kaske, who describes the structure as 'an emotional progression from sexual conflict to Christian-humanist resolution', the resolution being found in _Epithalamion_.[15]

Similarly, those who make numerological and calendrical inter-

pretations of the sequence usually suggest a relationship between this
symbolism and the lover's progress from an earthly to a higher form
of love. James Brown, for example, argues that the lunar and
calendrical symbolism of the sequence mark stages of progress in the
courtship, and defines that progress as 'the lover's education in the
meaning and necessity of true chastity'.[16] Hardison sees a calendrical
ordering of the sequence into units, which he describes as being like
panels on a triptych. He, too, argues that these stages represent
progress from conflict through reconciliation to a time when the
poet can explore what he has learned.[17]

Dunlop, who attempts to synthesize the insights of those who see
the sequence in a representational, historical context and those of the
numerological school, also sees the lover progressing 'from a state of
normal human ignorance to a state of relative wisdom concerning
love'. He takes the repeated sonnet (XXXV/LXXXIII) as part of his
evidence of the lover's progress in the education of love. Sonnet
XXXV is interpreted as a declaration of the lover's preoccupation
with the lady to the exclusion of all else, yet LXXXIII indicates to
Dunlop the lover's concern with spiritual rather than physical
beauty.[18] The different contexts apparently give the words their
different meanings. (It could, of course, equally well be argued that
the repeated sonnet suggests that the lover has made no progress of
any kind, and that he experiences the same frustration late in his
courtship that he experienced in its early stages.)[19]

These views depend on the assumption that the lover has to learn
how to love in the right way before he can be worthy of his mistress.
Yet the lover has shown himself to be aware of this knowledge from
very early in the sequence. He recognizes the meaning and necessity
of chastity as early as VI and VIII, and again in XXI and XXII; and he
is just as prone to sensual thoughts at the end of the sequence as he
was at the beginning, though he consistently shows himself aware
that such thoughts must be chastened.

He devises quite creative ways to deal with lustful thoughts
(LXXVI, LXXVII),[20] but his solutions are not entirely successful
and leave him with the problems only partially resolved. The point
at which he is most forceful with himself about his lust comes late in
the sequence (LXXXIIII), suggesting that the problem is continuing
to be troublesome:

> Let not one sparke of filthy lustfull fyre
> breake out, that may her sacred peace molest[21]

If anything, lustful thoughts increase towards the end, an increase which is in the order of things since the courtship itself is progressing, but the lover's determination to protect the purity of his mistress continues unabated (LXXVI, LXXVII, LXXXIIII). The things she would teach him – that true love knows nothing of lust and is a selfless emotion that puts the good of the beloved first – are things he has known all through the sequence, even though he often finds it difficult to live up to the standards imposed by that knowledge. These observations make it difficult to accept either Neo-Platonic or numerological views of the sequence which rest on the assumption that there is some significant improvement in the lover's moral outlook which ultimately makes him acceptable to his mistress.[22]

An examination of the paired sonnets, those which celebrate the same calendrical event on different occasions, also indicates that any change which occurs in the sequence has little to do with an improvement in the lover's moral attitudes. The New Year sonnets (IIII and LXII) both look forward hopefully to what is in store. The mood of IIII is light and carefree, whilst that of LXII is relatively serious and contemplative. Sonnet IIII is a poem of early courtship. The first 12 lines contain elaborations on the New Year's promise of 'new delight', and it is only in the couplet that the poet enjoins the mistress to prepare herself 'new love to entertaine'. There is no sense in this poem that the destinies of lover and mistress have become intertwined. The New Year is celebrated as a symbol of hope and new life, and the lover anticipates that it may encourage the mistress's response towards him. But in LXII the fate of lover and mistress is clearly viewed as being bound up together. The sonnet contains several indications of an established and rather stormy relationship:

> So let us, which this chaunge of weather vew,
> chaunge eeke our mynds and former lives amend,
> the old yeares sinnes forepast let us eschew

The promise of the New Year is to provide comfort for them both, and marks the lover's resolve that they will share a future without 'stormes'.

The positive gains in LXII are the sense of a shared past of lover and mistress, their more equal involvement, and their looking forward to 'peace and plenty' (with its biblical associations) rather than to 'new delight'. This in no way negates the 'new delight' of IIII (the phrase 'new delight' also forms the last two words of LXII), and it is expected that it will form a part of their future happiness. Although lover and mistress are more advanced in their courtship in the second sonnet, the quality of the lover's feelings for his mistress remains the same.

The paired Spring sonnets also suggest a progress in some senses, though not in others. The lover is hopeful and confident in the second Spring sonnet (LXX), whereas he held little hope that his 'rebell' would respond to his or anyone's guidance in the first Spring sonnet (XIX). He is also more tolerant of his mistress's silence in LXX than he was in XIX. In XIX he expressed his irritation with her for ignoring the call of Spring and love (though there is a hint of admiration for her being so distinctively herself, able to defy the pressures put upon her if she chooses). In LXX he feels sure she will awaken to love, given encouragement, so that he feels less need to chide her. Yet, as the sonnet progresses, his anxiety increases and in a Spenserian version of the *carpe diem* theme, the lover tries to be as persuasive as possible:

> Make hast therefore sweet love, whilest it is prime
> for none can call again the passed time.

The main difference lies in the change in her. In XIX it seemed she had deliberately chosen to ignore the call to love, whereas in LXX it seems more likely that she will respond to him, given time and encouragement.

The Lenten and Easter sonnets could appear to indicate progress in the lover's attitude (in that he has progressed from sacrificing his heart in flames 'of pure and chast desyre', to celebrating a Christian union), but, in fact, both sonnets suggest that the mistress, not the Maker, is of prime importance in the lover's scheme of things.[23] In XXII the mistress is the saint worshipped by the lover, to the exclusion of all else. *She* is the 'author of [my] blisse', not God, and as a result the lover offers her his devotion and sacrifices his heart to her as a relic. (The idea of his heart's becoming a relic has a humorous twist because she is the saint, not he.) She has replaced God, or the Virgin Mary, as the centre of his worship.

LXVIII begins with a celebration of the risen Lord, but gradually moves towards being a celebration of love. Instead of the mistress alone being the focus of the lover's attention, their union, of which she is a part, has the central place. He argues that their love is sanctioned by Christ's commandment to love one another, but, of course, Christ's commandment referred to all men, not one particular being.

> Most glorious Lord of lyfe that on this day,
>   didst make thy triumph over death and sin:
>   and having harrowd hell didst bring away
>   captivity thence captive us to win:
> The ioyous day, deare Lord, with ioy begin,
>   and grant that we for whom thou diddest dye
>   being with thy deare blood clene washt from sin,
>   may live for ever in felicity.
> And that thy love we weighing worthily,
>   may likewise love thee for the same againe:
>   and for thy sake that all lyke deare didst buy,
>   with love may one another entertayne.
> So let us love, deare love, lyke as we ought,
>   love is the lesson which the Lord us taught.
>   (LXVIII)

Petrarch had shown himself aware of the dangers of worshipping an earthly being in the *Canzoniere*, and many of the sonnets deal with attempts to resolve the conflict between his earthly and spiritual loves, and with the assuaging of his guilt about this subject:

> I'vo piangendo i miei passati tempi
> i quai posi in amar cosa mortale
> senza levarmi a volo, abbiendi' io l'ale
> per dar forse di me non bassi essempi.
>   (CCCLXV)

> I go weeping for my past time, which I spent in loving
> a mortal thing without lifting myself in flight, though
> I had wings to make of myself perhaps not a base example.

Towards the end of the *Canzoniere*, he replaces Laura with the Virgin Mary as the object of his worship, and tries to convince himself that his soul is out of danger:

Il di s'appressa et non pote esser lunge,
si corre il tempo et vola,
Vergine inica et sola,
e 'l cor or conscienzia or morte punge:
raccomandami al tuo Figliuol, verace
omo et verace Dio,
ch' accolga 'l mio spirto ultimo in pace.
(CCCLXVI)

The day draws near and cannot be far, time so runs and
flies, single, sole Virgin; and now conscience, now death
pierces my heart: commend me to your Son, true man and
true God, that He may receive my last breath in peace.

Petrarch's voice in dealing with conflicts between religious and
secular values is anguished and guilt-ridden. In contrast, there is an
edge of daring and challenge in the way in which Spenser's lover
asserts the congruity of his earthly and spiritual objects of worship.
Spenser's persona achieves a reconciliation between his love for
Elizabeth and his love for God, without self-flagellation or agony of
spirit, but he does it by making his religion accommodate his
mistress, and in so doing comes dangerously close to giving their
union more importance than he ought, particularly given the
Christian framework he is invoking.

The change from the Lenten to the Easter sonnet is not, then,
related to the lover's learning the nature and true meaning of
chastity. He was well aware of the importance of this in XXII (even
though he chose to be playful about sacrificing his heart to the
flames), just as he is aware of its importance in later sonnets. There is
no change in the way that the lover feels towards his mistress,
though there are changes in how he feels about her and about his
chances of success. The significant change is that instead of having
the worship of his mistress as the centre of his thoughts, their union
is now the centre of all his thoughts and endeavours. By the end of
the sequence he has 'kindle[d] new desire' 'that shall endure for ever'
in the mistress as he had hoped he would (VI), but his own love for
the mistress, which 'dint[s] the parts entire / with chast affects' (VI),
continues unabated, though it has gained the quality of greater
assurance.

The lover does not change in any fundamental way, but this is not
to say that the relationship remains static. The submission of the
mistress to the lover, which is heralded in LXIII and LXIIII, and is
formally acknowledged in LXVII, is prepared for over a number of

sonnets. It is difficult to pinpoint the moment when the change in direction which leads towards this moment begins, but it would seem to come much earlier in the sequence than most critics allow.

Commentators on the sequence have generally seen the turning point (that is the moment when a decisive change in the quality of the relationship and of the direction in which it is heading may be discerned) as occurring at about two-thirds of the way through. For Martz it occurs at the celebration of the New Year in sonnet LXII; Lever finds a new quality emerging after the kiss sonnet at LXIIII; Bayly chooses a slightly later point 'where the lady at last accepts his love in sonnet LXIX', and Neely mentions both the New Year and Easter sonnets (LXII and LXVIII) as the mark of the beginning of the second half of the sequence.[24] It can be argued, however, that a new note in the lover's address and the beginnings of a change in his attitude are discernible as early as LVII.

At the opening of LVII the lover insists that their 'war' has been going on for long enough, and it is high time that this was realized by the mistress:

> Sweet warriour when shall I have peace with you?
>   High time it is, this warre now ended were:
>   which I no lenger can endure to sue,
>   ne your incessant battry more to bear:
> So weake my powres, so sore my wounds appeare,
>   that wonder is how I should live a iot,
>   seeing my hart through launched every where
>   with thousand arrowes, which your eies have shot:
> Yet shoot ye sharpely still, and spare me not,
>   but glory thinke to make these cruel stoures.
>   ye cruell one, what glory can be got,
>   in slaying him that would live gladly yours?
> Make peace therefore, and graunt me timely grace,
>   that al my wounds will heale in little space.

The word 'warrior' has been previously used in the sequence as a pejorative epithet, to suggest unfair hostility on the part of the mistress. ('She cruell warriour, doth her selfe addresse / In battell', XI.) The change to the epithet 'sweet' here gives an entirely different complexion to the idea of her warrior-like character, softening the connotations of aggression and hostility. (Othello's address to Desdemona, 'O my fair warrior' (II.i.179), on their meeting at Cyprus conveys a similar feeling of warm salute.) This form of address sounds at once intimate and conciliatory, though there is also a note of determination in the line. The word 'peace', which occurs in the same line, is also referred to earlier in the sequence but always in such a way as to present the lover as a frustrated supplicant for peace to a hostile mistress (e.g. 'Dayly when I do seeke and sew for peace', XI.5; and 'Is there no meanes for me to purchace peace', XXXVI.5). In LVII the mistress is still a hostile figure, but the language employed in the lover's bid for peace suggests the hope of mutual agreement and happiness, goals which could be achieved by lover and mistress together ('when shall I have peace with you?'; 'Make peace therefore').

The second line of LVII, 'High time it is, this warre now ended were', expresses a mood appropriate to a relationship which has been long established. The lover is presented as having suffered the 'incessant battery' of the mistress's hostility for an intolerable period of time (in XIIII it was the lover who was responsible for the 'incessant battery', line 10, whereas here it is the mistress who is being accused of it), and as having an overwhelming desire for the resolution of their conflict. There is, however, a suggestion in this complaint of long-established familiarity. The complaint is also softened by compliment, not only in the first word of the poem, but also in line 8. The 'arrowes which [her] eies have shot' suggests the erotic power of the mistress, as well as conjuring up images of her proud hostility to the lover's importunities.

In the second quatrain, the language of the sonnet indicates, beneath its surface theme of desperate complaint, a degree of confidence and assurance in the lover's frame of mind. Although he describes himself as a helpless victim, the way in which he does this tends to belie his case. He gives a wryly exaggerated account of his suffering ('that wonder is how I should live a iot') and an amusing account of its cause – that she has launched a thousand arrows from her eyes into his heart. He manipulates the details of his story to make her guilt the greater (his accusation is placed immediately after the account of his wounds, for example), and to emphasize his innocence and long-suffering. This suggests someone who has a certain detachment from his plight, not a helpless victim.

The third quatrain seems to move back to the tone used in many previous sonnets in which thoughts of the mistress's cruelty aroused the lover's anger. He refers to her as 'ye cruell one', an address which is markedly different from 'Sweet warrior', yet in the immediately following question he uses a description of himself ('would live gladly yours') which is a more direct, more particular expression of his desire to belong to her than any he has previously offered. His earlier references to their union have been more general. He has envisaged 'greater meede' or 'endless pleasure', but not living as hers, as he envisages here.

The lover's tone in the couplet is warm and persuasive, with the note of authority carried by the imperatives ('Make peace', 'graunt'). The conflict is not over, but he is hopeful that its end might come 'in little space'. He is viewing the conflict as a stage in their relationship, a stage which may draw to a close, rather than as a battle that can never be won.

From this point until the union is assured, many of the sonnets display the growing confidence and assurance of the lover. In Sonnet LX he jokes about the mistress's 'shorting' her ways and ending his pain, a subject he usually complains of in more serious vein. He reassures and soothes his mistress in LXII and LXV, attitudes he has not previously adopted. In LXII he suggests they both make changes in order to make the second year of their courtship a happier, more fruitful one. In the past he has asked his mistress to change towards him, but he has not suggested they both make amends ('Let us . . . let us . . .'). The idea of their equal involvement continues in LXV, in which he sees them bound in a relation of mutual comfort, salving each other's wounds, instead of his wishing she would be his 'Lyfe's leach', as in L.

In LXVI his reference to his 'lowly state' suggests a consciousness of inferiority in his relation with her. Yet this sonnet needs to be seen in the context of all the other sonnets which deal with the theme of his lowliness, as well as in the context of the courtly love convention. At this point he is defining his humility as a positive contribution to their relationship – his lowliness and obscurity provide the perfect foil for her shining example:

> But ye thereby much greater glory gate,
>   then had ye sorted with a princes pere:
>   for now your light doth more it selfe dilate,
>   and in my darknesse greater doth appeare.
> Yet since your light hath once enlumind me,
>   with my reflex yours shall encreased be.

The hint of playfulness about a subject which has made him unhappy in the past is further indication that he is beginning to outgrow the role of inadequate suitor. Cummings recognizes that the poet is not completely self-deprecatory in these lines, but suggests different reasons for this. He finds in the lover's confidence 'a hint that his declarations of humility are not intended to be understood as totally sincere. The lover's pride in his conquest can not be fully disguised'.[25] It is true that the lover's attitude to the subject of his mistress's perfection and his own unworthiness is less serious than it has been in the past, but it is not sincerity that is the issue. He clearly feels humbled by his mistress's presence, but his attitude towards that humility is less earnest and anxious than it has been, indicating the more advanced stage of negotiation that they have reached in the process of courtship.

All these changes culminate in LXVII, the deer hunt sonnet. Spenser's sonnet is indebted to Tasso's 'Questa fera gentil', which is itself a version of Petrarch's 'Una candida cerva'.[26] Lever notes that Tasso changed the story by having the deer voluntarily submit to capture, and it was this which had appeal for Spenser.[27] It is remarkable that Spenser could fashion a sonnet which owes so much to imitation and tradition; which is magnificent in its own right; and which provides a particularly satisfying conclusion to a stage which has been developing to this moment within the sequence. It is a moment which has been well prepared for and which is structurally and psychologically satisfying. At the same time the moment is more dramatic than the lover's anticipation of it, so that it also has a quality of freshness and surprise:

> Lyke as a huntsman after weary chace,
>> seeing the game from him escapt away,
>> sits downe to rest him in some shady place,
>> with panting hounds beguiled of their pray:
> So after long pursuit and vaine assay,
>> when I all weary had the chace forsooke,
>> the gentle deare returnd the selfe-same way,
>> thinking to quench her thirst at the next brooke.
> There she beholding me with mylder looke,
>> sought not to fly, but fearelesse still did bide:
>> till I in hand her yet halfe trembling tooke,
>> and with her owne goodwill hir fyrmely tyde.
> Strange thing me seemd to see a beast so wyld,
>> so goodly wonne with her owne will beguyld.

The deer image, a favourite classical and Renaissance image (the doe was traditionally sacred to Diana), replaces the previous animal images (lion, tiger and panther) which have been used to describe the mistress. The deer is beautiful, submissive and gentle, and yet she has an inner strength which allows her to elude captivity if she chooses. She symbolizes beauty and purity of spirit. Her presence in the shady place provides what was previously lacking, and brings with it a feeling of fulfilment, for she intimates peace and contentment. When she chooses to return she places herself and all she symbolizes within the lover's reach.

The deer stands 'fearelesse', presumably encouraged by the 'mylder looke' of her huntsman. Casady interprets the deer's submission as a response to the milder look of rational rather than sensual love.[28] There is nothing in the poem to justify this interpretation. The only information which the poem provides as a possible cause of the mistress/deer's change of feeling towards the lover/huntsman is that he has ceased to be her relentless pursuer. When this occurs, she is able to submit to him quite willingly, and enter into a relationship in which good feeling abounds ('with her owne goodwill hir fyrmely tyde'; 'so goodly wonne'). The question as to whether the 'mylder looke' implies a distinction between rational and sensual love does not arise. That the deer seeks 'not to fly' carries great significance because it means that not only has the lover been successful in his wooing, but also that his mistress has freely chosen him to be her master.

Spenser's sonnet interestingly reverses the development of the relationship between the wild creatures and the poet/persona in the first stanza of Wyatt's 'They fle from me that sometyme did me seke'. Wyatt's poem begins with a description of a situation in which certain creatures, perhaps deer, who were formerly 'gentill tame and meke', and who 'put theimself in daunger / To take bred at [his] hand', have now forsaken him. In Wyatt's poem, the creatures return to their 'wyld' nature and become part of 'a straunge fasshion, of forsaking'. In Spenser's sonnet, to the wonder of the lover ('Strange thing me seemd'), the 'wyld' beast submits to captivity.

In Spenser's poem the moment has been reached when the mistress is responding in a way the lover has hoped she would, though her response overwhelms him in a way he could not have anticipated. It is an equal kind of union, for although he is master and ties her 'fyrmely' he does so with her goodwill. The sonnet suggests that to capture her without her willing submission would never have done, and would have been impossible (lines 2,4). The image of the capturing of the deer pinpoints what is essential about this moment in their relationship. The lover's interest is in what has happened between them, and in the mystery and wonder of his mistress's actions; he is not as self-absorbed as usual, or as concerned with his own role in the proceedings, because he is caught up in something miraculous which has taken place and of which he is a part. In most sequences the lover woos the mistress but fails to win her. It is not, however, customary for any explanation to be offered as to why the lover has failed to win his mistress's heart. The major difference between the *Amoretti* and other sonnet sequences of the period is that the lover is finally successful in his wooing of the mistress. But, just as in the other sequences there is no explanation of the mistress's obduracy, so in the *Amoretti* the change of heart on the part of the mistress is left unexplained. The discussion in this chapter of the structural organisation of the *Amoretti* shows that arguments concerning the lover's gradual education in chastity do not provide adequate explanations for the developmental changes discernible in the sequence. The development is rather to be defined in terms of the increasing intimacy and confidence of the lover persona both in his address to, and his thoughts about, his mistress. Most critics, as suggested above, recognize that indications of a change in the relationship of lover and mistress occur somewhere between LXII and LXVIII, but there is little acknowledgement of the earlier indications of this change. As has been argued here, the change in the relationship is hinted at from as early as LVII, though it is not given formal recognition until LXVII, the moment when the mistress accepts her lover as her suitor.

The sense of lover and mistress being committed to each other, which is evident in the deer hunt sonnet, underlies the rest of the sequence. There are moments when the mistress addresses the lover in tones that echo her spirited independence in former sonnets (LXXV), and moments where she has doubts about their union (LXV), but the lover has accustomed himself to things of this kind by this stage and meets her changes of mood with more tolerance than he has, in the past, been accustomed to offer. He himself does not remain entirely even-tempered during this period, but his dominant mood is of joyous confidence, a confidence which reflects the fact that their relationship is on surer ground.

One of the most important structural patterns of the sequence is, then, provided by the order suggested in the development of the courtship. The sequence begins with the lovers in relative isolation from one another and moves to a time when they share hopes and fears, and finally promise themselves to each other. The pattern of development within this framework is one of interruption and reversal, with quite some time passing before the direction in which the courtship is heading is finally confirmed. The betrothal sonnets which follow the confirmation of union deal with the doubts and setbacks, joys and triumphs, of the engagement period, though again not in any particular order. A lack of surface order is an important aspect of the whole (according to Hunter, 'a high proportion of casual elements is of the essence' of an English sonnet sequence),[29] though the underlying pattern of the developing courtship gives shape and direction to the sequence as a whole.

The cluster of sonnets about the mistress's absence at the end brings a mood of sadness and deprivation, one which is familiar from other sonnet sequences, though its cause is different from the usual one of the lover's rejection. Spenser implies that, with the return of the mistress, sadness will be replaced by joy. This creates a mood of anticipation which is unique amongst the closing movements of Elizabethan sonnet sequences.

NOTES: Chapter One

1. The paired sonnets are discussed below. See pp. 18–21.
2. Spenser makes use of a number of stock Petrarchan themes in the *Amoretti*. These include the notions that the mistress is a being of perfect beauty and saintly character who is relentlessly unresponsive to amorous courtship; that she inspires a quasi-religious adoration and reverence; and that she causes her admirer to experience a variety of symptoms in the name of love, such as burning, freezing, weeping and sighing. The idea of love as something which first strikes in the form of Cupid's arrow, through the eyes and thence to the heart, creating in the beholder a state of lovesickness from which there is no escape, is another notion to which Petrarch's poetry gave currency, and which is also employed in Spenser's sequence.
3. Petrarch includes many more sonnets on extraneous matters than does Spenser, though Petrarch's sequence is approximately four times longer. Petrarch makes no effort to link these sonnets to the main

themes of his sequence, whereas Spenser makes tenuous connections. See, for example, the *Canzoniere* XXVII and XL, and the *Amoretti* XXXIII and LXXX.

4. There are exceptions – sonnets XV, XVII, XXII, XXXIX and XL, are sonnets of praise, and in some sonnets neither complaint, praise nor blame is the centre of interest (XIX, XXVI, XXXIII). Others contain both praise and blame (XXI, XXIIII, XXXVIII). The sonnets of complaint also vary in intensity, with some being quite playful (e.g. XII, XVI, LI), whilst others include more extreme criticism (XXV, XXXVI, XLI, XLVII, XLIX, LIII, LVI).

5. There are two longish runs of unbroken complaint – sonnets XXXI–XXXVIII (with only XXXIII being about another subject) and XLVI–LVIII (though the subject of LV is both the cruelty and the fairness of the mistress).

6. There are sonnets in this last group which are not sonnets of praise – LXXX is about the writing of *The Faerie Queene*, and LXXXVI is an attack on the venomous tongue, and there are several sonnets which are only indirectly sonnets of praise, for their main theme is the loneliness of being without the mistress.

7. The so-called Anacreontic verses were bound (without separate title) between the *Amoretti* and the *Epithalamion* in both the octavo and folio editions of the *Amoretti*. (See *Works*, vol. 8, p. 455). The editors of the Variorum edition labelled the verses "Anacreontics" as they were apparently written in the manner of Anacreon, the sixth-century B.C. Greek lyric poet, known for his convivial, amatory verse. Spenser's verses include translations from the poetry of Ronsard, Belleau and de Baïf. These poets of the Pléiade had themselves been influenced by the publication of a collection of Anacreontic verse of unknown origin in Paris in 1554. A close study of the sources of the verses appended to Spenser's sequence has led Michael Hilton to conclude that they have very little to do with the poems of Anacreon. He casts considerable doubt on the idea that the poems are direct imitations of Anacreon and traces a number of different classical and post-classical influences in their themes and motifs. See Michael Hilton, "The Anacreontea in England to 1683", 2 vols., unpublished Ph.D. thesis, Oxford, 1981, pp. 206–215.

8. J. W. Lever, *The Elizabethan Love Sonnet*, 2nd. edn. 1966; rpt. Methuen, London, 1974, p. 128. See also B. E. C. Davis, *Edmund Spenser: A Critical Study*, Russell and Russell, Inc., New York, 1962, p. 48; and Don M. Ricks, 'Persona and Process in Spenser's *Amoretti*', *Ariel*, 3, October 1972, p. 13, footnote 1.

9. See, for example, J. C. Smith and E. De Selincourt, *Spenser: Poetical Works*, Oxford University Press, London, 1912, p. xxxvi, and A.C. Judson, *Works*, vol. 2, p. 170.

10. Carol V. Kaske, 'Spenser's *Amoretti* and *Epithalamion* of 1595: Structure, Genre, and Numerology', *English Literary Renaissance*, Autumn 1978, vol. 8, no. 3, p. 273.
11. Carol Thomas Neely, 'The Structure of English Renaissance Sonnet Sequences', *English Literary History*, vol. 45, 1978, pp. 368, 372, 374.
12. See, for example, pp. 20, 21.
13. E. Casady, 'The Neo-Platonic Ladder in Spenser's *Amoretti*', in *Renaissance Studies in Honor of Hardin Craig*, ed. Baldwin Maxwell, W. D. Briggs, Frances R. Johnson, and E. N. S. Thompson, Stanford University, California, 1941, p. 103.
14. Ricks, op. cit., p. 10.
15. See Ricks, op. cit., p. 9 and Kaske, op. cit., p. 272.
16. James Neil Brown, '"Lyke Phoebe", Lunar Numerical and Calendrical Patterns in Spenser's *Amoretti*'. *The Gypsy Scholar*, 1, 1973, p. 12.
17. O. B. Hardison, Jr, '*Amoretti* and the *Dolce Stil Novo*', *English Literary Renaissance*, vol. 2, no. 2, Spring 1972, pp. 209 and 214.
18. Alexander Dunlop, 'The Drama of *Amoretti*,' *Spenser at Kalamazoo, Proceedings from a Special Session at Kalamazoo*, Cleveland State University, Michigan, May 1978, pp. 274, 284.
19. Martz's explanation that the sonnet is a 'designed reminiscence and recurrence of an earlier mood of pining and complaint' (Louis L. Martz, 'The *Amoretti*: "Most Goodly Temperature"', in *Form and Convention in the Poetry of Edmund Spenser*, ed. William Nelson, Columbia University Press, New York, 1961, p. 151) has more to recommend it than Dunlop's account, but it must be noted that there is no precedent for this pattern of repetition in other sequences, and no particular reason in this sequence for a repetition of such a mood. The position of the sonnet, between one about the blessedness of the lover's lot and one about stamping out lustful thoughts, does not seem to be an appropriate place to repeat an earlier mood of pining and complaint.
    A difficulty with both Dunlop's and Martz's views is that they do not explain the minor alterations in the second sonnet. Lever's account of the repetition as a sign of carelessness in the preparation of the 1595 edition (Lever, op. cit., p. 101) has the advantage of accounting for this, and seems as reasonable as any explanation offered so far. The minor alterations in LXXXIII (e.g. the differences in spelling and 'having it' being replaced by 'seeing it') suggest two manuscript versions of the sonnet, a situation which would make its repetition by mistake quite feasible.
20. See below pp. 113–18.
21. For a fuller description of this sonnet, see below pp. 111–13.
22. The notion that Neo-platonism is a body of doctrine which Spenser accepts without reservation is challenged below in Chapter 5; it is argued in this chapter that it is difficult to substantiate the view that

progress in the lover's courtship depends on his spiritual and emotional development towards perfection.

23. For a fuller discussion of both these sonnets and of the idea that Spenser's lover challenges spiritual ideals by allowing his mistress the central place in his life, see below pp. 124–9.
24. Martz, op. cit., p. 167; Lever, op. cit., p. 124; P. Bayley, *Edmund Spenser: Prince of Poets*, Hutchinson University Library, London, 1971, p. 87 and Neely, op. cit., p. 373.
25. Peter M. Cummings, 'Spenser's *Amoretti* as an Allegory of Love', *Texas Studies in Literature and Language*, Summer 1970, p. 172.
26. Janet Scott points out that Tasso's poem 'Questa fera gentil' is a source for Spenser's sonnet LXVII. Janet Scott, 'The Sources of Spenser's *Amoretti*', *Modern Language Review*, vol. xxii, 1927, p. 195. The Petrarch sonnet is CXC. In that sonnet the deer wears the sign 'Nessun mi tocchi', but disappears leaving the lover alone. The Petrarch sonnet is also, of course, the model for Sir Thomas Wyatt's 'Who so list to hount'.
27. Lever, op. cit., p. 125.
28. There is some ambiguity in the syntax as to whether the 'mylder looke' belongs to the huntsman or the hunter, though, as Casady points out, the 'mylder looke' almost certainly modifies 'me' rather than 'she' (There she, beholding me with mylder looke'), Casady, op. cit., p. 100.
29. G. K. Hunter, 'Spenser's *Amoretti* and the English Sonnet Tradition' in Judith M. Kennedy and James A. Reither, *A Theatre for Spenserians*, University of Toronto Press, Toronto, 1973, p. 125.

2.   The Mistress

> Who is Silvia? what is she,
> That all our swains commend her?
>
> (*Two Gentlemen of Verona*, IV.ii.40–41)

The Elizabethan sonnet mistress is, generally speaking, a conventional figure whose main function it to provide a focus for poetic exploration of the emotional and spiritual predicaments of her forlorn suitor. The pattern is for the mistress to be of the fairest beauty and the highest virtue. She invariably fails to respond to her admirer's suit, and her cruelty, or what the lover sees as her cruelty, leaves him broken-hearted, wan and dispirited.

The sonnet mistress is often described as being without individuality – existing 'only as the sum total of her resemblances to other things'.[1] Giles Fletcher acknowledges this quality in the sonnet mistress when he describes his own mistress figure, Licia:

> If thou muse, what my LICIA is? Take her to be some DIANA, at the least chaste; or some MINERVA: no VENUS, fairer far. It may be she is Learning's Image, or some heavenly wonder: which the Precisest may not mislike. Perhaps under that name I have shadowed '[The Holy] Discipline.' It may be, I mean that kind courtesy which I found at the Patroness of these Poems, it may be some College. It may be my conceit, and pretend nothing. Whatsoever it be; if thou like it, take it![2]

Accounts of the mistress offered by sonnet lovers, at least in the minor sequences, are virtually interchangeable: golden hair, sapphire eyes, ivory skin, ruby lips, pearly teeth, lily-white hands, rosy cheeks and snowy breasts are the hallmarks of physical perfection. When a lover describes the whiteness of his mistress's hands, or the goldenness of her hair, for example, he is not usually describing the individuality of his mistress's beauty, but its excellence in a general sense. The whiteness of the hands of Constable's Diana, which causes the leaves of the lily to pale in envy, (Part I set 3, I)[3], is similar to that of Zepheria's 'lillie hands' (XII); to the 'snow-white hand' of Tofte's Laura (Part 1, XXI); and to those of Fowler's mistress, whose 'quhytnes graces and dothe glad my vewe' (XVII). Lodge's Phillis has golden hair ('And golde more pure then gold dothe guilde thy haire', XXII) which is indistinguishable from the golden hair of Griffin's Fidessa, except in terms of the purity of its goldenness ('My Ladies haire is threads of beaten gold', XXXIX).

Similarly, the saint-like spiritual perfection of one mistress is much the same as that of another. Samuel Daniel's Delia is 'Sacred on earth, design'd a Saint above' (VI), William Smith's Chloris is her lover's 'Sweet Saint' (XXII), just as Fowler's Bellisa is his 'sweit Sante' (VII). Drayton's mistress is 'my good Angell in my soule divine' (XVIII), and 'My soule-shrin'd saint' (LIII) whilst Griffin's Fidessa is worshipped as 'my saint, the gods and saints among' (XXXVI). Sometimes the saint-like, angelic exterior conceals a cruel heart. Drayton's angel is also his 'sweete Angell-divell' (XX), just as the 'angel's face' of Linche's Diella is a trap (XXII), and the saint-like qualities and graces of Barnes's Parthenophe are as weeds because of her mercilessness (XXVIII). Thus, in general, the descriptions of spiritual qualities in the minor sequences do no more than do the descriptions of physical qualities to differentiate one mistress from another.

Following the example of Petrarch, the minor sonneteers tend to cast the mistress in the limited role of one who is disdainful of, and who constantly rejects, her admirer's advances. Variations in the degree of disdain and rejection can occur: some sonnet mistresses appear to be more cold-hearted than others. Percy's Coelia is virulent in her rejection of her lover. On a chance meeting of their feet, for example, she moves her foot away 'as though, in very sooth, a snake had bit it.' Delia, on the other hand, shows some mercy by granting her lover a look:

> She thinks a looke may recompense my care
> And so with lookes prolonges my long'lookt ease. (XXI)

But despite variations in the intensity of rejection, the prevailing convention in the minor sequences is that the mistress is presented as a cruel fair, who continually meets her lover's advances with proud disdain.

It is, then, usually only the name of the mistress, or some small detail of background or behaviour which distinguishes her from other sonnet mistresses in the minor sequences of the period. Even the names that are chosen for the mistress usually deny her any special identity. The names are normally classical in origin (Diana, Parthenophe, Zepheria, Phillis), and/or they refer to some abstraction – Celia (heavenliness), Diella and Delia (presumably a play on the words *l'idée, idea or ideal*), and Fidessa (faithfulness). The names of the mistress figures tend to diminish rather than increase the sense of individuality conveyed in the figures' descriptions.

In the portrayal of the mistress in their sequences, Shakespeare, Sidney and Spenser all depart from convention in significant ways. In two of the sequences, the physical appearance of the mistress represents a deviation from the usual pattern. Shakespeare's mistress has black hair and dark eyes, and Stella's eyes are black. In all three sequences the behaviour of the mistress differs from the norm. The Dark Lady apparently grants sexual favours (as in sonnets CXXXVII, CXXXVIII); Stella is rather freer with her kisses than the usual sonnet mistress (as in sonnets LXXX and LXXXI); and Elizabeth eventually accepts her lover's advances, making their relationship a reciprocal one.

Shakespeare and Spenser differ from other sonneteers in the naming of the mistress and of the sequences themselves. Most sequences take their title either from the name of the mistress (*Delia, Diana*, etc.) or from the name of both lover and mistress (*Parthenophil and Parthenophe, Astrophil and Stella*). Shakespeare, in keeping with the enigmatic nature of his characters, does not name the mistress in his sequence, a fact which contributes to the sense that she is not one of the mere abstractions of many of the Elizabethan sonnet sequences. Shakespeare's sequence is also unnamed.[4]

Spenser's choice of title, the *Amoretti*, is unusual in that it refers to the poems themselves rather than to the character(s) of the courtship. His title is drawn from the contemporary Italian rather than the classical tradition, a fact which serves to link his sequence with the traditions of Dante and Petrarch. The title may mean simply 'love sonnets', a meaning which is now obsolete, but it may also have had the sense of 'little love offerings', or 'love tokens'.[5] The reference in the title to the poems themselves, draws attention to Spenser's notion of the sequence as an artefact of 'leaves, lines, and rymes' (sonnet I) which the lover is offering to his mistress as a gift or token of love.

Spenser's choice of name for his mistress (mentioned only once during the sequence, in contrast to Sidney's more frequent references to the name *Stella*) is also unusual in that the name is distinctively English, and of contemporary rather than classical reference. The name *Elizabeth* was not common in England until the end of the fifteenth century, but by 1560 it accounted for 16 per cent of female baptismal names, and by 1600 over 20 per cent. Its popularity was, of course, due to the length and success of the reign of Queen Elizabeth I.[6]

The name *Elizabeth* had both personal and political meaning for Spenser. It was the name of both his mother and his second wife, Elizabeth Boyle,[7] whom he married just prior to the publication of the sonnets. It was also the name of his sovereign, a fact acknowledged by Spenser within the sequence itself. The ways in which he refers to the queen in the poems do have a certain ambivalence. She is given several roles: that of a political leader who also has the powers of a divinity ('most sacred Empresse . . . my dear dred' XXXIII); that of his patron ('my sovereigne Queene most kind / that honour and large richesse to me lent', LXXIIII) and that of the object of worship and adoration of a humble suitor. In a sonnet begging leave from his labours of writing *The Faerie Queene*, Spenser asks permission to sing the praises of his mistress in the interval before he returns to his task. These praises, he acknowledges, will 'yet be low and meane, / fit for the handmayd of the Faery Queene' (LXXX). As Leonard Tennenhouse points out in his book *Power on Display*, 'to seek patronage came to be understood as an act of wooing', so that Elizabeth became the inspiration and the object of much love poetry.[8] Spenser's *Amoretti* provides a remarkably clear instance of the links between the Petrarchan idealisation of the mistress in Elizabethan poetry and complimentary courtship of the queen as supreme patron. It is, however, unusual for the queen to be given this position in a sonnet sequence, since it establishes her as superior to, or even a rival of, the mistress. Spenser's casting of the queen in this very elevated role is another way in which his attitude to the mistress figure can be differentiated from that of other sonneteers.

Critics have not always been willing to include Spenser's mistress in the company of the Dark Lady and Stella as one of the more individualised sonnet mistresses, and often see her as a merely conventional figure. Legouis, for example, claims that Spenser, in his most personal poems, the *Amoretti* and *Epithalamion*, 'offers us the picture not so much of a distinct and individual woman, as of the typical woman'.[9] Cruttwell, who is under the erroneous impression that the mistress is unnamed in Spenser's sequence, also claims that she is 'never analysed, never individualised',[10] whilst Ricks describes her role as 'passive'. He argues that she 'waits in Platonic serenity for her lover to be worthy of her'.[11]

Some critics have gone to the opposite extreme and seen Spenser's persona as a fully realized dramatic figure. Fowler describes her as 'a keenly intelligent witty person . . . an Elizabeth Bennet rather than a Penelope Rich – with a firm, unmistakeable character'.[12] Barthel compares her with the 'Shakespearean Beatrice confronted with a very forthcoming Benedick, though she may more clearly resemble Rosalind putting her Orlando through his lover's paces'.[13] Hallett Smith goes further and claims that she is not only more fully characterized than the lover of the sequence, but 'more elaborately presented, both physically and spiritually, than any of the Delias, Dianas, Phillises, Lauras, or even Stellas of the time'.[14]

Accurate description of the character of Elizabeth in the *Amoretti* necessarily involves a more analytical account than has so far been attempted of the ways in which the impression of a character is conveyed in the sequence. Comparison between Spenser's practice in this respect and that of his contemporary sonneteers is one of the means employed in the following discussion to help define the nature of his distinctive achievement in the creation of the mistress persona.

The persona of the mistress in Elizabethan sonnets is created in various ways. These include: descriptive accounts which the lover gives of his mistress's appearance, character or behaviour; the assumptions which Spenser indicates the lover makes about the mistress he is addressing; and occasional reports of what the mistress says, either by direct or indirect quotation. Spenser's sonnets display each of these means of presentation of the mistress figure. In some ways his methods are similar to those of the conventional sonneteers of the period, but there are also many ways in which the methods of presentation of the mistress in Spenser's *Amoretti* can be distinguished not only from the practices of the minor sonneteers, but also from those of Shakespeare and Sidney.

The descriptive accounts which a lover gives of his mistress's character and behaviour in any sequence need to be treated with caution. It is usual for the lover to be torn between contradictory impulses of praise and blame and to deliver exaggerated accounts of the qualities which inspire him to his celebration of, and lamentations about, the mistress. In the minor sequences the question of how deserving the mistress is of the praise or blame which is meted out to her by the lover rarely arises. She is presented as the cause of the extremes of emotion expressed by the lover: she is someone whose beauty and perfection inspire praise, and whose disdain arouses frustration and anger, but little or nothing is learned about her as a character in the drama.

Shakespeare, on the other hand, does bring into question the reliability of the lover's perceptions of his mistress. He presents the lover as someone who is confused about his own perceptions and who cannot be relied upon to throw any light on the degree of his mistress's worthiness. The lover continually ponders the question of whether the mistress deserves his flattery or criticism, but the reader is given little or no guidance as to the answer to this question.

Shakespeare's lover confesses that his eyes 'have no correspondence with true sight' (CXLVIII), that his reason 'hath left me' and that his senses and wits tell him one thing whilst his heart tells him another (CXLVII). It is as if each of the faculties, which normally cooperate and function harmoniously, takes on an independent existence. His faculties appear to influence each other in perverse and unexpected ways. At one time his eyes will see 'a thousand errors' in his mistress, whilst his heart 'loves what they despise' (CXLI). At another time, his eyes will encourage his heart to make judgements about his mistress which his heart knows to be false (CXXXVII). He has to struggle with a multitude of ideas in order to bring the evidence of his senses, what he judges to be true, and what tradition and the world tell him to be true into accord CXLVIII. In spite of the lover's attempts throughout the Dark Lady sonnets to view his situation from all possible angles, he is a victim of a 'false plague' (CXLVIII) of confused perceptions, and cannot see clearly or without bias.

The lover's conflicting feelings about the nature of the Dark Lady do settle into some kind of pattern (she has an individual beauty which he finds irresistible; his sexual attraction to her is overwhelming, but he fears, and is almost certain, that she is untrue to him in word and deed); but, even so, areas of uncertainty remain, and are left unresolved. Is she as dark as he sometimes thinks she is? And if she is dark, in the moral sense, then what is the degree of her darkness? Is she, like Cressida, guilty of infidelity but accused of being a whore, or is she, in fact, promiscuous 'the wide world's common place?'(CXXXVII).

Spenser's lover is less confused than Shakespeare's about the perceptions he has of his mistress. He displays a great deal of confidence in his own opinions, even when they are apparently contradictory. On the one hand, he offers his mistress the rarest of tributes and the highest of praise. The qualities which have special meaning for him are 'her mind adornd with vertues manifold' (XV), her 'gentle spright' (LXXXI) and her steadfastness (LIX).

On the other hand, there are a number of sonnets in which the lover makes far-fetched accusations against his mistress. It is conventional for a mistress to be accused of having a hard heart (XVIII, LI) and of behaving tyrannically (X), or cruelly (XI, XXXVI, XLVIII, XLIX), but Spenser's lover goes beyond this. He accuses her of being 'more cruell and more salvage wylde / then either Lyon or the Lyonesse' (XX); more harmful than 'beastes of bloody race' (XXXI); as deadly as the Cockatrice (XLIX); as devious as the panther (LIII) and as greedy and heartless as the tiger (LVI).[15]

Unlike Shakespeare, who leaves the reader's doubts about the lover's perceptions unresolved, Spenser positively counters many of his lover's perceptions, and suggests their absurdity. He usually leaves the lover's praise of his mistress uncommented upon, but Spenser uses the lover's criticism of the mistress as a way of highlighting the limitations of his judgements. Spenser has a number of ways of indicating that the lover's criticism of his mistress is ridiculously extreme and not to be entertained.[16]

The lover's presentation of the mistress as a predatory, bestial figure who enjoys her bloody massacres represents more extreme criticism than that offered by almost any other lover persona in an Elizabethan sequence, except for Shakespeare's. The extreme nature of this condemnation, particularly in the context of a sequence with a happy ending, tends to undermine the credibility of the lover's accounts. The fact that he nearly always presents his attacks on the mistress in a way which maximizes their dramatic impact[17] also suggests there is little foundation to his hostile descriptions of the mistress, and that it is his emotional response to her rejection of him that is being expressed. His accounts of her behaviour in these instances are certainly out of keeping with the mistress's character as it is described elsewhere in the sequence, and they are obviously at odds with the complete approval which is implied in his choice of her as his bride.

Sidney, similarly, chooses to counter Astrophil's views of Stella on several occasions during the sequence. He tends to use the sonnets of praise rather than the sonnets of blame to suggest a modification of the portrait Astrophil presents. There is very little direct complaint about Stella in the sequence.[18] Astrophil does not often indulge in violent arguments to express his feelings, but where he does express annoyance he usually directs it at some abstract idea (e.g. Reason (X), Love (LXV) and Thought (XCI)), or at the hated Lord Rich (e.g. XXIIII, LXXVIII). Astrophil's praise of Stella is fulsome, but Sidney has subtle ways of suggesting that she may be of more shallow and fickle nature than Astrophil perceives.[19] Neither Sidney nor Spenser presents perspectives of this kind consistently throughout their sequences, but there are many sonnets by both in which the lover's accounts of the mistress are undermined or positively challenged.

Some of the accounts of the mistress offered by Spenser's lover reveal as little about her as the descriptions offered by the minor sonneteers, described above. In many ways Spenser's Elizabeth conforms to the pattern of the conventional mistress in appearance and behaviour. She has 'golden tresses' (XXXVII; XV, LXXIII) and is of 'fayre cruell' disposition (XLIX). Her eyes are like sapphires, her skin ivory (XV), and her breast 'lyke lillyes, ere theyr leaves be shed' (LXIIII). Her voice makes its way through a 'gate with pearles and rubyes richly dight' (LXXXI); her hands are 'lilly hands' (sonnet I) and her cheeks are coloured with 'the rose' (LXXXI). She possesses saint-like spiritual perfection: she is an angel of 'blessed looke' (sonnet I), and a 'sweet Saynt' (XXII); yet her heart is 'stubborne' and 'hard', and is likened to steel, flint and marble (XVIII, LI).

These accounts of the mistress's appearance and behaviour may be indistinguishable from the descriptions offered by many of the other sonneteers. But there are occasions when Spenser moves beyond the limitations of stock description and conventional account.

In sonnets in which the mistress is described in a relatively conventional way, Spenser often introduces a thought which suggests that the mistress is something more than a sum of ideal qualities. The kiss sonnet (LXIIII), for example, expresses in catalogue form a tribute to the delights of the mistress's physical being. These are described through the metaphor of the fragrances of a garden of sweet flowers. The last line of the sonnet ('but her sweet odour did them all excell'), whilst staying within the terms of the metaphor, introduces a break in the catalogue and helps to establish the idea that the mistress has a distinct individuality. Her 'sweet odour' represents this individuality; it is something which cannot be located in the perfection of her outward form, or in the combination of her physical delights.[20]

Spenser's habit of having his lover praise some quality which is not ordinarily part of the conventional catalogue of compliments, usually in a position of importance in the sonnet, also helps to create the illusion that the mistress is different from a sonnet mistress of conventional mould. In sonnet XV, for example, after a catalogue of fairly conventional forms of praise, Spenser creates a delightful, capping compliment in the final lines:

> But that which fairest is, but few behold,
> her mind adornd with vertues manifold.

There is further praise for her mind in LV, where it is described as 'pure immortall hye'. The mistress of this sonnet is both cruel and fair, a conventional role for her, but her fairness is analysed not only in physical terms, but also in terms of the quality of her mind, an analysis which is less usual.

The sequence opens with a sonnet in which the mistress is described as a figure endowed with the conventional attributes of saintly perfection; an angel with lily hands, starry eyes, and power over her lover's life and happiness. Accounts of this kind occur intermittently throughout the sequence. Yet elsewhere the special power of the mistress's spiritual nature is described in a way that makes clear the personal value that nature has for the lover. In the sestet of VIII, for example, the light of the mistress's presence is described as something which touches every part of the lover's being. The mistress's presence, like light, transforms the lover's world from one which is chaotic to one which is calm, peaceful and meaningful. It is the unique power of his mistress's presence which brings about this miracle.[21]

Spenser suggests the mistress's individuality in other ways. The addresses the lover chooses to make to his mistress assume the existence of certain qualities in her as his audience. She is, after all, the reader of these 'leaves, lines and rymes', which were composed for her perusal (sonnet I), and at times the lover capitalizes on this fact. Sometimes he chooses to be daring in what he says to her, or he may exaggerate in a comical way, or again he may choose to make jokes at her expense.

It is indicated quite early in the sequence that the mistress is not simply a characterless recipient of her lover's addresses. In sonnet III, although the lover does not address his mistress directly, his description of the disastrous effects which her heavenly beauty and virtue have upon him suggests the presence of an addressee with a sense of humour, capable of appreciating the comedy of the lover's extravagant report of the paralysis of his powers of communication brought about by her transcendent qualities. The portrait he gives of himself exaggerates the way in which her beauty turns him into her utterly incapacitated and dumbstruck admirer:

> So when my toung would speak her praises dew,
> it stopped is with thoughts astonishment:
> and when my pen would write her titles true,
> it ravisht is with fancies wonderment.[22]

Again, in sonnet XII, a light-hearted sonnet about the lover's being ambushed and captured by forces residing in the mistress's 'hart- thrilling eies', the lover assumes a mistress attentive to the tone of his address. The argument he presents to extricate himself from his position of weakness is delivered with boldness and poise. He speaks directly to his mistress against her eyes, as though her eyes had a life of their own. He begs justice from her:

> So Ladie now to you I doo complaine
> against your eies that iustice I may gaine.

The request is disarmingly offered, and the tact and diplomacy he uses to phrase it, amusingly inappropriate, since it is, after all, her eyes which he wants to put on trial!

At other stages of the sequence the mistress's sense of humour is conveyed differently. In the embroidery sonnet (LXXI), for example, the subject of her embroidery (that of a bee in a garden of flowers, with a spider lurking in wait for it)[23] can be interpreted as an indirect statement of her view of their relationship. Her silently embroidering an emblematic account of their relationship which casts the lover in the role of predator comically contrasts with the lover's outbursts in which he describes the mistress as predator, and himself as helpless victim.[24] Her choice of image (the spider lurking in wait for the bee) is also in striking contrast to the images of domesticated, tamed animal life which the lover uses to describe their relationship near this point in the sequence: he uses the bird in the cage as an emblem of the 'bands' of marriage (LXV), and the deer in captivity as a symbol of the mistress's submission (LXVII); and he describes his heart as being like a bird who wants to be encaged in her (LXXIII). It is the lover who articulates the idea that the mistress is aware of the symbolism of her design, but even if he is crediting her with something she does not intend, his jokes about her intentions expressed in his development of the spider/bee image are directed at her.

It would be inaccurate to imply that the lover consistently addresses the mistress as though she were a figure of developed wit and sensitivity. There are some sonnets in which the lover complains of a mistress who is completely insensitive and impervious to his most strident complaint (e.g. X, XLI). But in most of the examples of sonnets in which the mistress is assumed to be the heartless recipient of her lover's address (for example, lines 3, 4 and 9–12 of XX, and all the occasions where comparisons are made between the mistress and predatory beasts), the statements which the lover makes are usually more a source of information about the lover's own moods and feelings than a source of information about the nature of the mistress. Her role as audience in these sonnets is not being invoked in order to suggest the qualities she possesses; she is, rather, the cruel fair who must be impressed by the extent of her suitor's frustration and unhappiness.

In most Elizabethan sonnet sequences the mistress is presented as the mute object of her lover's address. But in some sequences the poet employs, in the argument of certain poems, either direct quotation from a supposed speech of the mistress, or some reported statement by the mistress, such as that contained in Shakespeare's sonnet CXLIX 'Canst thou, O cruel, say I love thee not'.[25] The function of quoted and reported speech in the rhetorical strategies of individual sonnets is often complex in Elizabethan sequences, so that what the mistress says, or is reported to say, must be interpreted with extreme care.

In Shakespeare's sequence, for example, the context usually obscures, or casts doubt on, the meaning of the mistress's comments, and the syntactical arrangement of her statements increases their ambiguity. This is, in part, a projection of the lover's confused and tortuous thinking, and a reflection of his perpetual ambivalence about the nature of his mistress. Her words add to the ambiguity which surrounds her, rather than cast light upon the nature of her relationship with her suitor, or with his rivals.

In the opening of sonnet CXXXVIII, it is reported by Shakespeare's lover persona that his mistress swears she is the soul of truthfulness ('When my love swears that she is made of truth'). Such a statement by the mistress is also implied in the second line of sonnet CLII ('But thou are twice forsworn to me love swearing'). Both sonnets play with ideas of truth and falsehood, swearing and forswearing. The word 'swear' almost always appears in contexts which raise questions about the truth or value of what is sworn, or the degree of conviction with which the swearing has been undertaken. The lover repeatedly doubts the mistress's words, referring, for example, to her 'false-speaking tongue' (CXXXVIII). In such a context it is unwise to accept at face value the mistress's repeated oaths, or even the lover's claim that she has made such oaths.

Much of the amusement generated in sonnet CXXXVIII has its source in the lover's wittily proffered account of the elaborate procedures to which he and his mistress are silently committed in the cause of their union, and to the paradoxical notion that their relationship is given form and expression through a fabrication of lies and unspoken sentiments. As the sonnet unfolds, it is learned that the mistress's oath, according to the lover, is another of her lies, and part of their compact to flatter one another.

The narrator of Shakespeare's sonnet is placed in a much more vulnerable position than the mistress because he is the one who has confided his thoughts to the reader; the mistress's thoughts, in contrast, are unknown. She may be a willing conspirator with him in their games, but it is possible that he is deluded into thinking she is playing the game when she is not, or that she is playing a different game from the one he imagines engages her.[26]

The 'I hate . . . not you' of CXLV epitomizes the confusion and doubt which attach to the words of Shakespeare's mistress figure. 'I hate' occurs in line 2 and 'not you' in line 14, with the body of the sonnet in between (so that at one level the poem is a rather playful joke). The lips that utter the words in this sonnet are not the same as 'those lips of thine, / That have profaned their scarlet ornaments, / And sealed false bonds of love' (CXLII). Nor are they the lips of the woman of the previous sonnet (CXLIIII) who wooed purity to corruption. That fiend 'from heav'n to hell is flown away', and we have instead a mistress whose heart is suddenly filled with mercy and gentleness, or at least this is how the lover interprets her behaviour at this moment.

The lover treats her change of heart as though it were of major consequence, and speaks as though she has saved his life, drawing comfort and pleasure from her words. He describes her heart as merciful and biddable, yet all her heart actually encourages her to say is 'I hate . . . not you' – a rather doubtful compliment, that, at best, makes it clear that he is not the present object of her hatred. It is not, after all, that the mistress is confessing to loving, but just that, in a moment of pity, or some other emotion, she turns the force of her hatred away from him. Whatever the mistress feels, and the lover may be wrong about what she feels, her behaviour is still taunting (she takes her time about putting him out of his misery, if, indeed that is her intention), and relatively disdainful. The wordplay that has been associated with the couplet (*Hathaway* (maiden name of Shakespeare's wife) *hate away* and *Ann* (first name of Shakespeare's wife) / *And*)[27] also raises questions about how seriously the lover's interpretation of his mistress's words is to be taken.

The mistress's intentions or purpose in delivering her words in the fashion described, the precise meaning of her statement, and the degree of her positive or negative feeling towards the lover remain uncertain in this sonnet. Shakespeare consistently uses the words of his Dark Lady to deepen the confusion which surrounds her and confound any possibility of unravelling the mystery of her nature, or of the nature of her relationship with her lover(s).

Sidney uses Stella's words to rather different purpose in *Astrophil and Stella*. On the whole, what Stella says confirms Astrophil's growing concern that Stella is more interested in the game, the pursuit, than in love itself. Astrophil begins to detect a change of heart in Stella at sonnet LXXXVI, and in the Ninth Song he expresses his fears that Stella does not love him. This does not alter his feelings for her, and her tears give him hope that she suffers as he does (LXXXVII). His doubts, however, are there and tend to be confirmed from what we learn of Stella from her own words and behaviour as they are reported by Astrophil.

An example of the use of Stella's quoted speech occurs in the Fourth Song. Stella's refusal of Astrophil's requests 'No, no, no, no, my Deare, let be', is the refrain of every verse and so, in a sense, raises the problem of distinguishing between what is there to conform to the literary form of the song, and what is there as her response. Amusingly enough, Stella's denial is heard in the context of Astrophil's having playfully told her that 'two Negatives affirme' (LXIII).[28] In the earlier verses, Stella's 'let be' suggests that Astrophil should not ask her to take him to herself, ever again (unless four negatives make a very strong positive), but in the last verse there is something close to a volte-face on Stella's part. This is created by her same reply's being matched to different material:

> Wo to me, and do you sweare
> Me to hate? But I forbeare,
> Cursed be my destines all,
> That brought me so high to fall:
> Soone with my death I will please thee.
> 'No, no, no, no, my Deare, let be.'

In saying 'No' to his death, Stella is implicitly encouraging him to continue as before. Scanlon overlooks this when he quotes the verse, without including Stella's reply, to prove that Astrophil has realized his appetite's defeat.[29] For Stella, the game is paramount and there is no doubt that Astrophil enjoys the skill with which she plays, though he would like her to go further than she does.

There is a similar picture of Stella in the Eighth Song, in which she tells Astrophil of her love for him, but regrets that honour and fear of public disgrace demand she refuse him:

> Then she spake; her speech was such,
> As not eares but hart did tuch:
> While such wise she love denied,
> As yet love she signified.

> 'Astrophil' sayd she, 'my love
> Cease in these effects to prove:

Now be still, yet still beleeve me,
Thy griefe more then death would grieve me.

'If that any thought in me,
Can tast comfort but of thee,
Let me, fed with hellish anguish,
Joylesse, hopelesse, endlesse languish.

'If those eyes you praised, be
Half so deere as you to me,
Let me home returne, starke blinded
Of those eyes, and blinder minded.

'If to secret of my hart,
I do any wish impart,
Where thou are not formost placed,
Be both wish and I defaced.

'If more may be sayd, I say,
All my blisse in thee I lay;
If thou love, my love content thee,
For all love, all faith is meant thee.

'Trust me while I thee deny,
In my selfe the smart I try,
Tyran honour doth thus use thee,
Stella's selfe might not refuse thee.

'Therefore, Deere, this no more move,
Least, though I leave not thy love,
Which too deep in me is framed,
I should blush when thou art named.'

Therewithall away she went,
Leaving him so passion rent,
With what she had done and spoken,
That therewith my song is broken.

It is difficult not to share Astrophil's surprise at Stella's sudden
departure ('Therewithall away she went') after her long and ardent
declaration of love. Stella's protestations of love are somewhat
undermined by the reasons she gives for leaving Astrophil, as well as
by the abruptness of her departure. She is clever at deflecting blame

and claiming that 'Tyran honour' is the villain of the piece, rather than 'Stella's selfe'. Having removed the blame from herself, she begs Astrophil's trust and rewards it with a command that he cease his suit: 'Therefore, Deere, this no more move'. (The endearment sounds faintly patronizing at this point in the song, since it is attached to a command to leave her alone, and immediately precedes her obviously planned departure.) If Stella had been totally chaste during Astrophil's pursuit of her and so had demonstrated how highly she rated Honour, then it would have been easier to accept her submission to 'Tyran honour' at this stage as a genuine, though painful, choice, and to accept her sudden departure as the grievous experience she claims that it is. By raising doubts in the reader's mind about the genuineness of Stella's words, Sidney is able to hint that Astrophil may be deceived in his belief that

> While such wise she love denied
> As yet love she signified.

Astrophil himself eventually comes to the conclusion in the Ninth Song that Stella cannot love him because she is prepared to leave him helpless:

> Is that love? forsooth I trow,
> If I saw my good dog grieved,
> And a helpe for him did know,
> My love should not be beleeved,
> But he were by me releeved.

> No, she hates me, wellaway,
> Faining love, somewhat to please me:
> For she knowes, if she display
> All her hate, death soone would seaze me,
> And of hideous torments ease me.

There is further intrigue between Astrophil and Stella in the Eleventh Song. Stella shows herself ready to take up their bantering games again, at least until she thinks she hears someone coming. The setting is a suitably romantic one – a forbidden meeting on a dark night with Astrophil calling up to Stella's window. Her lively tone and willing involvement in their conversations do not suggest someone who is haunted by the pain of separation, but rather someone who confidently enjoys the flattery of her admirers, and who can safely question this particular admirer about the potential excitement to him of 'new beauties'. Once '_Argus_ eyes' are on the horizon, however, the game is over for Stella, and she insists that Astrophil leave her.

Stella does to a certain extent remain the 'black eyed effigy' that Martz describes, 'around whom Astrophil performs his brilliant Portrait of the Lover as a very young dog',[30] but she is not simply an effigy. As the songs in which she speaks indicate, she is presented as someone who is more interested in the games of courtship than in any possibilities of the achievement of its goals. Spenser's Elizabeth delights in the games of courtship, too, but her involvement is presented as a sign of willingness for a deeper commitment, whereas Stella's is not. It is difficult to avoid the conclusion that Stella's reason for leaving Astrophil is that she has tired of her games with him, and does not wish to continue them, except, perhaps, occasionally.

Spenser uses the words of his mistress or her reported speech in quite a different manner, and to different effect, from either Shakespeare or Sidney. The mistress's speech is reported rarely in Spenser's sequence, though the first occasion occurs relatively early, at sonnet XVIII, and the idea that she has been involved in exchanges with the lover is implied before this (VI, XI). In addition to this instance of reported speech, her words are quoted by the lover in XXIX and LXXV.

Sonnet XVIII deals with the idea that the mistress's hard heart is positively unnatural. The first two couplets are devoted to a fairly solemn exposition of the conventional complaint – that steel and flint are changed by wear and tear, but nothing the lover does will soften his mistress's hard heart:

> The rolling wheele that runneth often round,
> the hardest steele in tract of time doth teare:
> and drizling drops that often doe redound,
> the firmest flint doth in continuance weare.
> Yet cannot I with many a dropping teare,
> and long intreaty soften her hard hart:
> that she will once vouchsafe my plaint to heare,
> or looke with pitty on my payneful smart.

The use of 'hard' as though it had the same meaning when applied to her heart, as when applied to flint and steel, is the pivot of the lover's argument, and allows him to create the illusion that there is a logic to his comparisons of these different substances. The comparisons allow him to claim, with some conviction, that his mistress's heart is unnaturally hard, since her failure to respond to him represents virtually a defiance of the laws of nature: even steel and flint eventually show signs of being worn down. The lover claims that none of his entreaties makes any impression on his mistress's heart, as many lovers in sonnets have claimed before him, but it is clear from her responses that his entreaties do have an effect. His view of her reaction to him ('she as steele and flint doth still remayne') is contrasted with her actual responses as he describes them. He interprets her attitude as 'hard', and there is a sense in which she is unyielding, but she is not a distant or remote figure in this verse. She is presented as a good-humoured, witty, laughing figure, and the liveliness with which she plays her role makes her different from the stony-hearted figure he insists she is:

> But when I pleade, she bids me play my part,
>   and when I weep, she sayes teares are but water:
>   and when I sigh, she sayes I know the art,
>   and when I waile, she turnes hir selfe to laughter.
> So doe I weepe, and wayle, and pleade in vaine,
>   whiles she as steele and flint doth still remayne.

Her responses indicate that she is aware that his pleading, weeping, sighing, and wailing are strategies to win her. She sees through the pageants he is putting on for her benefit and teases him by refusing to be impressed by his emotional displays. She scoffs at his tears and laughs at his wailing; she chides him for not playing his part better or for playing it too well. This may not be the response he wanted from her, but nevertheless it is a response; she is not merely denying him as a matter of course.

In the 1611 and 1617 folio editions of the *Amoretti*, commas are placed after 'sayes' in lines 10 and 11, and 'teares' is spelt 'Teares'. This indicates, as the Variorum editors note, that the last four words in each line were treated in these editions as direct discourse.[31] This makes little difference to line 10, though the punctuation gives an added authenticity to what the mistress says. But in line 11, as the Variorum editors suggest, the commas, which function as inverted commas, make the antecedent of the second 'I' the lady rather than the lover ('and when I sigh she sayes, I know the art'). A declaration from the lady of this kind would confirm something that the lover has frequently claimed – that the mistress enjoys playing the games of courtship and is extremely artful at them.[32] Without the comma the statement is more likely to be about her recognition that the lover's sighs are part of the game that he is playing. The rhyme link with 'play my part' in line 9 tends to support the reading that she is accusing him of merely playing a role.

The positioning of the commas does not, in the end, make a great deal of difference to the interpretation of the sonnet, or of the sequence as a whole, as it does not suggest any new dimension to the mistress's character. The issue that is raised is the degree of the mistress's consciousness of her game-playing. She does consistently meet her lover's moves with countermoves, and so, to that extent, she is aware of the 'game' element in the courtship. The inclusion of the commas suggests a mistress who is a slightly more knowing, more deliberate participant in the courtship but it is a difference in degree, not in kind.

Sonnet LIIII reinforces the view of Spenser's mistress as a witty and involved participant in the courtship. In this sonnet the mistress's words are not reported, but her mockery and laughter are described in a pattern which is similar to that described in XVIII:

> Of this worlds Theatre in which we stay,
>   my love lyke the Spectator ydly sits
>   beholding me that all the pageants play,
>   disguysing diversly my troubled wits.
> Sometimes I ioy when glad occasion fits,
>   and mask in myrth lyke to a Comedy:
>   soone after when my ioy to sorrow flits,
>   I waile and make my woes a Tragedy.
> Yet she beholding me with constant eye,
>   delights not in my merth nor rues my smart:
>   but when I laugh she mocks, and when I cry
>   she laughes, and hardens evermore her hart.
> What then can move her? if nor merth nor mone,
>   she is no woman, but a sencelesse stone.

The lover uses the metaphor of the world as a theatre, himself the player and his mistress the audience/Spectator. He presents himself as a player engaged in a frenzied alternation of comic and tragic roles in order to impress the mistress, whilst she sits as an idle spectator. In her discussion of this sonnet, Judith Kalil assumes wrongly, I think, that the 'Spectator' of line 2 is a personification of the persona's love.[33] But it seems unnecessary to assume the presence of two audiences. The mistress is clearly the audience in the third quatrain, and also, surely, the 'Spectator' in line 2. The mistress's idleness contrasts with the lover's frenetic changes of mask,[34] and her reactions are the opposite of the ones he is hoping to elicit from her:

> but when I laugh she mocks, and when I cry
> she laughes and hardens evermore her hart.

A circular pattern is described, beginning with his laughter and ending with hers (though, of course, their laughter is differently motivated), and containing a chain of action and counteraction in between. The enjambement in lines 11–12 suggests the continuity of the action/counteraction pattern. Her wilful failure to be the audience he wants her to be eventually drives him to insult –

> no woman, but a sencelesse stone.

Yet, she is a participant in the game and shows constancy in playing it, and determination to win it. As Dunlop points out, she 'does not leave the performance',[35] and furthermore she manages to give the impression that she is positively enjoying it.

Another occasion when the mistress's words are quoted by her lover occurs in sonnet XXIX. What she has to say here again reinforces the idea of her, developed in XVIII and LIIII, as someone who deliberately plays at being contrary, rather than someone who is constantly disdainful as a matter of form. In XXVIII and XXIX, Spenser uses a series of shifts in the symbolic meaning of the laurel or bay, in order to create a context which makes it possible for lover and mistress to turn the arguments that are used against them to their own advantage.

In XXVIII, the lover tells of his hope that his mistress's wearing of the bay is a sign of her favour:

> The laurell leafe, which you this day doe weare,
>   gives me great hope of your relenting mynd:
>   for since it is the badg which I doe beare,
>   ye bearing it doe seeme to me inclind:

> The powre thereof, which ofte in me I find,
>   let it lykewise your gentle brest inspire
>   with sweet infusion, and put you in mind
>   of that proud mayd, whom now those leaves attyre:
> Proud *Daphne* scorning Phæbus lovely fyre,
>   on the Thessalian shore from him did flee:
>   for which the gods in theyr revengefull yre
>   did her transforme into a laurell tree.
> Then fly no more fayre love from Phebus chace,
>   but in your brest his leafe and love embrace.

At this stage, the leaf referred to is worn as an ornament by the mistress; but since it is also the 'badg' he bears (as poet), he interprets her wearing it as a sign of her relenting mind. The lover recounts the story of Daphne's fate to his mistress in the hope that she will take warning from the story of Daphne, who was turned into a laurel tree as a punishment for her pride. He instructs the mistress to become infused with inspiration from the laurel leaf as he does, though it is the leaf as a symbol of what happened to Daphne from which he expects the mistress to take inspiration.

Spenser's mistress would be unlikely to let pass an opportunity to reply to such moralizing, and her retaliation is recorded in the next sonnet. In XXIX, she challenges his interpretation that the laurel, or bay, is an indication of her favour and offers a different interpretation that quite cuts the ground from under his feet. Her account rests on the assumption that the bay (by this stage a wreath of bay leaves) is the trophy given to the victorious, who then adorn the heads of poets so that they may celebrate the victor's triumphs. The mistress's reference to 'poetes heads' is a general reference, which, in a sense, excludes the lover, or at least over-rides his assumption that the laurel is his rightful badge.

> The bay (quoth she) is of the victours borne,
>   yielded them by the vanquisht as theyr meeds,
>   and they therewith doe poetes heads adorne,
>   to sing the glory of their famous deedes.
> But sith she will the conquest challeng needs,
>   let her accept me as her faithful thrall,
>   that her great triumph which my skill exceeds,
>   I may in trump of fame blaze over all.

> Then would I decke her head with glorious bayes,
> and fill the world with her victorious prayse.

Thus, she ignores her lover's lecture, scorns his warning and claims that the wearing of the bay is an indication that he is *her* captive, rather than the other way around.

Barthel refers to this sonnet as evidence that the mistress is a more fully realized character than 'all their shadowy Stellas and Delias', adding that 'she is as capable as he of moralising over a laurel leaf'.[36] The sonnet does indeed provide evidence of the quick wit of the mistress, in the way in which she handles the lover's moralizing, as well as in her own comic retort to his pious lecture. He offers a moral lesson about the bay which he hopes will change her behaviour, whilst she outwits him with another piece of conventional folklore which gives the bay a different role altogether, and puts her in the role of victor and him in the role of vanquished.

In the final quatrain, the lover takes up her challenge and turns it back against her, though in a way which eventually heaps all the honours on her head. He picks up the idea of her casting him in the role of the vanquished, and claims a similar role, that of her faithful thrall, which makes it obligatory for her not to scorn him. As her thrall, he can acknowledge her triumph in his poetry. He will celebrate it in his verse, making the world ring with her praise, and decking her with the most glorious 'bayes' of all. (The bays are now metaphorical bays, far removed from the original laurel leaf.) The bays are returned, as it were, to the mistress, and the complicated game between them reaches a happy conclusion.

The other occasion on which the mistress's words are reported directly is LXXV, a sonnet with a more intimate setting than has been previously suggested in the sequence. Lover and mistress are engaged in walking on the strand together, the lover behaving in the manner of any romantic suitor and writing her name in the sand:

> One day I wrote her name upon the strand,
> but came the waves and washed it away:
> agayne I wrote it with a second hand,
> but came the tyde, and made my paynes his pray.
> Vayne man, sayd she, that doest in vaine assay,
> a mortall thing so to immortalize,
> for I my selve shall lyke to this decay,

> and eek my name bee wyped out lykewize.
> Not so, (quod I) let baser things devize
> to dy in dust, but you shall live by fame:
> my verse your vertues rare shall eternize,
> and in the hevens wryte your glorious name.
> Where whenas death shall all the world subdew,
> our love shall live, and later life renew.

She uses his failure to write her name without the tide's washing it away as an occasion playfully to chide him for his foolishness and vanity – an echo of his own earlier chiding of the doctor who thought he could cure the lover's spiritual illness with physical remedies ('Vayne man (quod I) that hast but little priefe' (L)).

The lover, however, is not rebuffed by the high tone of her criticism and simply takes her words about her mortality as opportunity for his rejoinder (as possibly she means him to): she shall live by his verse and her name shall be written in the heavens. His argument defeats time, woman and tide in one stroke! In the concluding couplet, he refers, not to his love for her, which he has referred to so often in the past, but to their love for each other:

> our love shall live and later life renew.

This conclusion provides a new emphasis to the often treated theme[37] deriving from Horace's ode, 'Exegi monumentum aere perennius', in that mutual love is finally stressed as the immortalizing and regenerative power, almost supplanting the poet's creative achievement.[38]

Elizabeth's reactions to her lover's various forms of courtship may, on the surface, seem akin to the disdain of the traditional sonnet mistress, but on closer examination her reactions are seen to represent involvement with, rather than detachment from, her lover. There are very few examples in other sequences of the presentation of a mistress in this way, though there are some presentations which have superficial similarities. Daniel's Delia, for example, meets her lover's tears, vows and prayers with mercilessness, but whilst her behaviour is similar in form to Elizabeth's, it is different in spirit:

> Teares, vowes, and prayers win the hardest hart:
> Teares, vowes, and prayers have I spent in vaine;

Teares, cannot soften flint, nor vowes convart,
Prayers prevaile not with a quaint disdaine.
I lose my teares, where I have lost my love,
I vowe my faith, where faith is not regarded;
I pray in vaine, a merciles to move:
So rare a faith ought better be rewarded.
Yet though I cannot win her will with teares,
Though my soules Idoll scorneth all my vowes;
Though all my prayers be to so deafe eares:
No favour though the cruell faire allowes.
Yet will I weepe, vowe, pray to cruell Shee;
Flint, Frost, Disdaine, weares, melts, and yeelds we see.

(XI)

Delia meets her lover's vows with scorn, and his prayers with deaf ears, but her failure to relent towards him seems based on indifference rather than involvement. There is nothing in Delia's reactions of the playful mind intent on winning in the game of courtship, though the lover is clearly hopeful of an eventual yielding.

Another example of similar kind occurs in Percy's *Sonnets to the Fairest Coelia*, a sequence with which it is likely Spenser was familiar since it was published the year before his own sequence, and by the same publisher, William Ponsonbie.[39] Percy's method of dramatizing his mistress's perversity is surprisingly like Spenser's. Coelia is every bit as perverse as Elizabeth, though in a less playful way. In sonnet XVI, each action of the lover is countered by an action from Coelia:

What may be thought of thine untowardness,
That movest still at every motion?
What may be hoped of so strange uncouthness,
That scorns all vows, scorns all devotion?
If I but sue, thou wouldst relieve mine anguish,
Two threatening arcs thou bendest rigorously!
Then if I swear thy love did make me languish,
Thou turn'st away, and smilest scornfully!
Then if I wish thou would'st not tyrannize;
Of Tyranny thou mak'st but a mockery!
And if I weep, my tears thou dost despise!
And if I stir, thou threatenest battery!
Frown on! Smile on! mock me! despise me! threat me!
All shall not make me leave for to intreat thee!

She threatens with her eyes, scorns with her smiles, mocks, despises and 'threatens battery'. (In Spenser, it is the lover who 'threatens battery' (XIV), not the mistress.) Even so, her responses are not the finely balanced, intelligent reactions of Elizabeth, for Coelia appears to be less discriminating in her choice of response, and to be generally more threatening and unkind.[40]

Spenser, in contrast to Daniel and Percy, uses the occasions when the mistress speaks to establish an image of her that is contrary to the image, often projected of her by the lover, of the hardhearted recipient of his suit. Those critics who have seen her as a Rosalind, or an Elizabeth Bennet, recognize the spirit with which Spenser's mistress plays her role, but they exaggerate the degree to which her personality is developed, and overstate their case by assuming that she is consistently presented in this way. On the other hand, the views which stress the mistress's lack of individuality underestimate the extent to which her character is developed. She is not simply a re-creation of the Petrarchan Laura, nor a Neo-Platonic goddess who waits for her lover to pass through his trial of fire. Such views do not acknowledge her liveliness, wit and independence of spirit.

Spenser does not, of course, present a fully rounded characterisation of the mistress in his sequence. He does, however, suggest that she is a charming, intelligent individual who is capable of involving herself in an intimate relationship, though human enough to be nervous about its outcome. The presentation of her in this light is not entirely uniform, for there are many sonnets in which she is treated as though she were merely the rhetorical occasion for the lover's feelings and frustrations. In such instances she is presented in much the same way as a conventional mistress figure. But the glimpses that are offered of her as a lively, wilful, yet responsive, human being affect even these moments. The image of the mistress which emerges from the sequence as a whole is that of a person of intelligence, spirit and wit.

NOTES: Chapter Two

1. Don M. Ricks, 'Persona and Process in Spenser's *Amoretti*', *Ariel*, 3, October 1972, p. 7.
2. From Fletcher's 'To the Reader', which precedes his sequence *Licia*. See *Elizabethan Sonnets*, 2 vols., ed. Sidney Lee, Archibald Constable and Co., Ltd, Westminster, 1904, vol. 2, p. 32.

3. Henry Constable's sonnet sequence *Diana* is arranged in an unusual way. The text which is used here, Joan Grundy's edition of *The Poems of Henry Constable*, is based on the Todd manuscript (Victoria and Albert Museum, MS. Dyce 44). In the Todd manuscript the sonnets are divided into three 'parts' each of which contains three sets of seven poems. References in the present work follow the Todd/Grundy arrangement.

4. The 1609 quarto edition of the sonnets appears to have been published without the authorisation of Shakespeare. The title page records 'Shake-Speares Sonnets. Never before Imprinted.'

5. Louis Martz defined *Amoretti* as 'intimate little tokens of love'. See Martz, op. cit., p. 156.

6. E. G. Withycombe, *The Oxford Dictionary of English Christian Names*, 2nd edn, 1945; rpt. Clarendon Press, Oxford, 1977, p. 99.

7. This is not to suggest that the Elizabeth of the sonnets is a representation of Elizabeth Boyle, though it seems likely that she provided a model for the figure of Elizabeth, at least in some of the sonnets.

8. L. Tennenhouse, *Power on Display: The Politics of Shakespeare's Genres*, Methuen, New York and London, 1986, pp. 30, 31.

9. Emile Legouis, *Spenser*, J. M. Dent and Sons Ltd., New York, 1926, p. 94.

10. According to Cruttwell, 'Spenser does not name his lady'. P. Cruttwell, *The English Sonnet*, published for the British Council and the National Book League by Longman, London, 1966, p. 18. For the claim that she is 'never analysed, never individualised', see P. Cruttwell, *The Shakespearean Moment and its Place in the Poetry of the Seventeenth Century*, Random House, New York, 1960, p. 16.

11. Ricks, op. cit., p. 8.

12. Alastair Fowler, *Edmund Spenser*, Writers and their Work, ed. Ian Scott-Kilvert, Longman for the British Council, Harlow, 1977, p. 20.

13. Carol Barthel, *'Amoretti*: A Comic Monodrama?', *Spenser at Kalamazoo, Proceedings from a Special Session at the Thirteenth Conference on Medieval Studies in Kalamazoo, Michigan*, 5–6 May 1978, Cleveland State University, p. 292.

14. Hallett D. Smith, *Elizabethan Poetry: A Study in Conventional Meaning and Expression*, Harvard University Press, Cambridge, Massachusetts, 1952, p. 166.

15. For a more detailed discussion of his attacks upon the mistress see below pp. 70–73.

16. The next chapter is devoted to a fuller analysis of the techniques Spenser uses to distance the persona from the point of view presented in an individual poem, or from the sequence as a whole.

17. The dramatic impact of some of these attacks on the mistress is referred to below. See p. 73.

18. It is only in the Fifth Song that Astrophil attacks Stella with any vehemence, and there he accuses her of everything (theft, murder, tyranny, rebellion, cowardice and being a witch and a devil), making it impossible to take his charges seriously. The song does not appear in any of the MS. texts, and this fact, coupled with the unusual theme, has led some editors to conclude it is out of place in *Astrophil and Stella*. See, for example, *Sir Philip Sidney: Selected Poems*, ed. Katherine Duncan-Jones, Clarendon Press, Oxford, 1973, p. 222. She notes that Ringler suggests the song belongs with Sidney's Philisider–Mira poems.

19. This is discussed more fully below. See pp. 44–48.

20. For a fuller discussion of this sonnet, see below pp. 119–21.

21. The sestet of VIII is discussed below. See pp. 101–2.

22. For a fuller discussion of these lines, see below pp. 150–1.

23. The coupling of the spider and the bee occurs frequently in literature of the period, though Spenser's treatment of this theme is more light-hearted and playful than is usual. See, for example, *The Complete Works of George Gascoigne*, ed. John W. Cunliffe, 2 vols., Cambridge University Press, Cambridge, 1907, vol. 1, p. 12; and G. Whitney, *A Choice of Emblemes, and other Devises*, 1586, p. 51.

24. Martz makes a similar point about this sonnet: 'This is the sonnet where the lady, in a witty reversal of the poet's complaints, has woven into her embroidery a fable of the Bee and the Spyder; the poet picks up the imagery with joy and develops it with a deeply affectionate humour'. Louis L. Martz, op. cit., p. 154.

25. 'I love thee not' could be the reported words of the mistress about her own feelings towards the lover, or could be her account of his feelings for her. The rest of the sonnet throws little light on the ambiguity of the line.

26. Martin Seymour-Smith comments that part of the point of the sonnet 'is the need sensitive people have to talk like this while making illicit love. It provides a kind of comfort, a semi-hysterical insulation against their own feelings of guilt and dishonesty'. *Shakespeare's Sonnets*, ed. Martin Seymour-Smith, Heinemann, London, 1967, p. 183. This reads too much into the situation which is being described and assumes the perspective of a psychologist considering the motivation of his subject, rather than the perspective of a literary critic.

27. Andrew Gurr suggests a pun on *Hathaway* in 'Shakespeare's First Poem: Sonnet 145' in *Essays in Criticism*, XXI, 1971, pp. 221–26. Booth suggests the possibility of a pun on Shakespeare's wife's first name, *Ann*, since '*And* was regularly pronounced "an".' See Stephen Booth, op. cit., p. 501.

28. Wendy Goulston's argument that in this sonnet (LXIII) Astrophil's games with grammar and logic are a sign of his corruption, surely rests on too solemn an interpretation: 'Instead of respecting study, and using

grammar, rhetoric and logic to speak "truth" and to persuade to goodness Astrophil misuses his poetic licence, making things true by calling them so, trying to persuade his lady to an immoral physical love he knows to be vain . . . In Astrophil's words which abuse grammar and Stella, we see the rhetorical self-delusion against which Du Bartas warned his readers . . .'. Wendy Goulston, 'The "Figuring Forth" of Astrophil: Sidney's Use of Language', *Southern Review*, vol. XI, November 1978, p. 235.

29. James Scanlon, 'Sidney's *Astrophil and Stella*' in *Studies in English Literature*, 16, 1976, p. 70.
30. Louis Martz, op. cit., p. 153.
31. See *Works*, vol. 8., p. 426. *Amoretti* and *Epithalamion* was published with a separate title page, with various other works of Spenser, in a volume entitled *Colin Clouts Come Home Againe*, 1611. For a full description of the history of folio publications of Spenser's works in the early seventeenth century, see Francis R. Johnson, *A Critical Bibliography of the Works of Edmund Spenser Printed before 1700*, The Johns Hopkins Press, Baltimore, 1933, pp. 33–48.
32. Other sonnets in which the lover indicates that she is artful include XXXVII, in which he accuses her of 'guile', and XXI, which concludes with the lines

> Thus doth she traine and teache me with her lookes,
> Such art of eyes I never read in bookes.

33. Judith Kalil states: 'The setting is "this worlds Theatre" where the persona's "love lyke the Spectator idly sits". The imagery saliently points to the speaker's comic condition by inferring (because his "love . . . idly sits") that he, unlike the active lover, is not primarily a man of deeds'. J. Kalil, '"Mask in Myrth Lyke to a Comedy": Spenser's Persona in the *Amoretti*', *Thoth*, Spring 1973, p. 25.
34. There is probable wordplay on three different senses of 'mask' in the clause 'and mask in myrth lyke to a Comedy' in the sixth line of the sonnet involving:
1. *O.E.D.* mask, verb, intrans., sense 5 (obsolete) 'to be or go in disguise; to hide one's real form or character under an outward show' (a usage in Spenser's *Shepheardes Calender*, January, l. 24 is cited).
2. The verbal form of the noun 'masque' (*O.E.D.* mask, verb, intrans., sense 4 'to take part in a mask or masquerade').
3. A reference to the masks of Greek theatre.
35. A. Dunlop, 'The Drama of *Amoretti*' in *Spenser at Kalamazoo, Proceedings from a Special Session at the Thirteenth Conference on Medieval Studies in Kalamazoo*, Michigan, 5–6 May 1978, p. 277.
36. Barthel, op. cit., pp. 291, 292.

37. See, for example, Shakespeare's sonnets LV and CVII.
38. Fuller notes the difference between Spenser's and Shakespeare's use of this theme, but he sees the difference to lie in Spenser's couplet not being 'dignified by wit'. Spenser's couplet is described as 'a melodious game', whilst Shakespeare's use of the theme is said to be presented with 'assertiveness'. Spenser's couplet is clearly melodious, but it also makes a contribution to the argument of the poem, and provides a different twist to a familiar theme. See John Fuller, *The Sonnet*, Methuen and Co. Ltd, London, 1972, p. 21.
39. Lee claims that 'Spenser's publisher, William Ponsonby, undertook the publication' of *Sonnets to the Fairest Coelia*. Sidney Lee, op. cit., vol. 2., p. c.
40. Other examples in Percy's sequence of Coelia's perversity are similarly threatening, though the techniques Percy uses to describe her behaviour have little in common with Spenser's techniques. See, for example, sonnets IIII, XVI and XXX in Percy, *Sonnets to the Fairest Coelia*, op. cit.

3. The Author and Lover/Persona Relation

Many critical approaches to the *Amoretti*, including quite recent ones, fail to recognize the presence of irony and playfulness in Spenser's treatment of the persona of the lover. The speaking voice of the poems is often simply identified with that of Spenser himself, with the result that many of the complex effects which he achieves in the poems are overlooked.

In his influential study of the Elizabethan sonnet, first published in the 1950s, J.W. Lever indicates that he sees no distinction between Spenser and the speaking voice of the *Amoretti*. He says of the *Epithalamion*, the *Hymnes* and the *Amoretti* that 'personal experience, subject always to the necessary moral qualifications was directly voiced', and in his discussion of individual poems he always refers to the narrating voice as Spenser's: 'Spenser's response to the lady's beauty is admittedly sensuous . . . to a degree which he would never have permitted himself in the earlier phases of courtship'; 'Spenser thanks his lady for the gifts of mind she has conferred on him'.[1] Approximately 20 years later, Waldo McNeir's attitude is similar:

> The person speaking is nearly always Spenser himself, in his own character, without disguise – whatever the variety of his feelings – speaking as a particular man to a particular woman.[2]

It is understandable, of course, that a strong association between Spenser and the speaking voice of the sonnets has been assumed in critical commentary. Spenser himself encourages the reader's belief in this idea by including details in his lover persona's 'biography' which correspond with known facts about his own life. Both, for example, are approximately 40 years old at the time of the composition of the sequence (LX), both are courting someone whose name is Elizabeth and both pay homage to their queen, who is named Elizabeth (LXXXIIII). Lodovick Bryskett, Spenser's close friend, is the namesake referred to by the lover persona in sonnet XXXIII, and it is *The Faerie Queene*, Spenser's epic poem, which is referred to as being in the process of composition during the courtship (XXXIII, LXXX).

It is quite possible that Spenser walked with Elizabeth on the strand of Youghal, which was near her home at Kilcoran, County Cork, and that some such occasion might have provided inspiration for his sonnet 'One day I wrote her name upon the strand', though, of course, this cannot be established with any certainty.[3] There are several other incidents, such as the mistress's sending her lover home in a storm (XLVI), or her burning of his letter (XLVIII), which convey the impression of actual experience.

One indication of the power of the tradition that Spenser and the lover persona are one and the same is to be found in the reliance which Spenser's biographers place on the sonnets as a source of information about his life and marriage to Elizabeth Boyle. Judson remarks in his 'The Life of Edmund Spenser', for example, that 'Much that we know about Spenser's marriage to Elizabeth Boyle is found between the covers of a small octavo volume published in 1595 by William Ponsonby with a title page bearing the words: "*Amoretti* and *Epithalamion*".[4] Smith and de Selincourt similarly state that 'The inner history of this courtship and its consummation is recorded in idealized form, in the *Amoretti* and *Epithalamion*'.[5]

Because of the number of fixed biographical reference points in the *Amoretti*, it will, perhaps, never be possible or reasonable to establish a complete dissociation of the author, Spenser, and the speaking voice of the poems. But in some recent critical discussion of the sequence, there has been increasing recognition of the presence of a lover persona who is not simply identifiable either with Edmund Spenser, the historical personage, or with some authoritative voice of 'the poet' who is the author of the poems.

Dunlop, in an article which attempts to mediate between traditionalist and numerological criticism of the *Amoretti*, provides a clear articulation of the essential point that 'Spenser is speaking to us not directly but indirectly through the persona of the poet-lover, and that the persona is 'a semifictional dramatic character'. But Dunlop rather overstates the case when he goes on to argue that the lover persona is consistently presented as a dramatic figure: 'Each individual sonnet represents not the completeness of vision of Spenser the author, but the emotional state of the lover at one stage of his development'.[6]

Barthel makes a comparable assumption when she describes the sequence as a monodrama, a play in which 'the poet arranges his actors in the stylized and extravagant postures that literary lovers assume'.[7] Barthel's analysis of the sequence puts emphasis on its dramatic qualities, an aspect which is repeatedly underestimated by other commentaries, but her account assumes that the distance between the author and the lover persona is regularly maintained throughout the sonnets of the *Amoretti*.

Judith Kalil also sees a uniform distinction between the author (poet) and lover persona: 'Spenser's speaking voice in the sequence, the voice which takes on various roles in order to relate the sonnet's "story", is always separate from that of the poet'. Kalil adds, though almost in passing, the valuable insight that the mask adopted by Spenser, as lover persona, alters in its masking or covering ability from sonnet to sonnet.[8]

Critical approaches which draw a distinction between the author and the lover persona certainly constitute a more sophisticated way of coming to terms with the complexity of the sonnets than is found in the work of ealier commentators such as Lever, who tend simply to identify Spenser and the lover persona. But none of the more recent critics just mentioned explores this aspect of Spenser's artistry in adequate detail, and there are important reservations to be made, not only about many aspects of the critical accounts which they offer of individual poems, but also about their larger conclusions.

In the accounts of Dunlop, Barthel and Kalil it is suggested that a distinction between author and lover persona is present in each sonnet. Such a description does not recognize the irregular manner in which this distinction occurs in Spenser's sequence. It is simply not true to say that every sonnet in the sequence presents us with a clear example of a dramatically realized lover persona who is clearly distinguishable from the creating poet. There are some sonnets in which there is no readily discernible distinction between Spenser and his lover persona, and there are others in which Spenser, the historical personage, is in evidence as the speaking voice of the poems. In many sonnets, however, it is clear that an ironic distance between Spenser and his lover persona is established.

The sonnets in which Spenser has the narrator of the poems mention details and events which are clearly recognizable as referring to Spenser's public life allow no room for making a distinction between poet and persona. Sonnet XXXIII, for example, is about Spenser's anxiety, expressed to his friend Lodowick Bryskett, that work on *The Faerie Queene* has not been finished because the poet's spirit is troubled by a 'proud love'. Two of the sonnets reflect Spenser's interest in, and quest for, patronage from Queen Elizabeth. The speaking voice of sonnet XXXIII is unequivocally that of Spenser the public poet, with his values, priorities and interest in patronage uppermost. Again, sonnet LXXX is about Spenser's satisfaction in completing six books of *The Faerie Queene* and his plan to sing his love's sweet praise in a manner befitting his queen. The concerns expressed here are inseparable from those of Spenser as public figure and poet. Kalil's observation that the masking function of the persona is not consistently maintained in the sequence does not acknowledge the fact that in poems such as these the mask appears to be completely absent.

There are other sonnets, or parts of sonnets, in which it is virtually impossible to establish the presence of effects which create a sense of distance between Spenser and his lover persona. One of the methods which Spenser often uses to create this distance is hyperbole, but in sonnet I, for example, although hyperbole is used, it is not employed to provide a comic or ironic light on the speaking voice of the poem. The hyperbole serves to heap compliments upon the mistress and to establish the inferiority in which the lover holds himself and his verse, in relation to her:

> And happy lines, on which with starry light,
> those lamping eyes will deigne sometimes to look
> and read the sorrowes of my dying spright

The speaking voice in this example is not identifiable with Spenser the public poet but belongs, rather, to an earnest, humble, relatively conventional suitor. It is a voice which is used in a number of sonnets in the sequence (eg. VIII, XXXIX, LXIII, LXXXI). The ways in which this voice is similar to, as well as distinctive from, that of the conventional lover figure of Elizabethan sonnets is explored in the next chapter.

Occasionally there are borderline examples where it is extraordinarily difficult to determine whether or not irony is present. In
sonnet LI, for example, it is difficult to decide whether the author is
displaying his superior abilities and knowledge at the expense of his
lover persona, or whether the persona partly, or wholly, shares in his
wisdom:

> Doe I not see that fayrest ymages
> of hardest marble are of purpose made?
> for that they should endure through many ages,
> ne let theyr famous moniments to fade.
> Why then doe I, untrainde in lovers trade,
> her hardnes blame which I should more commend?
> sith never ought was excellent assayde,
> which was not hard t'atchive and bring to end.
> Ne ought so hard, but he that would attend,
> mote soften it and to his will allure:
> so doe I hope her stubborne hart to bend,
> and that it then more stedfast will endure.
> Onely my paines wil be the more to get her,
> but having her, my ioy will be the greater

The description of the lover as 'untrainde in lovers trade' could be
interpreted as showing him to be *either* actually naive *or* engaging in
playful self-deprecation for the purposes of argument. Similarly, the
shift in the meanings of 'hard', which allows the lover to move to the
conclusion he wants, may be part of his (the lover's) assigned
rhetorical strategy, or it may be a device of the author to indicate that
the lover is comically caught up in his own rhetoric, the victim of his
own faulty logic. There is nothing in the poem as a whole to resolve
these issues, so that one does not know whether irony is present.[9]

These examples aside, there are many examples of sonnets in
which irony is present. Essentially, the irony involved in the creation
of a separately identifiable lover persona is akin to Sophoclean irony
in drama, which occurs when the playwright supplies the audience
with information or understanding withheld from one or more of
the *dramatis personae*. The audience can thus see a character comically
deluded (like Malvolio in *Twelfth Night* or Orlando in *As You Like It*)
or tragically ignorant of the full circumstances of his situation like
Oedipus or Othello.

The analogy with the theatre has of course, certain limitations. In a sonnet, the author creating such effects of irony (in which author and reader possess superior intelligence in comparison with the lover persona) has to rely almost entirely on the speech of the persona himself to reveal the gap of intelligence between author and reader on the one hand, and persona on the other. Furthermore, a sonnet sequence rarely maintains a regular distance between author and persona of the kind maintained in a Shakespearean play.

The sonnets, or parts of sonnets, which provide the clearest examples of the ways in which Spenser creates distance between himself and his persona are those in which he makes use of a range of ironic effects. These encourage the identification of different perspectives from which statements contained within the sonnets can be viewed. Some of the techniques Spenser draws upon for these purposes will now be considered, though it must be remembered that in some sonnets several techniques may be used simultaneously, whilst in others a particular technique may be dominant.

One of the methods Spenser uses to create distance between himself and his persona is hyperbole. Elizabethan sonneteers frequently use hyperbole as a means of describing the depth and extent of a lover's feelings for his mistress, and to honour the nature of her absolute perfection. Sonneteers compete to offer the most extravagant descriptions of their miseries, or to devise excessive forms of compliment. Spenser uses hyperbole in the *Amoretti* for these purposes. But he also uses it in his sonnets for ironic effect, a much less common practice.

Hyperbole is often used to create distance between the persona's view of his situation and the reader's perception of it. In the sonnets in which Spenser uses hyperbole in this way, the lover persona is usually made the butt of the humour. Spenser has several comic roles for his lover figure in sonnets of this kind – the automaton, the bewildered victim of forces that relentlessly oppose him, and the love-struck fool. The lover persona is presented as naively unaware of the foolishness of the figure he cuts. The exaggeration he employs to describe his condition, or situation, reveals the seriousness of his problems as he perceives them; but at the same time his extravagant accounts suggest a certain ridiculous and clown-like dimension to his behaviour.

In order to suggest the first of these roles, the automaton-like nature of the lover's behaviour, Spenser has his lover exaggerate the brevity and pace of his exchanges with his mistress. The pattern of

their interaction in these instances suggests a speeded up comic
film in which great energy is expended, but little or nothing
achieved. In lines 9–12 of XXI, for example, the mistress is said to
give alternating stop/go messages with her eyes, and frequently to
change her facial expression, with the result that her demented lover
goes backwards and forwards, from death to life:

> With such strange termes her eyes she doth inure,
>   that with one looke she doth my life dismay:
>   and with another doth it streight recure,
>   her smile me drawes, her frowne me drives away.

With the mistress's smiles and frowns, the lover is alternately
drawn towards her and sent away from her as though he were a
puppet. There is a close relation between her action and his response,
a discrepancy in the effort each exerts (she merely making facial
gestures, he responding with his whole being), and an illusion of
their actions alternating with ever-increasing speed. The increase in
speed is suggested in the gradual paring down and refining of the
way their exchanges are described. Line 12 of XXI represents the
culmination of the process whereby the mistress's contrary actions
and his immediate responses, which have been dealt with indi-
vidually in the previous two lines, are drawn together in neat,
contrasting, but parallel syntactical units.

The lover gives this account as though unconscious of the comic
dimensions of his mechanical behaviour. He is obsessed with the
confusion and frustration of being at the beck and call of 'such art of
eyes' and is, in this quatrain, intent on delivering his complaint about
this aspect of his treatment by the mistress. The reader, on the other
hand, is not subject to the mistress's relentless 'training' methods,
and so more readily responds to the comedy of the description he
offers.

There is a similar use of hyperbole in XXIII, a sonnet which is
discussed below in relation to the playful use of analogy. The lover's
frustration increases as he dwells on his lack of success in comparison
with Penelope's competence in achieving her goals of being faithful
to Ulysses, and deceiving her suitors. No matter how long-suffering
and patient the lover is in his efforts towards his mistress, she
destroys the progress of his suit with a minimum of effort. His
frustration reaches a climax in the third quatrain:

> So when I thinke to end that I begonne,
> I must begin and never bring to end:
> for with one looke she spils that long I sponne,
> and with one word my whole years work doth rend.

That his activity is futile and unproductive is suggested in the word patterning of this quatrain. The lover thinks 'to end' (line 9), but never brings 'to end' (line 10), and just as he thinks he can end what he has 'begonne' (line 9), he must begin again (line 10). His ceaseless labour, and his 'whole yeare's work', so intimately familiar to the reader from other sonnets, is destroyed by 'one looke' (line 11) or 'one word' (line 12). Things that usually have distance between them or are ordinarily unrelated (the beginning and the end; a brief action and a year's work) are comically telescoped in their temporal relation. At first, it took the mistress 'one short houre' to undo his weaving of many days (in contrast with Penelope, who spent the night unravelling the labours of the day), but now she undoes his whole year's work with a single word.

The injustice of the situation obsesses the lover and blinds him to the humour of the picture he presents of himself. He expends an alarming amount of energy getting nowhere (spinning endlessly), but has absolutely nothing at the end of all his endeavours to show for his arachnidan efforts.

The lover's bewildered-victim role is also created by the employment of hyperbole, in conjunction with other poetic devices. In sonnets in which the mistress responds to the lover, it is often the pattern of their interaction which is exaggerated. The mistress responds with almost mathematical precision to her lover's every move; she neatly counters his actions with actions of her own, and never gives him the response he is trying to win from her. The difference between what is desired by the lover and what he actually achieves, as well as the regularity with which he achieves the opposite of what he wants, becomes the basis for humour in sonnets of this kind.

The lover's excessive efforts to win his mistress almost always prove to be counterproductive. In XVIII, for example, she meets his pleading, weeping and sighing with scorn and laughter, and in LIIII she meets his mirth with indifference, and his laughter with mockery.[10] In the third quatrain of XXXII, the process is comically precise in its reciprocative dynamics:

> But still the more she fervent sees my fit
> the more she frieseth in her wilfull pryde:
> and harder growes the harder she is smit,
> with all the playnts which to her be applyde.

His mistress's opposition is described as mechanical and relentless ('the more . . . the more', 'and harder growes', 'the harder'), and the lover's slightest striving to make her change towards him achieves the very opposite of the effect he wants. The more he tries, the less he succeeds.

There is a similar pattern in XXX – the more fiery the lover's ardour, the colder the mistress's response:

> My love is lyke to yse, and I to fyre;
> how comes it then that this her cold so great
> is not dissolv'd through my so hot desyre,
> but harder growes the more I her intreat?
> Or how comes it that my exceeding heat
> is not delayd by her hart frosen cold:
> but that I burne much more in boyling sweat,
> and feele my flames augmented manifold?

In this sonnet the lover perceives himself to be a victim of the laws of nature, which appear to be deviating from their usual patterns in order to make him the more helpless. The reader perceives that it is not the laws of nature that are at fault, but the lover's view of the situation. He is, in fact, describing the operation of a different set of laws – the Petrarchan oppositions of passion/fire/heat and disdain/ice/cold.[11] In relation to that set of laws, things are proceeding as would be expected. Hence, the reader is placed in the position of having the superior knowledge: s/he has the explanation which the lover seeks but cannot find, and the lover remains the bewildered victim of forces he cannot understand.[12]

The mistress's response in all of these sonnets is swift, automatic and inevitable. Consequently, any move the lover makes towards the mistress is certain to bring results; but the results are diametrically opposed to those he desires. He is, more or less, the victim of his own actions – any increase in passion on his part ensures an increase in her resolve against him.

In other sonnets the lover plays quite a different role – that of the 'stupid stock' (XLIII), or the dumbstruck fool (III, XLIII). Instead of responding immediately to his mistress's commands, or courting her with diligent, but futile industry, he finds himself impotent, reduced to 'silence'. In sonnet III, he describes himself as being struck dumb by his mistress's great beauty. He opens his mouth to praise her, but finds he is unable to utter any words at all. He is similarly incapacitated when he picks up his pen to write.[13]

In the octet of XLIII, the lover finds himself struck dumb for other reasons. He is unable to decide whether to speak and risk his mistress's wrath, or to stay silent and have his heart choke on his 'overflowing gall'. His indecision leaves him tongue-tied, unable either to think or speak:

> Shall I then silent be or shall I speake?
>   and if I speake, her wrath renew I shall:
>   and if I silent be, my heart will breake,
>   or choked be with overflowing gall.
> What tyranny is this both my hart to thrall,
>   and eke my toung with proud restraint to tie?
>   that nether I may speake nor thinke at all,
>   but like a stupid stock in silence die.

He is lost in dilemmas that threaten to incapacitate him, but apparently unconscious of the humour of one ordinarily so eloquent being reduced to a block.[14]

For the most part, in the sonnets which employ hyperbole for ironic purposes, the lover persona is presented as the victim of apparently irrational forces and behaviour. He makes superhuman efforts to reverse or control the processes that defeat him, but his endeavours frequently end in failure. His frenzied, unproductive activity and his stupefied inaction are treated humorously by Spenser. Nevertheless, the ways of love and mistresses are shown to be powerful and exacting in their operations, and a certain sympathy is elicited for the lover's plight as a love-struck fool.

Another method which Spenser uses to create ironic perspectives in his treatment of the lover persona is the creation of a context which provides a counter to the views and attitudes expressed by the lover. As will be shown, the context of the sequence as a whole, or the wider context of Renaissance poetry, may be drawn upon for this end.

The sonnets in which Spenser's lover engages in excessive criticism of his mistress, claiming, for example, that her behaviour is comparable with that of predatory beasts, provide evidence of this process at work. The notion that the mistress uses her beauty in extremely cruel and heartless ways occurs as early as XX, and is repeated on a number of occasions (XXXI, XLI, XLVII, XLIX, LIII, LVI). After sonnet LVI the notion is supplanted by one which was also expressed very early in the sequence, and which contradicts it: that the mistress is of irreproachable virtue. In the last third of the sequence, the lover's anger is not directed against his mistress, and their proposed union makes it clear that he is confirming his view of her as someone worthy of his admiration and worship.

From this perspective, it is clear that the lover's excessive criticisms of his mistress are not to be viewed as attacks upon her character. They are, rather rhetorical strategies employed by the lover in his attempts to persuade the mistress to change her ways towards him. In XX, for example, the lover's first ploy is to present himself as the humble pleader for mercy and his mistress as the heartless victor:

> In vaine I seeke and sew to her for grace,
>   and doe myne humbled hart before her poure:
>   the whiles her foot she in my necke doth place,
>   and treat my life downe in the lowly floure.
> And yet the Lyon that is Lord of power,
>   and reigneth over every beast in field:
>   in his most pride disdeigneth to devoure
>   the silly lambe that to his might doth yield.
> But she more cruell and more salvage wylde,
>   then either Lyon or the Lyonesse:
>   shames not to be with guiltlesse bloud defylde,
>   but taketh glory in her cruelnesse.
> Fayrer then fayrest let none ever say,
>   that ye were blooded in a yeelded pray.

His striking visual portrait of their relationship, with himself prostrate on the ground whilst her foot is on his neck in a manner reminiscent of a figure in an attitude of victory, is designed to portray the mistress's unfeeling and callous nature. But the static quality of the image he describes, and the incongruity of the postures he complains about, have their amusing side for the reader, who perceives that Spenser's attitude to these complaints is less earnest than that presented by his lover persona.

The lengthy description of the behaviour of the lion and the lioness, which are used as comparisons with the mistress's behaviour in the next two quatrains, are presented authoritatively by the lover, and offer detailed information about animal behaviour, which, at the time, would have been accepted animal lore.[15] The notions that the lion spares the submissive and weak, and that the lioness is more cruel than the lion, for example, had currency from the works of Pliny and Aristotle, as well as from the bestiaries – works which represented scientific opinion in the Elizabethan period.[16]

The lover is presented as one engaged in building up the reader's faith in him as an accurate reporter of factual information, so that this belief in him as a recorder of the truth can be transferred to the things he has to say about the mistress's behaviour. The information the lover uses is chosen to discredit the mistress and to prove her merciless nature. He implies that since even the cruellest of beasts have their rules of behaviour, the mistress ought to have some rules to regulate her cruelty. Yet, he states, she has none, and so is more contemptible than the beasts. It is this which he seizes upon as justification for attempting to change her ways and for offering reproofs of her behaviour.

The lover's assumption of the role of one who dispenses moral judgement, using animal lore as his text, creates a further twist in the sonnet. Conventionally, it is the mistress who is the figure of perfection and who is seen as undeserving of any reproof. And it is the lover whose shortcomings would ordinarily place him in need of moral guidance. In wittily reversing the traditional roles, Spenser alerts the reader to the idea that the lover's harsh condemnation of the mistress should be regarded with caution. The lover's rather pious reliance on a text of animal lore as the basis of his sermon is a parody of the ways in which writers of emblem books and bestiaries, so popular in the period, made use of 'truths' about animal behaviour as the basis of their didactic lessons. Spenser's comic treatment of the lover's inept applications of examples of animal lore, in which he adopts a pious moral attitude towards the mistress, occurs in a number of sonnets of this kind – XXXI, XXXVIII, XLVII, LIII and LVI.[17]

Other sonneteers make use of images of predatory creatures rather less frequently than does Spenser. Fletcher's Licia is 'tiger-like' (VIII), Griffin's Fidessa has the mind of a griffon, with the play on *Griffin*, (XXXIX), and Linche's Diella has a 'tigress' heart' (XVI).

Barnes accuses his mistress of being lion-like (XXXVI) and of hiding 'craftie clawes and Lyon's heart' beneath 'chast vayles of single life' (XXXVII). But for the most part the comparisons are in the form of occasional epithets which are not a significant part of the argument of the sonnet.[18] In Spenser's poems the references to predatory creatures generally have a prominent place in the overall argument of the poems. This is illustrated in the opening of LVI, for example, where the lover's accusation is voiced without any apologies to tender sensibilities:

> Fayre ye be sure, but cruell and unkind,
>   as is a Tygre[19] that with greedinesse
> hunts after bloud

In XX, discussed above, the accusation of savagery occurs at the climax of the poem, in the third quatrain, where the lover's indignation explodes in vehement denunciation.

Thus, there are a variety of ways in which Spenser relies on the context of the sequences, and the wider context of Renaissance poetry to reveal the dramatic, rhetorical nature of his lover's accusations, and indicate detachment from the lover's opinions. The distance created between the author and the lover persona in sonnets of this kind allows a perspective on the lover which encourages the reader's amusement at his wily strategies and far-fetched arguments, but which does not detract from the recognition that the lover's accusations are offered with vehemence and heartfelt complaint.

The lover does not, of course, confine himself to comparisons with animal behaviour to establish his mistress's treachery. On several occasions the lover accuses his mistress of deliberately using her beauty to cause him pain so she can enjoy the spectacle of his suffering. In the golden hooks sonnet (XLVII), for example, he draws on images of death and decay to frame his accusations of treason, hypocrisy and cruelty. His attack on his mistress is mitigated by the fact that she is given something of the quality of a legendary figure in this sonnet – a cruel princess who dispenses 'charm'.[20] But the main counter to the view the lover expresses here occurs elsewhere in the sequence. It is his final assessment of the mistress as a figure of sanctity and worthiness which eventually belies judgements of this kind.

A more complicated example of Spenser's evocation of the

context of the sequences itself, as well as of the larger context of Renaissance poetry and literary tradition, occurs in XXXVII. In this poem, the golden hair sonnet, the lover sets out to warn of the trap of his mistress's golden hair and of her guile and cunning in using that trap to catch her victims. The lover's critical attitude towards the mistress and his accusation of 'guile' are not positively endorsed by Spenser at any point in the sonnet. Indeed, in criticising the intention of his golden-haired mistress, Spenser's lover is challenging the traditional associations of fairness and virtue, as well as the notion that outward fairness is a manifestation of inner fairness. These time-honoured associations are assented to elsewhere in the sequence, as well as being familiar from love poetry through the ages, including Elizabethan poetry.

In Spenser's sequence an association between fairness and goodness is firmly established. At several points the mistress's outward beauty is seen as a manifestation of her inner goodness. In LXXXI, for example, a sonnet which is the culmination of tributes to her outward fairness, her beauty and incomparable nature are seen as inseparable. The notion of the 'cruel fair', which is a part of the sequence, does not really conflict with this idea, since the cruelty is found to be more in the eye of the beholder than in the nature of the mistress. As Sidney's persona confesses in the poem 'To the tune of a Neapolitan Villanell', it is his lady's refusal or acceptance of him that determines whether he sees her fairness as 'Thy faire haire my heart enchained', or 'Thy haire not worth a haire esteemed'.

In both the classical and Renaissance literary traditions, the ideally beautiful woman is golden-haired and fair-skinned. Ogle notes that the reign of the blonde in literature

> is but a continuation of her reign in the literature of Greece and Rome . . . the Greek heroes and heroines, gods and goddesses, with one or two prominent exceptions, are described as blondes by Homer and the early poets, and continued to be so described by succeeding writers, in spite of the fact that the Greeks of the classical period had dark hair and dark eyes.[21]

This tradition includes the idea of the lady's outward fairness being a reflection of her pure and virtuous inner nature. The association of outward fairness and inner beauty also has a long history, being found in the earliest folk and fairy tales, in which the heroine is golden-haired, and the wicked sister dark-haired.[22]

The association between golden hair and virtue, is not, of course, confined to folk tales. There are numerous literary examples, which include Petrarch's fair and virtuous Laura, who provided an immediate model for the mistress of the Elizabethan sonnet sequences. Most lyrics of the medieval period reserve their praise for fair-haired beauty, and Elizabethan sonnet mistresses are almost always both fair and virtuous.[23]

Hence, the lover's defiant dismissal of traditional assumptions, in a context in which they are usually endorsed, is one of the first things that alerts the reader to the idea that the lover's version of events may be suspect. The values implied in the lover's account of his mistress's intentions do not tally with the values endorsed in the rest of the sequence, or with those established in the literary tradition itself.

The familiar Renaissance conceit of the net of hair as a trap that captures the beholder[24] is also treated in an unusual way in this sonnet. Spenser's lover implies that the mistress deliberately sets out to create this trap for her victims, an assumption which runs counter to ideas expressed elsewhere in the sequence, as well as to those that are ordinarily associated with the use of the conceit in the literary tradition.

In LXXIII of the *Amoretti*, the lover views the fair tresses of his mistress's golden hair as bonds which enslave him because of his own helplessness in the face of his mistress's beauty, and not because she is deliberately laying a trap. The final acceptance of each other by the lover and his mistress at the end of sequence contains no suggestion that the mistress has trapped him. Their bonding is seen to be a voluntary submission of the one to the other.

Petrarch uses the image of the net of hair several times in *The Canzoniere*,[25] though Pebworth traces it much further back to the Biblical *Song of Songs*:

> The head of you is like Carmel
> And your tresses like purple threads
> A King could be caught by their coils. (7:5)[26]

In neither of these sources of the conceit does the beholder blame the mistress for his captivity, or potential captivity. In the Petrarchan sonnets, for example, the persona sees Love itself as responsible for his being bound to Laura:

Tra le chiome de l'or nascose il laccio
al qual mi strinse Amore

Amid the locks of gold, Love hid the
noose with which he bound me. (LIX)

Although Laura's hair is described as a snare, or trap, it is not so by
her intention. She does not set out to rob her admirer of his liberty by
displaying her hair.[27]

Renaissance examples of the use of the conceit follow a similar
pattern. When Bassanio looks at Portia's portrait in *The Merchant of
Venice*, he holds the painter responsible for reproducing the beauty
that entraps the hearts of men; there is no implication that it is
Portia's intention to trap:

> Here in her hairs
> The painter plays the spider, and hath woven
> A golden mesh to entrap the hearts of men
> Faster than gnats in cobwebs.
> (III. ii. 120–3)

The 'amber locks' of Daniel's Delia are a medium through which
Love's weapons of assault operate on her admirer; but, again, it is not
suggested that Delia guilefully sets out to capture her lover.[28]

The usual pattern, then, is for the lover to blame something other
than the mistress for his being trapped by the net or lure of her hair.
There are two notable exceptions to this pattern: the sonnet 'Of his
Ladies vayle wherewith she covered her' from Constable's *Diana*,
and sonnet XXXVII of the *Amoretti*. Although it cannot be
established with any certainty, it is possible that Spenser may have
been influenced by Constable in using the image to imply blame.
The Constable poem opens with a quatrain which presents a thinly
veiled analogy in the natural world to the experience of entrapment
which the lover feels he is undergoing in his relations with the
mistress.[29] This pattern, which is rather unusual in Renaissance
sonnet sequences, is followed by Spenser in several of the poems in
the *Amoretti*.

Spenser's and Constable's use of the conceit is strikingly similar,
but Spenser offers a more dramatic and more lively exposition of the
idea. In Constable's sonnet, Diana's hair is seen as a trap which she
deliberately uses to ensnare the victim, but the persona is not

interested in condeming his mistress's actions. As he points out, if Diana were trying to trap him, she need only put out her hand, since he is already caught:

> Of his Ladies vayle wherewith she covered her
>
> The fouler hydes as closely as he may
> The net where caught the sillie byrd should be
> Least that the threatning prison it should see
>   And so for feare be forst to flye away
>
> My Ladie so the while she doth assay
> In curled knotts fast to entangle me
> Puts on her vayle to th'end I should not flee
> The golden net wherein I am a pray
>
> Alas (most sweete) what need is of a nette
> To catch a byrd which is allreadie tame
> Sith with youre hand alone yow may it gette
> For it desires to fly into the same
>
>   What needs such arte my thoughts then to intrap
>   When of them selves they flye into youre lap.

In the Spenser sonnet the emphasis is on accusation – the lover implies his mistress *has* set out to trap by arranging her hair in its most alluring fashion:

> What guyle is this, that those her golden tresses,
>   She doth attyre under a net of gold:
>   and with sly skill so cunningly them dresses,
>   that which is gold or heare, may scarse be told?
> Is it that mens frayle eyes, which gaze too bold,
>   she may entangle in that golden snare:
>   and being caught may craftily enfold
>   theyr weaker harts, which are not wel aware?
> Take heed therefore, myne eyes, how ye doe stare
>   henceforth too rashly on that guilefull net,
>   in which if ever ye entrapped are,
>   out of her bands ye by no meanes shall get.
> Fondnesse it were for any being free,
> to covet fetters, though they golden bee.

In allowing the lover to assume his mistress is being 'guilefull', Spenser follows Constable; but in allowing the lover to accuse and blame his mistress for trying to trap many victims in her net, Spenser is departing from Constable's emphasis, and radically departing from traditional use of the conceit. Hence, the context of the sequence, and the associations that are brought into play from the wider context of literary tradition suggest that the mistress of the golden hair sonnet is unlikely to be guilty of the crimes of which she is accused.

The weight of literary tradition and of the sequence itself, then, provides a counter to the lover's accusations. Spenser's mistress is not an exception to the rule: she is no 'dark' lady. It is her lover who momentarily finds faults with her. As the sequence develops, it becomes clear that the lover's accusations have little or no foundation, and that his complaints represent his attempts to blame his mistress for the situation in which he finds himself, and provide opportunities for him to use rhetorical techniques to make her change her ways towards him.

That the lover is deliberately seeing his mistress's actions in a critical light is also conveyed in the choice and arrangement of language in this sonnet. The question with which the sonnet opens is phrased so that 'guyle' and 'golden tresses' are seen in opposition to each other.[30] As the quatrain develops, 'guyle' is linked by assonance with words that point to the mistress's insidious cunning in dressing her hair as she does. The vowel sound of 'guyle' is echoed in 'attyre' (which refers to the dressing of her hair, as well as implying that this is how she sets her trap), and in 'sly', which refers to the skilful method she uses to dress her hair, but also to her deceit and treachery in so doing.[31] (There is a similar ambiguity in 'craftily' in the second quatrain.)

In the second quatrain the real net which was described in the first quatrain is merged with the metaphorical notion of hair as a net which traps ('that golden snare'). The words that are chosen to describe the way the net traps, also convey its sensual allure. The 'snare' is 'golden', and to be 'entangled', 'caught' or 'enfolded'[32] in it could be a pleasurable experience, though this does not cancel the element of censure in the lover's choice of words. The rhetorical question he asks makes use of the critical connotations of the words in a way that points to his mistress's deliberate cunning and cruelty. Furthermore, she wields her charms over the helpless victims with 'frayle' eyes and 'weaker' hearts. When the lover sees himself in relation to the trap (as he does in the sestet), he is much sterner about the danger, as though he thinks he can prevent himself from entanglement if only he is harsh enough with himself. His warning is voiced in the imperative in contrast with the questioning of the previous quatrains, and is a personal, particular admonition. The terms he uses to describe the danger to himself are similar to earlier terms, but the connotations are different. 'Guylefull net' (line 10) suggests an object to be avoided, while in line 2 'net of gold' sounds more attractive; to be 'entrapped' is more final, hopeless and less sensual than to be 'entangled' or 'enfolded'; to be entrapped in bonds or fetters is presumably more dangerous than to be snared in hair. (At a later point in the sequence the lover assures his mistress that bonds 'are sweet' (LXV), but this is when she is in *his* trap.)

In the couplet the lover censures the foolishness of those who desire the very thing which will deprive them of their liberty. He is of course describing his own state. His wistfulness of tone as his thoughts dwell on her hair ('though they golden bee') puts the emphasis on the beauty and allure of the fetters, rather than on their imprisoning quality. Spenser uses the couplet to bring home the irony of the lover's self-deception. As the lover's thoughts formulate themselves into a moral dictum against the 'fondnesse' of coveting fetters, he is at his most vulnerable; for in describing the allure of her hair, and the foolishness of coveting it, he betrays his own captivity. His knowledge of the powers of her golden-netted hair is much too intimate for one who is supposed to have evaded those powers. In these ways Spenser suggests it is the lover's own 'fondnesse' (foolishness and perhaps lovesickness) that has trapped him, and bound him to his mistress.[33]

Lever points out that the sestet of sonnet XXXVII implies 'that the poet still regards himself as a "free man" with hopes of escaping love's entanglements', whereas earlier in the sequence 'he has protested many times against his intolerable thraldom'.[34] The criticism that an anachronistic attitude is displayed by 'the poet' loses much of its force when it is recognized that the sestet of the sonnet presents the views of a lover persona created by Spenser, and that these views are countered within the poem in various ways. The lover persona is annoyed with the mistress for looking so alluring, and in his irritation he chooses to present himself as someone who has ecaped the trap of her 'guilefull net', and who can see through her cunning. He is, of course, manifestly deceiving himself, for his entanglement is demonstrated by his obsession with her golden hair;

he refers to its colour five times and repeatedly describes its allure. His warning to himself, in the sestet about the trap which her golden hair represents, comes too late, for he is already ensnared, and his 'intolerable thraldom' demonstrated once more.

The playful treatment of analogy is another of the techniques Spenser favours to provide different perspectives upon his persona lover. A common pattern in the *Amoretti* is for a part of the sonnet, usually the first quatrain, to be devoted to a story, anecdote or idea, whilst the remainder provides an explanation of its application and relevance to the lover's experience.[35] The lover's choice of anecdote or story usually suggests to the reader likely ways in which the lover will apply it to his experience. Spenser often deals with these expectations in unexpected or surprising ways in the rest of the sonnet, where the application is made.

Spenser's usual method, in sonnets of this kind, is to have the lover counter, or fail to meet, the expectations which have been set up, and to adopt a different method of application (often startling or surprising in itself), from the one that has been anticipated. The unexpected nature of the course of argument that the lover takes, in contrast with the course the reader has been led to anticipate he will take, is an important source of humour. The lover seems to have enormous faith in the efficacy of the comparisons he draws, and in the logic of his application of them. He acts as though he is unaware of certain connections, makes links between sets of ideas that are not really justified, and changes details of comparisons in an illogical way when it suits his purposes. Other sonneteers use the method of relating an anecdote in the first quatrain, and then using the rest of the sonnet for its application.[36] The distinctive mark of Spenser's use of this kind of analogy, however, is his playful manipulation of the details of the comparison.

Spenser draws on classical legends as a source for some of the four-lined analogies he employs. Misapplied or untenable analogies between the situation of heroical figures in classical literature and the lover's own situation are an essential part of the comedy of several of the poems of the sequence. Sonnet XXIII opens with a reference to Penelope and Ulysses:

> *Penelope* for her *Ulisses* sake,
>   Deviz'd a Web her wooers to deceave:
>   in which the worke that she all day did make
>   the same at night she did againe unreave;

The immediate assumption in line 1 is that the lover intends to reveal some parallel between his mistress and Penelope, or between Ulysses and himself – presumably to criticize his mistress for not behaving as Penelope did towards Ulysses.

As the lover's account of the story proceeds, however, there is more emphasis on Penelope's deception of her suitors than on her fidelity to Ulysses. This creates a change in expectations: it seems as if the lover intends to identify himself with the deceived suitors rather than Ulysses, so that a complaint from him in the role of wooer is anticipated.

When the story is applied to the lover's own experience, some of these expectations are met; but he also surprises the reader by dividing the role of Penelope between himself and his mistress. The lover equates himself with the one who does the weaving in the story, allowing the virtues of fidelity and perseverance ordinarily associated with Penelope to be associated with him, and making the injustice of his mistress's treatment of him seem all the more unfair. His mistress is given the other part of Penelope's role, that of doing the unravelling, so that the more doubtful virtue of 'craft' can be accorded to her:

> Such subtile craft my Damzell doth conceave,
>   th' importune suit of my desire to shonne:
>   for all that I in many dayes doo weave,
>   in one short houre I find by her undonne.

The play on 'craft' in line 5 (i.e., Penelope's unweaving, as well as her wily plan, *and* his mistress's cunning) allows a slide from the description of Penelope's activity (craft) to an accusation about the mistress's skill or craft in outwitting him. Whereas Penelope, in undoing her weaving, was both honouring her true love and outwitting her suitors, his mistress in undoing his weaving is not acknowledging his love at all, and is laying waste his hopes. The time it takes his mistress to wreak her havoc is negligible when compared with the time it takes him to weave his suit.

The comedy of the lover's behaviour is highlighted by its resemblance to the behaviour of the spider – a role far removed from that of Ulysses anticipated earlier, and one that the lover is to play again in sonnet LXXI. Although the lover himself does not explicitly make the comparison with the spider until line 13 ('Such labour lyke the Spyders web I fynd, / whose fruitless worke is broken with least wynd'), the use of 'sponne' in line 11 (with a play on the sense of spinning as in weaving, and spinning in the sense of making the thread that is used to make a spider's web) encourages this association a little earlier. The association was also prepared for as early as line 2, where the 'web' that Penelope makes is referred to. The literal meaning of 'web' at this point is woven fabric,[37] but the term 'web', of course, is repeated in line 13, and on this occasion refers simply to the spider's web.

The analogy with the spider's labour which the lover uses to reach his conclusion about his own fruitless labour in the couplet, is not related to the story of Penelope's weaving with which the sonnet began, though the structure, ideas and vocabulary of the sonnet suggest that it is. The ideas of the couplet have a proverbial, folkloric quality. The truth the lover is drawing upon to support his conclusion is similar to the moral that would be found in an emblem book, or a book of animal lore. Theobaldi's *Physiologus*, a medieval didactic verse bestiary, for example, gives information akin to the kind the lover uses:

> Huic placet illud opus tenue
> Sed sibi nil valet ut fragile:
> Quelibet aura trahit patulum;
> Rumpitur et cadit in nihilum.
>
> 'The Spider is pleased with that fine-spun work,
> but it is to no avail to it because it is fragile:
> the first breath of air pulls it and spreads it out;
> it is broken and falls into nothing.'[38]

The lover relies on this undeniable truth about the spider's web being broken by the least wind to suggest the truth and poignancy of his own conclusion that what is laboriously created by one person can be effortlessly destroyed by another. Thus, at the end of the sonnet, the lover's vulnerability when he is at the mercy of the mistress, becomes the focus of attention, and the comedy of the lover in his spider role recedes.

Spenser's deployment of analogy in the lover's speech in this sonnet produces complex poetic effects. On the one hand, there emerges in the poem the image of an abject lover, desperately twisting the well-known details of a classical legend to suit the purposes of his argument of complaint. But behind this image is that of another intelligence, the witty creator of the poem, who shares with the reader an awareness of other more straightforward and logical possible applications of the Penelope/Ulysses story, and whose inventiveness in creating the lover's variations on the story is recognizable as an essential part of what distinguishes him from his creation.

A similar pattern of comic manipulation of analogy can be observed in XXXVIII. This sonnet opens with a reference to another classical legend, that of Arion, a poet and musician, who was cast into the sea by sailors and rescued by a dolphin. This story was recorded by Pliny, and was a favourite subject of emblematic motifs in the sixteenth century.[39] The extraordinary nature and magical power of Arion's music, the reponse of the dolphin to the charm of the music, and the gallantry of the dolphin's rescue in a dangerous sea are celebrated in these accounts.

Spenser selects some aspects of this story to use as points of comparison with the lover's situation. The parallels between Arion's story and the lover's (apart from the obvious link that both Arion and the lover are 'music' makers) are not immediately anticipated by the reader, as the parallels were in XXIII. The connections which are established between the two stories in this sonnet are, however, both surprising and amusing:

> *Arion*, when through tempests cruel wracke,
>   He forth was thrown into the greedy seas:
>   through the sweet musick which his harp did make
>   allur'd a Dolphin him from death to ease.
> But my rude musick, which was wont to please
>   some dainty eares, cannot with any skill,
>   the dreadfull tempest of her wrath appease,
>   nor move the Dolphin from her stubborne will . . .

The lover compares his 'musick' with Arion's ('my rude musick'), but at the same time complains that his music has failed to achieve for him any of the things which Arion's music achieved. He attributes the cause not to the inferiority of his music, but to the ears which have listened to his music and found it wanting. Other 'dainty eares', he claims petulantly, have responded with pleasure to his song. His attitude suggests that the responsibility for the failure of his music belongs to his mistress, not himself. The lover's irritation, his less than magical music, and his placing of the blame for his failure upon the mistress draw attention to the differences between himself and Arion. Arion is a far more successful and heroic figure – a conclusion the lover chooses not to emphasize, but which is unlikely to be overlooked by the reader.

The next stage of the application of the analogy is the comparison of the mistress to two of the things referred to in the Arion story – the tempest and the dolphin. The comparison of the mistress to two things in the classical analogy reverses the pattern in XXIII, where it was Penelope, the heroine of the classical legend, whose role was shared between lover and mistress. The lover's equation of his mistress's wrath with the tempest's 'cruel wracke' provides an exaggerated account of the mistress's anger, which the lover has had to endure, and which he has failed to appease. Once the mistress's wrath has been compared with the tempest in line 7, the reader does not expect any further parallel, so that her appearing as 'the Dolphin' in line 8 comes as an amusing surprise.

The reference to the mistress as 'the Dolphin' implies there is a similarity between her qualities or behaviour and that of the dolphin in Arion's story; yet there is none. She is, in fact, quite undolphinlike (in terms of the story) in her reactions to her lover. The comparison, however, allows the lover to express his irritation with the mistress, and to use the label as a term of criticism. Whilst his name-calling ('Dolphin', 'stubborne') expresses his annoyance, it also indicates a close familiarity with, and knowledge of, his mistress's ways. The fact that he calls her a dolphin, rather than some crueller animal (dolphins in Spenser's time had a reputation for being extraordinarily good-natured and cooperative[40]), softens the critical note. The tone of his address, then, is a mixture of exasperation and affection.

In the sestet, the analogy with Arion's story is discarded as a yardstick for the lover's experience, though a shadowy reference to the story remains in the terms 'save or spill':

> But in her pride she dooth persever still,
>   all carelesse how my life for her decayse:
>   yet with one word she can it save or spill,
>   to spill were pitty, but to save were prayse.
> Chose rather to be praysd for dooing good,
>   then to be blam'd for spilling guiltlesse blood.

The sestet of this sonnet is rather disappointing, in that the witty play with the Arion story, which characterized the octave, descends to flat complaint.

Another example of the use of analogy for witty purposes occurs in LIII, a sonnet in which the lover compares his mistress to the panther, in order to show how merciless she is in her treatment of him:

> The Panther knowing that his spotted hyde
>   Doth please all beasts but that his looks them fray:
>   within a bush his dreadfull head doth hide,
>   to let them gaze whylest he on them may pray.
> Right so my cruell fayre with me doth play:
>   for with the goodly semblant of her hew,
>   she doth allure me to mine owne decay,
>   and then no mercy will unto me shew.
> Great shame it is, thing so divine in view,
>   made for to be the worlds most ornament:
>   to make the bayte her gazers to embrew,
>   good shames to be to ill an instrument.
> But mercy doth with beautie best agree,
>   as in theyr maker ye them best may see.

The first quatrain refers to the cunning of the panther, which allows the outwitting of his victims. The reader immediately assumes, in this case correctly, that it is the mistress's behaviour which has inspired this detailed account of the panther's habits and the concentration on his deceptive ways. Earlier in the sequence the lover has complained of his mistress's 'cunning' and her cruel treatment of her victims as 'spoil' or 'pray'. The reference to the panther's 'looks' and his victim's 'gaze' also brings to mind the relationship between lover and mistress.[41]

The lover's account of the panther's behaviour is an accurate rendering, according to contemporary beliefs. Lievsay, in attacking the Elizabethan popular author Robert Greene's shortcomings as a recorder of panther lore, quotes Spenser's sonnet as evidence of notions of the panther which were current in the Renaissance period.[42] Numerous sources mention the panther's habit of hiding his frightening head and alluring beasts to him, either by his 'painted skinne', or his 'sweet breath'.[43] In keeping close to the truth in his descriptions of the panther's habits, the lover is preparing the way for the readers's acceptance of his next point – that his mistress's actions resemble the panther's behaviour. The lover's bid for a reputation as an earnest recorder of the truth is, of course, doomed to failure. The reader cannot help but be sceptical in view of the outrageousness of the comparison the lover has chosen.

According to the lover, panther and mistress act from the same motive, to lure prey; they use the same methods of displaying their outward attractions, and when they successfully trap their victims by this means, they behave mercilessly towards them. In order to draw these parallels the lover successfully glosses over impricisions and inaccuracies in the details of correspondence between the mistress's and the panther's behaviour. The mistress may look attractive and lure admirers to her, but this does not establish that she intends to do this, or that she plans to trap her victim once he is a confirmed admirer of her. The panther's and the mistress's merci-lessness is similar in that they treat their victims in cruel ways, but the nature of their mercilessness is quite different. The panther responds to his victim by treating him as his 'pray', whereas the mistress is disdainful of her victim, and will not respond to him at all. The analogy between the panther and the mistress breaks down on the crucial point that, whereas the panther, after his first enticement of his victims remains very much interested in them, the mistress's attitude, after the allurements of her 'goodly semblant' have had their effect, is one of disdain and rejection. The reader of the poem is left with a sense of the radical difference between the panther's and mistress's behaviour at the same time that the lover persona is absurdly attempting to assert the exact similarity of their ways: ('Right so my cruell fayre with me doth play').

In the sestet the lover continues his rhetorical strategies by introducing the moral of his panther exemplum – that 'good shames to be to ill an instrument' – in an attempt to shame the mistress into more 'merciful' behaviour. The couplet reinforces this with its further homily and scriptural reference. But the lover's pious adoption of the role of moral critic in these circumstances is amusing rather than edifying, and cannot be taken very seriously.

In the sonnets discussed here, the lover chooses analogies which allow him to demonstrate similarities with his own situation, and to deliver moral advice as a corrective to the wayward behaviour of his mistress. But Spenser's purpose is not the same as his lover's rhetorical design. Spenser employs the analogies as a way to demonstrate their failure as parallels and the lack of correspondence between the details of the analogies and those of the lover's situation. In drawing attention to the gap between the lover's failed attempts to woo his mistress and the successes of the hero/heroine figures of the analogies, Spenser emphasizes the comic aspects of his lover's behaviour: he spins endlessly and gets nowhere, resorts to childish name-calling, invents ridiculous comparisons to describe his mistress's 'evil' ways, and dresses himself in the ill-fitting garb of a pious moralizer.

Although the lover is repeatedly thwarted in his efforts to win his mistress in these sonnets, the note of sad resignation that is characteristic of, say, Petrarch's *Canzoniere* or Daniel's *Delia* is noticeably absent. The comic treatment of the lover does not undermine his presentation as a figure of serious purpose. The comedy of the lover's behaviour and complaints is stressed, but it is balanced against the determination and imaginative energy with which he confronts his predicament, and the buoyancy of his spirit in the face of his mistress's determined opposition. The lover is amusing in his failures and in the tactics to which he resorts to impress his mistress, but he is also an earnest, purposeful suitor whose potential as a worthwhile partner for the mistress is not really in question.

In the sonnets just discussed a fairly clear distinction is established between author and lover persona by the use of broadly ironical effects produced by hyperbolical complaint, obvious clashes between the local statement of the poem and the overall narrative or context of the sequence, and the far-fetched use of analogy.

Close study of the *Amoretti* shows that Spenser has deliberately created a lover persona with characteristic, often comical, ways of dealing with his experiences of love, and that the speaking voice is not simply that of Spenser the public poet, or some objectively viewed aspect of the author's self. It is true that there are sonnets in which the ironical, distancing effects such as are evident in, say, XXIII or XXXVIII, are absent altogether, or only doubtfully present, and that in some sonnets there is a temporary identification of author and lover persona. These examples confirm that the distinction between author and persona is not consistently and clearly maintained throughout the sequence. But the exceptions do not bring into question the idea that the presentation of a lover persona is part of the overall design of the sequence. The character of the lover persona as it is developed in the sequence as a whole is the subject of the next chapter.

Notes: Chapter Three

1. J.W. Lever *The Elizabethan Love Sonnet*, 2nd edn. 1966; rpt. Methuen, London, 1974, p. 95; p. 127; p. 126. Other critics who write as though there were no distinction between poet and persona include Sidney Lee, editor of *Elizabethan Sonnets* 2 vols., Archibald Constable and Co. Ltd., Westminster, 1904; W.L. Renwick, *Daphnaïda and Other Poems*, The Scholartis Press, London, 1929; Edwin Casady, 'The Neo- Platonic Ladder in Spenser's *Amoretti*' in *Renaissance Studies in Honor of Hardin Craig*, ed. Baldwin Maxwell, W.D, Briggs, Frances R. Johnson and E.N.S. Thompson, Stanford University, California, 1941; Waldo McNeir, 'An Apology for Spenser's *Amoretti*', in *Essential Articles for the Study of Edmund Spenser*, ed. A.C. Hamilton, Archon Books, Hamden, Connecticut, 1972, p. 531. Robert Ellrodt, *Neoplatonism in the Poetry of Spenser*, 1960; rpt. Folcroft Library Edn. 1978; O.B. Hardison, Jr, '*Amoretti* and the *Dolce Stil Novo*', *English Literary Renaissance*, vol. 2, Spring 1972, no. 2; and G.K. Hunter, 'Spenser's *Amoretti* and the English Sonnet Tradition', *A Theatre for Spenserians*, ed. Judith M. Kennedy and James A. Reither, University of Toronto Press, Toronto, 1973.
2. W. McNeir, 'An Apology for Spenser's *Amoretti*' op. cit.
3. Judson remarks that it is pleasant to believe 'that Spenser's seventy-fifth sonnet . . . has a basis in fact, [and] refers indeed to the famous three-mile beach at Youghal, to this day called the Strand'. 'The Life of Edmund Spenser' vol. 2 of *The Works of Edmund Spenser*, A Variorum edition, 9 vols., ed. E. Greenlaw, C.G. Osgood, F.M. Padelford and R. Heffner, 1947; rpt. The Johns Hopkins Press, Baltimore, 1966, p. 169.
4. Ibid. p. 166.
5. J.C. Smith and E.P. de Selincourt, *Spenser: Poetical Works* 1912; rpt. Oxford University Press, London, 1975, p. xxxv.
6. A. Dunlop, 'The Drama of *Amoretti*' in *Spenser Studies: A Renaissance Poetry Annual*, ed. P. Cullen and T.P. Roche, Jr, A.M.S. Press, Inc., New York, 1978, vol. IV, pp. 107, 108.
7. Carol Barthel, '*Amoretti*: A Comic Monodrama?' *Spenser at Kalamazoo, Proceedings from a Special Session at the Thirteenth Conference on Medieval Studies in Kalamazoo*, May 1978, Cleveland State University, 1978, p. 293.
8. J. Kalil, '"Mask in Myrth Lyke to a Comedy"; Spenser's Persona in the *Amoretti*', *Thoth*, Spring 1973, pp. 20, 25.

9. For a fuller discussion of this sonnet, see below pp. 105–6.
10. For a fuller discussion of these sonnets, see above pp. 48–50; 50–51.
11. See, for example, sonnets CXXII and CLIII in *Petrarch's Lyric Poems, The 'Rime Sparse' and Other Lyrics*, trans. and ed. Robert M. Durling, 2nd edn, 1976; rpt. Harvard University Press, Cambridge, Massachusetts, 1981.
12. Failing to appreciate Spenser's deliberate use of hyperbole for comic effect in this sonnet, Crutwell complains that 'the hackneyed antithesis of ice and fire . . . topples to the ludicrous with "but I burne much more in boyling sweat"'. P. Crutwell, *The Shakespearean Moment and its Place in the Poetry of the Seventeenth Century*, Random House, Inc., New York, 1960, p. 17.
13. The syntactic and rhythmic patterns which emphasize the comic aspects of his behaviour are discussed below, p. 151.
14. The sense of the adjective 'stupid', which Spenser uses in line 14, is 'having one's faculties deadened or dulled; in a state of stupor, stupefied, stunned; esp. *hyperbolically*, stunned with surprise, grief, etc.' (*O.E.D*, sense *1*, now obsolete except in archaic poetic uses.) The *O.E.D.* also cites Spenser's use of 'stock' as an example of the meaning of 'stock', sense *lc.*: 'As the type of what is lifeless, motionless or void of sensation. Hence, a senseless or stupid person'.
15. As Anne Clark points out, 'For much of recorded history – from ancient times until the late seventeenth century – knowledge of the animal kingdom consisted of a curious mixture of travellers' tales, fable and extravagant invention . . . splendidly absurd notions accepted as true facts less than three hundred years ago'. Anne Clark, *Beasts and Bawdy*, J.M. Dent and Sons Ltd., London, 1975, p. 13.
16. Pliny declares that 'the lion alone of wild animals shows mercy to suppliants'. Pliny, *Natural History*, ed. T. Page, E. Capps, W.H.D. Rouse, L.A. Post and E.H. Warmington, 10 vols., Loeb Classical Library, Harvard University Press, Cambridge, Massachusetts, 1967, vol. 3, book VIII, p. 37.

   Edward Topsell, a Renaissance compiler of animal lore, maintained that the lion's 'clemencie in that fierce and angry nature is also worthy commendation, and to be wondered at in such beasts, for if one prostrate himselfe unto them as it were in petition for his life, they often spare except in extremitie of famine'. Topsell also remarks that 'There is no beast more vehement than a shee or Female-lyon, for which cause *Semiramus* the Babilonian tyranesse, esteemed not the slaughter of a Male Lion or Libbard, but having got a Lyonesse, above all other she rejoyced therein'. This information about the lion is printed in *The Elizabethan Zoo: A Book of Beasts Both Fabulous and Authentic*, ed. M. St. Clare Byrne, Nonpareil Books, Boston, 1979, p. 42 and p. 39.
17. For a discussion of the use of animal lore in XXXVIII and LIII, see

above, pp. 83–6.

18. An isolated example in Daniel's sequence, sonnet XVIII, has something of the impact of Spenser's accusations since it comes after a long line of compliments (as does Griffin's criticism of his mistress, though more playfully because of the pun):

> But yet restore thy fearce and cruell minde
> To *Hyrcan* Tygers, and to ruthles Beares.

19. Phipson notes that the tiger was generally considered 'the personification of remorseless cruelty'. She adds that Lear calls Goneril and Regan 'tigers, not daughters' (*King Lear* IV. ii.40), and York calls Margaret 'O tiger's heart, wrapt in a woman's hide' (*King Henry VI Part 3*, 1. iv.137). Emma Phipson, *The Animal Lore of Shakespeare's Time*, Kegan Paul, Trench and Co., London, 1883, p. 20.

20. Two senses of 'charm' are being used here:
    1. The *O.E.D.* sense 1 – 'magic spell'
    2. The *O.E.D.* sense 3 – 'any quality, attribute, trait, feature etc. which exerts a fascinating or attractive influence exciting love or admiration'.

21. M.B. Ogle, Classical Origin and Tradition of Literary Conceits', *American Journal Of Philology*, vol. 34, February, 1913, pp. 126–7. In another article ('The White Hand as Literary Conceit', *Sewanee Review*, vol. 20, February, 1912), Ogle discusses examples of the use of the 'golden hair' motif in Chrétien de Troyes' *Arthurian Romances*, Chaucer's *Canterbury Tales*, Lydgate's *Reson and Sensuallyte* and *Troy Book*, Ariosto's *Orlando Furioso*, Desportes' *Diane* and Marlowe's *Hero and Leander*.

22. Gertrude Jobes records that golden hair usually signifies purity and wisdom. G. Jobes, *Dictionary of Mythology, Folklore and Symbols*, Scarecrow Press, Inc., New York, 1961, pp. 71, 73. The power of the association between fair hair and virtue in the European literary tradition is illustrated in the changing attitudes to the morality of the intruder in the Goldilocks story, who was first a wicked fox called Scapegoat and finally a sweet-natured girl called Goldilocks. See Iona and Peter Opie, *The Classic Fairy Tales*, Oxford University Press, London, 1974, pp. 199–200.

23. See, for example, 'A Catalogue of Delights', 'The Beauty of his Mistress III', 'To His Mistress, Fairest of Fair' etc. in *Secular Lyrics of the Fourteenth and Fifteenth Centuries*, ed. Rossell Hope Robbins, Oxford University Press, London, 1964, pp. 120, 126 and 202. There are, of course, some exceptions. The medieval lyric 'In Praise of Brunettes' offers a light-hearted defence of dark hair:

> blac wol do as god a nede
> as þe wyte at boud & bedde;

> & per-to also treu in dede,
> & per-to y ley my lyf to wedde.
> *Ibid.*, p. 30.

Among those of Elizabethan sonnet mistresses, Stella's dark eyes and less than virtuous behaviour provide something of an exception. But the more notable exeption is Shakespeare's dark lady. Shakespeare also includes some dark-haired, virtuous heroines in his plays. Ogle points to 'Biron's rhapsodies over the fair beauty of his dark lady (Rosaline)' in *Love's Labour's Lost*, for example, and mentions other instances from *A Midsummer Night's Dream*. See M.B. Ogle, 'The White Hand as Literary Conceit'. op. cit., p. 461.

24. See, for example, Sidney's 'What toong can her perfection's tell'; *Astrophil and Stella* XII; Fletcher's *Licia*, LII; and Tofte's *Laura*, Part III, sonnets VI and XVI.

25. Examples of Petrarch's uses of this conceit occur in LIX, CXCVI, CXCVII, CXCVIII and CCLIII. Another poem of Petrarch's where the veil or net is admired in addition to Laura's golden hair is LII, though in this poem the hair is not directly referred to as a trap. The image of the hair as a trap in Petrarchan poetry is pictorially represented in the illustration (reproduced overleaf) of 'La Belle Charité' by the Dutch lithographer Crispin de Passe (1560–1637), which is included in Charles Sorel's satirical novel *Le Berger Extravagant*. 'La Belle Charité' represents the perfections of the mistress as they are extravagantly described by Petrarchan poets: her eyes are suns, there are roses and lilies in her cheeks, and her hair is represented as consisting of chains of gold which are furnished with hooks or lures.

26. 'Purple' originally meant scarlet, the royal colour, but here it means bright-hued, or brilliant. The quotation Pebworth refers to is from the Revised Standard Version of the Bible, the translation which he claims is closer to the original Hebrew than the King James version. See T.L. Pebworth, 'A Net for the Soul: A Renaissance Conceit and the Song of Songs' *Romance Notes*, 13, 1971, pp. 160, 163.

27. A further example of the conceit of the mistress unconsciously ensnaring the lover's heart with her beautiful hair is provided in Petrarch's sonnet CXCVI:

> et le chiome, or avolte in perle e 'n gemme,
> allora sciolte et sovra or terso bionde,
>
> le quali ella spargea sì dolcemente
> et raccogliea con sì leggiadri modi
> che ripensando ancor trema la mente.
>
> Torsele il tempo poi in più saldi nodi
> et strinse 'l cor d'un laccio sì possente
> che Morte sola fia ch'indi lo snodi.

(Reprinted with permission of the Bodleian library from Charles Sorel, *Le Berger Exravagant*, Touen, 1629, vol. I, plate opposite p. 63. [Douce S 387].) [See note 25]

> . . . and her golden locks
> now twisted with pearls and gems, then loosened
> and more blond than polished gold,
>
> which she let loose so sweetly and gathered again
> with such a charming manner that as I think
> back on it my mind still trembles.
>
> Time wound them afterward into tighter knots
> and bound my heart with so strong a cord
> that only Death will be able to untie it.
> (*Petrarch's Lyric Poems*, op. cit., pp. 342–3.)

28. See Daniel's *Delia*, XIIII:

> Those amber locks, are those same nets my deere,
> Wherewith my libertie thou didst surprize:
> Love was the flame, that fired me so neere,
> The darte transpearsing, were those Christall eyes.
>   Strong is the net, and fervent is the flame;
> Deepe is the wounde, my sighes do well report:
> Yet doe I love, adore, and praise the same,
> That holdes, that burnes, that wounds me in this sort.
>   And list not seeke to breake, to quench, to heale,
> The bonde, the flame, the wound that festreth so;
> By knife, by lyquor, or by salve to deale:
> So much I please to perish in my wo.
>   Yet leastlong travailes be above my strength,
> Good *Delia* lose, quench, heale me now at length.

29. Joan Grundy discusses the dating of the manuscripts of Constable's
     sonnets in *The Poems of Henry Constable*, Liverpool University Press,
     Liverpool, 1960, pp. 50–51, 60. His sonnets were first published in 1592
     and most of them circulated in manuscript before 1591. The sonnet
     referred to here was included in the Todd manuscript. Spenser's
     sonnets were not published until 1595, and as the title page indicates
     they were 'Written not long since'. It seems unlikely that many would
     have been circulated before that date. See *Works*, vol. II, appendix VII,
     p. 632. Thus, Spenser could have read the Constable poem before
     writing his sonnet.
        Pebworth offers a different suggestion for the source of Spenser's
     sonnet XXXVII. He singles out LIX from the other examples he notes
     of the use of the conceit in Petrarch (CXCVI, CXCVII, CCLIII), for in
     the sonnet Laura's hair serves 'not as the net itself, but as a camouflage
     for it', whereas in the other examples the hair itself is the net. See

Pebworth, 'A Net for the Soul', op. cit., pp. 160–1. However in Spenser's sonnet there is a real net, not simply a metaphorical one, and it is difficult to say whether the net camouflages the hair, or the hair the net:

> that which is gold or heare may scarse be told.

Thus Petrarch's sonnet LIX does not seem to have particular claims to be considered the source of Spenser's sonnet.

30. 'Guyle' and 'golden' are linked by alliteration (the 'g' and 'l' link) and separated by another group of alliterative sounds ('½', and 's' or 'z'). They are positioned symmetrically ('guyle' towards the beginning of the line, 'golden' towards the end), and they are important words in the line.

31. 'Skilful' is a meaning of *sly* that is now obsolete. (*O.E.D.* adj. sense 1.) The motif of failing to detect the difference between golden thread (or netting) and golden hair, a motif which is suggested in line 4, may go back to Chrétien de Troyes's *Cligès*, in which Soredamois inserts a strand of golden hair amongst the golden threads of embroidery. See Chrétien de Troyes, *Arthurian Romances*, trans. W.W. Comfort, Everyman's Library, Dent, London, *Cligès*, lines 1147 to 1196, p. 106. Ogle quotes *Cligès* as possible inspiration for Petrarch's use of the image. He notes that Petrarch was the first to make the change from eyes as a snare, to hair as a snare. See Ogle, *The Classical Origins*, op. cit., p. 130.

32. 'Enfolded' had the sense of 'involved', but it could also mean 'plunged into disaster' (*O.E.D.*, 3b).

33. The *O.E.D.* mentions affectionateness as a meaning for 'fondnesse' as early as 1603, and the adjective in that sense is earlier.

34. Lever, op. cit., p.99.

35. Examples of this pattern include XVIII, XXIII, XXXII, XXXIIII, XXXVIII, LIIII, LXVII, LXIX and LXXI. Spenser does not play with expectations in all of these examples.

36. Although this pattern occurs in Elizabethan sequences, it is not particularly popular with other sonneteers. There are very few instances of its use in Daniel's *Delia*, or Constable's *Diana*, for example. A more favoured method, but one which Spenser rarely uses, is the related pattern of the long anecdote with its relevance being made explicit towards the end of the sonnet, or in the couplet. See, for example, *Astrophil and Stella*, XIII, XXX, XXXIX, and *Shakespeare's sonnets*, CXXIX, and CXLIII.

37. The *O.E.D.*'s definition of 'web', sense 1, makes reference to figurative uses of the term from 1576. Spenser's use of 'web' in 'Unwisely weaves that takes two webbes in hand' from *The Shepheardes Calendar*, (October, line 102) is given as an example of this usage.

38. Theobaldi, *Physiologus*, ed. P.T. Eden, E.J. Brill, Leiden, 1972, p.53.

Other than his name Theobaldi, virtually nothing is known about the author of this work.

39. Alpers notes that Arion was thought to be a real person, rather than a legendary figure. The Corinthians said his adventure took place about 600 B.C., and his story was recorded about 200 years later by Herodotus. A. Alpers, *Dolphins*, Pauls Book Arcade, Auckland and Hamilton, 1963, p. 16. The story is also recorded in Pliny, *Natural History*, op. cit., pp. 183–4. Examples of the use of the Arion story in emblems can be found in Andreas Alciatus, *Emblematum*, Libellus Wissenschaftliche Büchgesellschaft, Darmstadt, 1967, Emblem XI, p. 38 XXI; p. 58; LXXV, p. 168.

Whitney also includes an Arion emblem. See G. Whitney, *A Choice of Emblems and other Devises*, Leyden, 1586, p. 144. It is reproduced below.

No mortall foe so full of poysoned spite,
  As man, to man, when mischiefe he pretendes:
The monsters huge, as druers aucthors write,
  Yea Lions wilde, and fishes weare his frendes:
    And when their deathe, by frendes supposd was fought
    They kindnesse shew'd, and them from daunger brought

> Arion lo, who gained store of goulde,
> In countries farre; with harpe, and pleasant voice:
> Did shipping take, and to Corinthus woulde,
> And to his wishe, of pilottes made his choise:
> Who rob'd the man, and threwe him to the sea,
> A Dolphin lo, did beare him safe awaie.

40. W.M. Carroll notes that the dolphin's gentleness and affection for mankind were recorded by Aristotle, Pliny, Euphues, Lodge and Greene. See W.M. Carroll *Animal Conventions in English Renaissance Non-Religious Prose 1550–1600*, Bookman Associates, New York, 1954, p. 100. Aelian records similar information about dolphins in his *De natura animalium*, a work which influenced 'that remarkable compound of animal lore and pious allegory known as "the Bestiary"' (xxiv). See Aelian, *On the Characteristics of Animals*, trans. A.F. Scholfield, 3 vols., Harvard University Press, Cambridge, Massachusetts, 1958, vol. 1, pp. 95 and 99. Shakespeare's use of the expression, 'Why, your dolphin is not lustier' ('lustier' meaning 'merrier'), in *All's Well That Ends Well* (II.iii.31) also suggests the dolphin's reputation for good nature.

41. Example of sonnets, in which the lover complains of the mistress's treatment of her victims as 'spoil' or 'prey' include X, XI, XX, XXXI and XLVII.

     The 'looks' of the panther may refer to his glances since the panther had a reputation for his lynx-eyed sight:

> It is thought that of all beastes they see most brightly, for the poets saine, that their eie/sight pierceth through every solid body, although it be as thick as a wall.

     (This quotation is from Edward Topsells' *Historie of Foure-Footed Beastes*, as recorded in M. St. Clare Byrne, *The Elizabethan Zoo*, op. cit., p. 30.) On the other hand, the 'looks' may refer to his appearance, since this was traditionally thought to have a hypnotic effect on animals. (See footnote 43 below). The reference to 'looks' in relation to the mistress, however, suggests looks or glances. The lover has 'gazed' at his mistress in XVI ('as I unwarily did gaze') and mentions her 'gazers' later in the sonnet. He is often in a gazing posture in relation to her.

42. John L. Lievsay, 'Greene's Panther' in *Renaissance Studies in Honor of Hardin Craig*, ed. Baldwin Maxwell, W.D. Briggs, Francis R. Johnson, and E.N.S. Thompson, Stanford University Press California, 1941, p. 111.

43. See Greene's 'Carde of Fancie' (1587), *Works*, IV, 82, quoted in Lievsay, op. cit., p. 107. Spenser refers only to the beautiful skin, but the sweet

breath was also thought to be a powerful lure. Lievsay also quotes Thomas Nashe's reference to 'sweete-breathing Panthers that would hyde their terrifying heads to betray . . .' in *The Unfortunate Traveller* (1594), p. 110. Anne Clark notes that 'On awakening, he [the panther] emits a loud belch which smells so sweet that it draws all animals after him. His voice sounds like a bell, and though his head is so terrifying that he has to hide it, the colours of his body are diverse and beautiful, so that other beasts cannot help being hypnotised by them. In this way the panther is able to lure his prey' (Anne Clark, op. cit., pp. 92, 93). See also Pliny, *Natural History*, op. cit., vol. III, book VIII, p. 49.

4. The Lover Persona

> I am melancholy, myself, divers times, sir, and then do I no more but
> take pen and paper presently, and overflow you half a score, or a dozen of
> sonnets, at a sitting.
>
> (Jonson, *Every Man In His Humour*, III, i)

The fashion in sonnet cycles of the 1590s was for the lover to wallow
in the woes of unrequited love. His most frequent complaints
included the bitter-sweet pain of love and the excessive degree of the
suffering it entailed; the failure of the lover's reason to keep control
over his will and desire; the debilitating effects of unrequited love on
the lover's physical well-being and the cruelty of the mistress's
rejection of him.

The language in which the lover in an Elizabethan sonnet
expresses these complaints was heavily indebted to the example of
Petrarch, whose influence held sway over English and Continental
love poetry throughout the early Renaissance period. In tune with
Petrarch in the *Canzoniere*, the lover in an Elizabethan sonnet is
commonly found to burn, freeze, pine, groan, weep, wail, and be
full of grief, sorrow and sighs – for love's wounds afflict him with an
anguish from which he feels he can never recover.

In many respects, the presentation of the lover persona in the
Amoretti is in accord with the conventional Elizabethan pattern, and
the language Spenser uses is similar to that found in most Elizabethan sonnet sequences. His mistress's rejection of him causes
'sighes' (II.3), and 'sorowe' (XXXIIII.14; XLVI.9), causes him to
'weepe' (XVIII.13) and 'waile' (LIIII.8), to 'burne . . . in boyling

sweat' (XXX.7) and to spend his days in 'pining languor' (XXXVI.3; L.1,10), to mention but a few examples.

There are, however, several ways in which the lover persona of Spenser's *Amoretti* is different from the conventional lover of the Elizabethan sonnet sequences. One major point of difference is that the lover in Spenser's sequence is not left forsaken, as other lovers are, and he is able to look forward to the consummation of the wooing of his mistress in marriage, a prospect not in view for any of his counterparts in the sonnet sequences of the Renaissance period. The complaint of Spenser's lover comes to an end, and complaint is replaced by expressions of pleasure and anxiety about problems which arise from his new status as an accepted suitor. The unique narrative line of the sequence, with its happy ending, is responsible for most of the distinguishing marks of Spenser's lover persona described to this point. But there are other equally important ways in which Spenser establishes the individuality of his lover figure.

As indicated in the previous chapter, certain details of the lover persona's 'biography' correspond roughly with known facts about Spenser's life. The lover is approximately 40 years old (LX) and is courting a woman named Elizabeth (LXXIIII). The *Amoretti* provides an account of the progress of this courtship. His pursuits and interests mark him as a suitor of intelligence and sensitivity. He is a poet who is engaged in writing an epic poem which is to honour his queen and country (XXXIII, LXXX). He has a knowledge of classical legends (XXIII, XXVIII, XXXVIII, XLIIII); is familiar with Christian doctrine (e.g. XXII, LXVIII) and Platonic doctrine (e.g. XXXV, XLV, LXXVIII);[1] and takes pride in his bond with queen, mother and mistress, showing willingness to do duty by them all (LXXIIII). These aspects of the lover's background and interests are not distinctive in themselves, but taken together they define a figure who is different from other sonnet personae.

In many ways the lover's emotional and intellectual attitudes (at times difficult to separate from one another) are similar to those of the typical lover figure. He does, however, have certain emotional and intellectual attitudes which are distinctive. One of the more distinctive habits of the lover persona in the *Amoretti* is the excessive degree of criticism which he offers his mistress, and the extreme, and sometimes vicious nature of his verbal attacks. His use of predatory animal imagery, in this regard, has been discussed above.[2] Most

sonnet lovers engage in heartfelt criticism of the mistress figure; but
Spenser's lover clearly has less justification than do others to indulge
himself in this way. He never, for example, reaches the absolute
depths of despair which Shakespeare's persona conveys in sonnets
CXLVII and CXLVIII. Another significant point of difference is
that the lover persona of the _Amoretti_ does not suffer for as long, or in
such perpetually wearying ways, as the protagonists of the more
conventional sequences. But the accusations which Spenser's
persona heaps on his mistress are more vehement and extreme than
those offered by almost any other sonnet persona, except for
Shakespeare's.[3] As has been suggested above, the lover's vehement
accusations in Spenser's sequence can usually be seen as rhetorical
devices used by the lover to persuade his mistress to his own point of
view. Reliance on, and use of, rhetorical powers in the pursuit of the
mistress is common practice for the persona of an Elizabethan sonnet
sequence. Sidney's Astrophil, for example, describes his search for
these powers (powers which he ultimately rejects in favour of
simplicity and truth) in the opening sonnet of _Astrophil and Stella_:

> Loving in truth, and faine in verse my love to show,
> That the deare She might take some pleasure of my pain:
> Pleasure might cause her reade, reading might make her know,
> Knowledge might pitie win, and pitie grace obtaine;
> I sought fit words to paint the blackest face of woe,
> Studying inventions fine, her wits to entertaine:
> Oft turning others' leaves, to see if thence would flow
> Some fresh and fruitfull showers upon my sunne-burn'd
> braine.
>
> (I)

Spenser indicates a similar awareness in his persona of the possible
value of rhetorical accounts of his woes, but Spenser's persona goes
further, in that he indicates a readiness to feign various emotions if he
thinks it opportune to do so. In XIIII, for example, Spenser's lover
lists the tactics he is planning to use to win his mistress's love:
'playnts, prayers, vowes, ruth, sorrow and dismay.' In earlier
sonnets he has explained how he has made use of some of these
devices, but now he plans to use them together as part of an
'incessant battery' against her heart. In XVIII, he complains that his
pleading, weeping, sighing and wailing fail as tactics in his battle to

win her. He is clearly trying out these various displays of emotion to achieve the end he wants. The possibility that he can produce these emotions to order, can turn them on and off, as the occasion demands, is firmly implied. There is a mind at work calculating the kinds of 'battery' that will best achieve his end.[4]

The extent to which the lover is prepared to engage in role-playing in order to break down his mistress's opposition to him as a suitor is further underlined in LIIII. The metaphor of the theatre, applied to the relationship between lover and mistress, indicates that the lover is courting his mistress as an actor courts his audience. The 'pageants'[5] he acts out may, or may not, have a basis in how he is feeling. At times, he disguises his 'troubled wits', whilst at others, the reader is led to believe, his 'merth' or 'smart' has a basis in his feelings. His determination to provide a winning performance for his mistress is, however, of paramount importance.

Another of the distinctive traits of the lover persona of the *Amoretti* is his ability to recognize and appreciate his mistress's special qualities in a manner which is both passionate and reverent. It is to be expected that a lover figure in an Elizabethan sequence will value the beauty and perfection of the mistress, but few respond in as sensitive and articulate a manner as Spenser's lover. The sestet of VIII, for example, contains an account of how essential the persona feels his mistress is to him:

> You frame my thoughts and fashion me within,
> you stop my toung, and teach my hart to speake,
> you calme the storme that passion did begin,
> strong thrugh your cause, but by your vertue weak.
> Dark is the world, where your light shined never,
> well is he borne, that may behold you ever.

At this point in the sonnet, the lover is concentrating on a single idea: that the mistress transforms his world and makes it meaningful for him. The shift to a single subject in the sestet, from the more diverse pattern of thought of the octave,[6] is heralded by the placing of the pronoun 'you' in the first position in lines 9, 10 and 11. 'You' is the unstated subject of the second half of lines 9 and 10, and the reference continues in the 'your' of lines 12 and 13 and the 'you' of line 14. More integral than this, however, is the way in which the extent of her importance to the lover is central to every line of the sestet. She affects his being through and through, and his contemplation of life without her suggests terrible deprivation:

> Dark is the world, where your light shined never.

In the couplet, Spenser extends the use of the image of light, first mentioned in line 1 of this sonnet ('More then most faire, full of the living fire'), to indicate that the mistress is someone whose qualities are of universal importance. The 'living fire' that fills her, and the implicit connection of her light with Christ as the Light of the World (line 13), suggest the spiritual dimensions of her power, and its effect on him. In the couplet of the next sonnet her 'powrefull eies', which lighten his dark spirit, are said to have the same kind of power as the Creator's:

> Then to the Maker selfe they likest be,
>   whose light doth lighten all that here we see.
>   (IX)

The light that shines from her has other dimensions as well: life, comfort, hope, virtue and knowledge. The qualities which she represents fill his life, as they would any man's, with light and meaning:

> well is he borne, that may behold you ever.

The lover of an Elizabethan sonnet sequence frequently engages in rationalization about the problems of love, or makes use of the skills of argument and rhetoric in order to gain control of the experiences which cause him such torment. Both Shakespeare and Spenser, for example, create lover personae who make heavy demands on reason in their struggle to deal with the problems of love. But whilst both these figures make use of reasoning processes for this purpose, each displays quite distinctive qualities in his intellectual approach to the problems of love.

In general terms, Shakespeare's persona tends to be far more cynical and world-weary, in his attitude to language and argument as a means of dealing with the torments of lust and love, than Spenser's persona. Extravagant displays of sophisticated wit, such as that found in Shakespeare's 'Will' sonnets (CXXXV, CXXXVI), in which the persona engages in facetious wordplay and spurious argument[7] in order to persuade his mistress to 'accommodate' him, are indicative of the contempt in which he holds logic as a means of coming to terms with his problems, as well as the low regard in which he sometimes holds his mistress. In sonnet CXXXVIII, the persona analyses the state of his relationship with his mistress by concentrating on the validity of his arguments whilst steadfastly ignoring the truth of his situation. This sonnet is, amongst other things, about the ways in which language and argument can be cleverly manipulated to confirm any perception of reality.

Spenser's persona has a much higher regard for the power of language and argument as a means to help him deal with love's difficulties. The occasions when lover and mistress argue and try to outdo each other by playing with words and ideas suggest the value of a relationship based on the mutual pleasure of witty exchange. Spenser's persona, like Shakespeare's, uses illogical arguments and wordplay in order to convince himself that he is in control of things, as well as to persuade his mistress to change her ways towards him. But he does not become the victim of the tortuous path of logic, as Shakespeare's persona often does.[8] His manipulation of language and argument helps to create a more bearable reality for himself, or is employed in his attempts to change his mistress's behaviour.

Spenser's persona tends to rationalize more often and at greater length than does Shakespeare's about the pain of love. Shakespeare's persona does occasionally tell himself that the pain of love has its rewards, albeit somewhat pessimistically:

> Only my plague thus far I count my gain,
> That she that makes me sin awards me pain.
>
> (CXLI)

On the whole however, he is more likely to lose himself in a confusion of doubts and anxieties about his love than to console himself that there is pleasure in his pain. Spenser's persona, on the other hand, often uses skilful and persuasive arguments to convince himself that pain and suffering are positively valuable things. In XXVI, for example, the lover begins by listing a number of growing things, an apparently careless selection. Each of the things he has chosen has qualities both of sweetness and nonsweetness, pleasure and pain, so that he is able to view pain as something which necessarily accompanies pleasure:

> Sweet is the Rose, but growes upon a brere;
>> Sweet is the Iunipere, but sharpe his bough;
>> sweet is the Eglantine, but pricketh nere;
>> sweet is the firbloome, but his braunches rough.
> Sweet is the Cypresse, but his rynd is tough,
>> sweet is the nut, but bitter is his pill;
>> sweet is the broome-flower, but yet sowre enough;
>> and sweet is Moly, but his root is ill.
> So every sweet with soure is tempred still,
>> that maketh it be coveted the more:
>> for easie things that may be got at will,
>> most sorts of men doe set but little store.
> Why then should I accoumpt of little paine,
>> that endlesse pleasure shall unto me gaine?

(XXVI)

Although, at one level, there appears to be a balance between pleasure and pain, the emphasis is, in fact, on the pain. The sweet things are described with the single term 'sweet', whilst a whole range of painful or unpleasurable sensations is drawn upon. The relationship between the two halves of each line becomes more strongly antithetical as the sonnet develops and the degree of pain increases. The relentless sequence of 'buts' and the heavy use of end-stops add further emphasis to the reminders of pain which recur in the second half of each line.

In the early lines of the octave, the 'soure' quality which is described ('So every sweet with soure is tempred still') is something which is unpleasant to the touch, but the later examples are more distasteful – 'bitter', 'sour', and 'ill'. The 'ill' or poison of moly is more dangerous and threatening than the thorn or the briar.[9] The pain, then, is described more vividly than the pleasure, and this suggests its power, though throughout the course of the sonnet, the lover is bent on convincing himself that he is quite able to deal with his pain, and that it is something which he ought not to mind.

In the sestet he consoles himself with generalization and cliché about the value of pain, and the rewards which come from enduring it.[10] In line 9 he views pleasure and pain as part of each other, but in lines 11–14 he shifts to thinking them sequential. In the couplet, pleasure and pain are also seen in terms of the proportions which he has to suffer. This makes it easier to bear present pain, since endless pleasure shall be his in the future. In these ways the lover places pain in perspective which helps him to deal with its severity.

In LI, the lover's powers of rationalization are presented more comically. The sonnet is about the lover's determination to find advantages in his mistress's having so hard a heart – an amusing reversal of the traditional complaint:

> Doe I not see that fayrest ymages
>   Of hardest Marble are of purpose made?
>   for that they should endure through many ages,
>   ne let theyr famous moniments to fade.
> Why then doe I, untrainde in lovers trade,
>   her hardnes blame which I should more commend?
>   sith never ought was excellent assayde,
>   which was not hard t'atchive and bring to end.
> Ne ought so hard, but he that would attend,
>   mote soften it and to his will allure:
>   so doe I hope her stubborne hart to bend,
>   and that it then more stedfast will endure.
> Onely my paines wil be the more to get her,
>   but having her, my ioy will be the greater.
>
> (LI)

The Pygmalion legend, in which Galatea, Pygmalion's ivory statue, loses its hardness and grows soft under his wooing, hovers in the background, providing a model against which the lover's unsuccessful efforts to 'bend' his mistress's stubborn heart are to be seen. Ovid records that the statue which Pygmalion sculpted eventually comes to life; 'at this touch the ivory lost its hardness, and grew soft: his fingers made an imprint in the yielding surface, just as wax of Hymettus melts in the sun and, worked by men's fingers is fashioned into many different shapes, and made fit for use by being used'.[11]

In the first quatrain a link is established between hardness and endurance, so that in the second quatrain the mistress's hard-heartedness can be approved, and the lover can comfort himself that his apparently fruitless courtship will eventually succeed. The second stage of the argument depends on the assumption that the marble images and the mistress share the same quality of hardness, when, in fact, two different kinds of hardness are involved. Similarly, in the second quatrain, there is a slide from 'hardnes' in the sense of relentlessness, to 'hard' in the sense of difficult. This allows the argument to be taken a stage further, so that the lover can convince himself that the challenge to persevere is both necessary and desirable. Other facts which the lover glosses over for the purpose of his argument include the fact that the mistress and the marble are not comparable materials of 'trade', in that they set different problems for the skill of those who would shape them; that the figure of the lady is the end product for the sculptor, whereas the figure of the lady is the material the lover is working with; and that the 'trades' of lover and sculptor are not really comparable, though there is the verbal illusion that they are because of the play on 'untrainde', 'trade', 'hardnes', 'excellent' and 'bring to end'.

The lover imposes rigorous questions upon himself, as if the discipline will force him to repress his irritation with his mistress. His irritation with her hard-heartedness surfaces, however, in line 11, where he refers to her 'stubborne hart' which he hopes to 'bend'. ('Bend' is being used figuratively here to mean 'cause to relent', but there may also be a play on 'to bind, to constrain, to make fast',[12] and if so, line 12 refers to his hopes about their long-term relationship.) This is reminiscent of an earlier moment in the sequence where the lover's irritation leads him to call his mistress a dolphin, whose 'stubborne will' cannot be altered (XXXVIII).

There is another change of tone in the couplet, and here it seems that the lover is experiencing a feeling of confidence that joy is going to be his, rather than simply convincing himself that he should be glad of his pain. The 'paines' he has to take will be the greater because of her hard heart, but once she is his, his joy will also be greater. ('Paines', in the sense of taking pains, provides a link back to the sculptor, but also has the sense of the pain he will experience in his wooing of her.) His joy will be greater than it would have been if he had not experienced pain, or if he had not had to take such care to woo her, or if she had yielded at once. The humour of the lover's determined rationalizing about his hardship fades as his anticipation of joy gains in strength, and the sonnet ends on a more serious note.

Both Spenser's and Shakespeare's personae attempt in several sonnets to camouflage something which is of concern to them, with a show of logic or argument about something else. The way in which each of the personae approaches this deception (or possibly self-deception) reflects quite differently on each of them. In CXXXIII and CXXXIIII of Shakespeare's sequence, for example, the persona wishes to draw attention to the impropriety of his friend's behaviour, and to highlight the generosity of his own. He disguises this intention beneath a show of concern for his friend, and a flourish of complaint about the mistress on his friend's behalf. In sonnet CXXXIII he asks that the mistress confine her torture to himself and let his friend go free:

> Beshrew that heart that makes my heart to groan
> For that deep wound it gives my friend and me.
> Is't not enough to torture me alone,
> But slave to slavery my sweet'st friend must be?
> Me from myself thy cruel eye hath taken,
> And my next self thou harder hast engrossed.
> Of him, myself, and thee, I am forsaken –
> A torment thrice threefold thus to be crossed.
> Prison my heart in thy steel bosom's ward,
> But then my friend's heart let my poor heart bail;
> Whoe'er keeps me, let my heart be his guard,
> Thou canst not then use rigor in my jail.
>   And yet thou wilt, for I being pent in thee
>   Perforce am thine, and all that is in me.

He presents himself as a humble victim, one who has been tortured, rejected and forsaken, but who yet has enough humanity to feel the pain of his friend. However, it is a mock compassion, and even, to some extent, a mock humility, which he expresses, for clearly his own feelings are at the centre of his interest. The frequency of 'me', 'my', 'myself', 'I', is some indication of this, as is his reference to his friend in terms of himself – 'my next selfe'. (A variant of the first-person pronoun occurs at least once in every line except line 8.) The friend's suffering is cited mainly because it is something which increases his own suffering, and because it is a part of his torment which he would dearly like to be without. Thus, all his remarks about wishing to free his friend from the position he is in have a double edge, just as his compliments to him have an undertone of criticism. (In this light, the word 'sweet' in 'my sweet'st friend' could mean that the friend is alluring or enticing to the mistress, rather than to the lover.)

In XXXI of the *Amoretti*, the impression that the lover is seeking a rational explanation for Nature's role in creating such a cruel being as his mistress is indicated in the phrasing and formal language of the opening question (in contrast with its subject matter), as well as in the steady progression of the arguments. The clear purpose of the sonnet, however, is to persuade the mistress to desist from her cruel behaviour:

> Ah why hath nature to so hard a hart,
>> given so goodly giftes of beauties grace?
>> whose pryde depraves each other better part,
>> and all those pretious ornaments deface.
> Sith to all other beastes of bloody race,
>> a dreadful countenaunce she given hath:
>> that with theyr terrour al the rest may chace,
>> and warne to shun the daunger of theyr wrath.
> But my proud one doth worke the greater scath,
>> through sweet allurement of her lovely hew:
>> that she the better may in bloody bath
>> of such poore thralls her cruell hands embrew.
> But did she know how ill these two accord,
>> such cruelty she would have soone abhord.

The arguments are founded upon premises which are blatantly false (she is not a beast 'of bloody race', nor is she comparable with a beast in the sense the lover suggests: she does not lure men to destroy them 'in bloody bath' as such beasts do). The premises have been chosen so that the lover can lead up to the explanation he has wanted to offer from the beginning, one which allows him to chastise her and present her with powerful reasons for changing her behaviour.

Similarly in XLI, Spenser's lover attempts to disguise his fears that the mistress will plague him unmercifully, and never allow him any relief, by appearing to carry out an objective analysis that will provide him with an answer as to what makes his mistress cruel. The patterning of the thought processes which the lover uses to pursue this question (is it . . . or is it, if . . . then, if . . . then, but if . . . then) helps create the illusion of his objectivity. The plea/warning of the couplet is also made to sound as though reason and fair play are on the lover's side (the play on 'faire', the balancing of 'fayre' against 'fowly'), and that it would be unfair and short-sighted of the mistress to refuse his request.

The personae of both authors attempt to disguise the concerns which obsess them, but they have different ways of doing so. The approach of Shakespeare's persona is hypocritical, and emphasizes the calculating side of his nature. His attempt to deceive his friend, for ends of his own, shows him in a particularly bad light. Spenser's lover persona, on the other hand, is more a naïve sophist than a devious deceiver. His attempts to disguise his underlying desire to complain and persuade (these themes are an obvious subtext of these sonnets) with philosophizing about the ways of nature are comically transparent, and have the effect of encouraging the reader to be amused by, rather than to despise, his unsuccessful attempts.

Throughout the sequence, Spenser's lover persona displays a stubborn, and often comical, determination to rationalize his problems, and a relentless use of logic and argument to force the mistress to see things as he wishes her to see them. He refuses to admit defeat in argument, however daunting the evidence against him. He is reluctant to acknowledge that the solutions he finds bear little relation to his experience of pain and suffering, which only serves to emphasize the stubbornness and optimism which characterize his approach to love.

A further distinguishing feature of the persona in the *Amoretti* lies in the manner in which Spenser presents the lover's attitude towards moral aspects of the love relation. Spenser's persona is presented, in many sonnets, as a figure engaged in inner conflict between certain ideals of moral conduct and his amorous desires. This in itself is not unique, in that other personae, especially, for example, Astrophil and the lover in Shakespeare's sequence, are clearly engaged in similar struggles between conscience and desire. But the presentation of the conflict in Spenser's sequence has a quite different character from that of other sequences.

The view of love offered by the persona in Spenser's *An Hymne in Honour of Love*,[13] combines Petrarchan, Platonic and Christian elements of thought and encompasses most of the standards the lover feels obliged to honour in relation to love:

> For love is Lord of truth and loialtie,
> Lifting himselfe out of the lowly dust,
> On golden plumes up to the purest skie,
> Above the reach of loathly sinfull lust,
> Whose base affect through cowardly distrust
> Of his weake wings, dare not to heaven fly,
> But like a moldwarpe in the earth doth ly.

> His dunghill thoughts, which do themselves enure
> To dirtie drosse, no higher dare aspyre
> Ne can his feeble earthly eyes endure
> The flaming light of that celestiall fyre,
> Which kindleth love in generous desyre,
> And makes him mount above the native might
> Of heavy earth, up to the heavens hight.

> (ll. 176–189)

True love is ennobling, causing the lover to deny all that is low and base within himself. To love in a worthy way, he must create in himself a selfless devotion, in which desire is turned toward 'heavens hight'. Lust is unequivocally outlawed as a selfish, destructive emotion which plays no part in love.

The sonnets provide the drama of the lover's attempts to deal with the feelings and passions he experiences in loving, in relation to these ideals. He is relentless with himself in denying his lustful feelings and in being determined to stamp them out.

In the late sixteenth century, the term 'lust' was sometimes used to refer to pleasure or desire in a positive sense, though Spenser rarely uses the noun in this way. He does occasionally use 'lustful' or 'lusty' with this meaning.[14] The term 'lust' was more commonly used pejoratively to refer to sinful forms of desire and ungoverned sexual appetite.[15] Shakespeare uses the term in this way in *Venus and Adonis*:

> Love comforteth like sunshine after rain,
> But lust's effect is tempest after sun;
> Love's gentle spring doth always fresh remain,
> Lust's winter comes ere summer half be done;
> Love surfeits not, lust like a glutton dies;
> Love is all truth, lust full of forged lies.
>
> (II. 799–804)

His powerful account of the pain and lure of lust in sonnet CXXIX ('Th'expense of spirit in a waste of shame / Is lust in action') provides other examples of this sense of 'lust'. Spenser, who shared Shakespeare's loathing of, yet fascination for, lust as it is described in this sonnet, makes frequent use of the word in pejorative senses in his poetry. In book 11 of *The Faerie Queene*, for example, when Guyon and the Palmer are journeying towards Acrasia to capture her and destroy the Bower of Bliss forever, Guyon is distracted from his purpose by two 'wanton Maidens' (*F.Q.*, II. XII. lxvi. l) who bring 'the secret signes of kindled lust' to his face (*F.Q.*, ll. XII. lxviii. 6). It is only by denying the lust aroused by the sensual power of the maidens (a power which Spenser evokes in tantalizing and erotic detail), that Guyon can complete his vital task of destroying the Bower. Acrasia's lovers who have fallen prey to lust serve as examples of what happens to those who do not avoid sensual snares. Her lovers are turned into wild beasts, each one in the shape for which his bestial nature is most appropriate:

> . . . these seeming beasts are men indeed,
> Whom this Enchauntresse hath transformed thus,
> Whylome her lovers, which her lusts did feed,
> Now turned into figures hideous,
> According to their mindes like monstruous.
> Sad end (quoth he) of life intemperate,
> And mournefull meed of ioyes delicious.
>
> (*F.Q.*, II.XII.lxxxv. 1–7)

Even when Guyon has the beasts turned back into men, after Acrasia is captured, none of them can find contentment, and Grill, of 'hoggish forme' (*F.Q.*, II.XII.lxxxvi.9), has sunk so low as to bemoan his return to his natural form, preferring his hoggish existence. Elsewhere in Spenser's writing, lust is treated with similar contempt. It is labelled 'disloyall' (*Colin Clout*, l.892), 'lawlesse' (*F.Q.*, II.II.xviii.5), 'filthy' (*F.Q.*, II.III.xlii.5), 'licentious' (*F.Q.*, II.VII.xvi.8) and 'carnall' (*F.Q.*, II.XI.xiii.7).

In the *Amoretti*, lust is described as 'base' (VI.3), 'impure' (XXI.8) and 'filthy' (LXXXIIII.l). In sonnet LXXXIIII, both lust and sensual desire are referred to directly as things of harmful consequence, and lust is spoken of as if it were wholly damaging. Any part of it would molest the sacred peace of the lover's mistress;

> Let not one sparke of filthy lustfull fyre
> breake out, that may her sacred peace molest:
> ne one light glance of sensuall desyre
> Attempt to work her gentle mindes unrest.
> But pure affections bred in spotlesse brest,
> and modest thoughts breathd from wel tempred sprites,
> goe visit her in her chast bowre of rest,
> accompanyde with angelick delightes.
> There fill your selfe with those most ioyous sights,
> the which my selfe could never yet attayne:
> but speake no word to her of these sad plights,
> which her too constant stiffenesse doth constrayn.
> Onely behold her rare perfection,
> and blesse your fortunes fayre election.

This sonnet opens dramatically with a firmly delivered imperative about the harmfulness of lust. The biblical ring of the lover's tones, and the severity of his attitude (lust is filthy; even a spark of it is damaging) imply his absolute condemnation. When he moves on to sensual desire, he is still strongly critical, but his vehemence has abated a little. The consequences of a light glance of desire are less harmful than a spark of lust; a glance of desire would disturb, or put into turmoil, her gentle mind, rather than 'molesting' her sacred peace. ('Molest' would have had the meaning, now obsolete, of 'troubling, grieving or vexing'.)[16]

It is uncertain from this sonnet whether lust and sensual desire are different in nature or in degree. If, in the lover's scheme of things, it is a matter of degree, then it would be difficult for him to admit sensual desire as part of the higher love which he approves. Yet this is something he must do since he is contemplating marriage and a sexual relationship with his mistress. His solution to the problem is to see desire as legitimate when it is modified or 'wel tempred', so that it can be presented to the mistress without guilt or anxiety. The lover does not envisage himself enjoying sexual union in the sonnets (as he does in *Epithalamion*, in which he mentions procreation as a hope and joy), but he does hint that sexual pleasures await him if he can only modify, restrain and purify his desires in the proper way. This is somewhat removed from the way the Platonist would deal with desire, and quite different from Petrarch's self-castigation about the subject:

> Oi me, lasso! e quando fia quel giorno
> che mirando il fuggir de gli anni miei
> esca del foco et di si lunghe pene?
>
> Vedro mai il di che pur quant' io vorrei
> quell' aria dolce del bel viso adorno
> piaccia a quest' occhi, et quanto si convene?
>
> Ah me alas! and when will that day be when gazing
> at the flight of my years I may come out of the fire
> and out of so long a sorrow?
>
> Will I ever see the day when the sweet air of that
> lovely face will please these eyes only as much as I
> wish and as much as is fitting?
>
> (CXXII)

The lover's solution may be possible in theory but he still has the problem of making the sensual element of his feelings part of more acceptable emotions. Although they are never explicitly expressed, questions about the relation between sensual desire and spiritual purity seem to underlie many of the lover's dilemmas. How can the

sensual be subsumed into the sacred? Is it to be purified out of
existence? If it remains, in what form is it to remain? If it remains as
physical desire, how can the guilty feelings associated with ordinary
sensual desire be avoided when experiencing it, even if it is part of a
larger emotion?

It is noticeable that the lover is far more troubled by sensual
thoughts towards the end of the sequence than he was in the
beginning, something which is to be expected, given the progressive
nature of courtship. As his sensual thoughts and desires become
more insistent, however, he devises means to deal with them which
can leave him feeling relatively guiltless, though not entirely so.

Sonnets LXXVI and LXXVII are about the sensuous pleasure the
lover finds in dwelling on the delights of his mistress's bosom. He
begins most circumspectly in LXXVI, presenting his pleasure as
though it were hallowed by being a part of his total admiration for,
and love of, his mistress:

> Fayre bosome fraught with vertues richest tresure,
>   The neast of love, the lodging of delight:
>   the bowre of blisse, the paradice of pleasure,
>   the sacred harbour of that hevenly spright

He is simultaneously aware of his mistress's inner qualities and her
outward beauty, as though her form were the manifestation of the
heavenly spirit within. This is akin to ideas about the relation
between spiritual purity and physical beauty in *An Hymne in Honour
of Beautie*:

> So every spirit, as it is most pure,
> And hath in it the more of heavenly light,
> So it the fairer bodie doth procure
> To habit in, and it more fairely dight
> With chearefull grace and amiable sight.
> For of the soule the bodie forme doth take:
> For soule is forme, and doth the bodie make.
>
> (ll. 127–33)

The first quatrain of sonnet LXXVI contains a further idea about
his mistress's beauty. However sacredly and acceptably he may
describe the effects of the sight of his mistress's bosom upon himself,
there is a sensual element in his response. Her bosom is many things

to him, beautiful, comforting, sensuous and sacred. The set of images that imply her bosom is a home ('neast, 'lodging', 'bowre') has associations of comfort, rest and safety which are mingled with the more erotic pleasures suggested in 'love', 'delight', 'blisse', and 'pleasure'. 'Bowre', as well as being a home, and so a logical transition from 'lodging', has more intimate associations (a lady's private appartment, an idealized abode, a place of intimacy) that are picked up in the phrase 'paradice of pleasure'. The idea that her breasts evoke physical delight in the beholder is mingled with a different, more spiritual set of associations that 'blisse', 'paradice' (in its more spiritual sense), 'sacred harbour' and 'heavenly spright' set up as a group. The complicated transition between sets of associations serves to indicate the inseparable nature of the sacred and the sensual in his attitude at this point.

The balance achieved in the first quatrain is not sustained for the rest of the sonnet. The thought of his mistress's physical attractions can no longer be kept in check, for he feels his physical desires are dominating in a way that they ought not to be. He deals with this in an extraordinary way, by attempting to separate himself from his thoughts and speaking as though he and his thoughts had independent existences:

> How was I ravisht with your lovely sight,
>   and my frayle thoughts too rashly led astray?
>   whiles diving deepe through amorous insight,
>   on the sweet spoyle of beautie they did pray.
> And twixt her paps like early fruit in May,
>   whose harvest seemd to hasten now apace:
>   they loosely did theyr wanton winges display,
>   and there to rest themselves did boldly place.
> Sweet thoughts I envy your so happy rest,
>   which oft I wisht, yet never was so blest.

It is a legitimate response for him to be ravished (transported, carried away) with her 'lovely sight'. But 'frayle thoughts' are 'rashly led astray' and 'pray' on the 'sweet spoyle of beautie', an interesting reversal since preying on spoil is usually *her* crime. Whilst he is critical of his thoughts' behaviour (it is 'rash', 'wanton', and 'bold'), he finds delight and pleasure in that very rashness. He appears to move between finding satisfaction in being sensuous and condemning that same pleasure.

That the lover's moral attitude is distinctly ambiguous is a fact which critics tend to play down. Brand felt that Spenser gave this sonnet Neo-Platonic modifications, and that he stressed the triumph of virtue over temptation in its companion sonnet (LXXVII), in order to avoid the dualism of sensualism and idealism that was implied in the Tasso model for both sonnets.[17] The first quatrain of LXXVI (and the couplets of both sonnets) do imply that temptation has been overcome, but the rest of sonnet LXXVI describes the heady pleasures of temptation and the lover's vicarious delight in those pleasures. In LXXVII, Spenser does not specifically make the link between apples and Adam's fall as Tasso does, and the lover's thoughts do not entirely avoid temptation.

In his discussion of LXXVI, Lever deals with the possibility of moral ambiguity in sonnets LXXVI and LXXVII in a different way. He notes that Spenser is embarrassed about his truant thoughts, but feels this is resolved in the couplet when those thoughts calm down, and 'after their initial frolic' go safely to sleep in the lady's bosom. Lever is making an equation here between happy rest and innocence: 'Indulgently the poet envies them their happy rest: they have entered Love's paradise and recovered their first innocence'.[18] He quotes from *An Hymne in Honour of Love* (lines 287–91) to support this view.

There is no reason to assume the lover's thoughts are asleep on the mistress's bosom. After so boldly placing themselves (line 12), they rest there, presumably enjoying their pleasures. The lover is envious: his thoughts can behave in ways that are unseemly for him. In the couplet, he humorously confesses that he wishes he could behave as his thoughts do. He is expressing a wry envy for their freedom and the fact that they are not culpable for what they do.

Spenser deals with the tensions between sexuality and innocence in this sonnet in a manner which is different from the way in which he treats them in *An Hymne in Honour of Love*. It is necessary to include the previous verse, as well as the one Lever quotes, to demonstrate this:

> There thou them placest in a Paradize
> Of all delight, and ioyous happie rest,
> Where they doe feede on Nectar heavenly wize,
> With *Hercules* and *Hebe*, and the rest
> Of *Venus* dearlings, through her bountie blest,
> And lie like Gods in yvorie beds arayd,
> With rose and lillies over them displayd.

> There with thy daughter *Pleasure* they doe play
> Their hurtlesse sports, without rebuke or blame,
> And in her snowy bosome boldly lay
> Their quiet heads devoyd of guilty shame,
> And full ioyance of their gentle game,
> Then her they crowne their Goddesse and their Queene,
> And decke with floures thy altars well beseene.
>
> (ll.280–93)

The surface similarities are marked – the sonnet lover's thoughts 'rest' 'boldly' on his mistress's bosom, whilst the lovers in the *Hymne* are 'at rest' and 'boldly' lay their heads in Pleasure's 'snowy bosome'. But in the *Hymne* the lovers actually engage in 'their hurtlesse sports, without rebuke or blame', whereas in the sonnet the lover remains something of a voyeur, unable to imitate his thoughts in their achievement of pleasure. Thus the lover of the *Amoretti* is left in a state of tension not experienced by the lovers of *An Hymne in Honour of Love*.

This passage in the *Hymne* solves the problem of sensual pleasure being part of the higher love by describing very generalized sensual pleasures (lovers feed on nectar, lie about like gods, sport and play with Pleasure), rather than specific sexual pleasures. Lust is clearly excluded, but there is ambiguity as to whether sporting and playing with Pleasure are sexual but innocent, or not specifically sexual because they have been transformed into a higher emotion. Given our knowledge of other instances where sexual pleasure is described in a similar way (e.g. *Epithalamion*, ll.296–314, and 352–71), the former, that the pleasures are sexual but innocent, is the more likely. As Enid Welsford comments, the lover's thoughts 'are not the dunghill thoughts of base borne mynds' but nor are they very 'like the thoughts of dedicated Christians or aspiring Neo-Platonists'.[19] They presumably hover somewhere in between.

The thoughts of the lover in sonnet LXXVI can similarly be described, but there is the difference that his thoughts (i.e. not himself) enjoy experiences that he cannot legitimately enjoy at this stage of his courtship. He is enjoying in his fancy what he should only enjoy with his whole being, and to that extent the sensuality he enjoys is something of an indulgence.

In LXXVII, the lover also distances himself from having responsibility for his desires by transferring that responsibility to his thoughts. He recalls a vision of a richly spread table upon which is placed a dish containing two golden apples:

> Was it a dreame, or did I see it playne,
>   a goodly table of pure yvory:[20]
>   all spred with iuncats, fit to entertayne
>   the greatest Prince with pompous roialty?
> Mongst which there in a silver dish did ly
>   twoo golden apples of unvalewd price:
>   far passing those which Hercules came by,
>   or those which Atalanta did entice.
> Exceeding sweet, yet voyd of sinfull vice,
>   That many sought yet none could ever taste,
>   sweet fruit of pleasure brought from paradice
>   by Love himselfe and in his garden plaste.
> Her brest that table was so richly spredd,
>   my thoughts the guests, which would thereon have fedd.[21]

Until the third quatrain the visual element of the allegory is particularly strong and the lover's feelings and thoughts about the meaning of his vision, and the effect it has upon him, are very much in the background. But in the third quatrain his attitudes towards the sight he is recalling emerge more strongly. He emphasizes the sweetness (with the play on 'sweet') of the apples (her breasts), but indicates an awareness of the possibility of the sin associated with such contemplation. Whilst the apples themselves are linked with the golden apples of classical myth,[22] they are also referred to as being 'voyd of sinfull vice'. This implies an indirect association with the apple of paradise, so that Adam's sin of partaking of the apple is hinted at. The lover's attitude is a mixture of reverence and wonder for the beauty of the sight so vivid in his imagination, yet this does not remove the desire he feels to 'taste', or enjoy the pleasures before him.

The couplet, which nominally explains the allegory, provides him with a place for his confession. His tone is circumspect, in accordance with the propriety of the rest of the sonnet, though the sentiments he is expressing are far from circumspect. He has two things, as it were, to confess: the first is that he has been thinking of his mistress's breasts all along (as is indicated, though not stated), and the second is that he, or at least his thoughts, would like to 'have fedd' on the sight further. In this context, 'fedd' means a range of things: be nourished by, gaze longingly at, taste, savour, and devour.[23] The confessional tone suggests guilt, though he makes it clear he is not guilty in any way.

The mood of determination to enjoy pleasant thoughts of his mistress's bosom changes in sonnet LXXXIIII, in which the lover feels an earnest and heartfelt need to stamp out any 'light' (unchaste) or 'lustful' desires. The kind of thoughts he would like to present to his mistress in this mood are 'modest' (chaste and moderate). His reference to 'modest thoughts breathd from wel tempred sprites' seems to be in opposition to the behaviour of his thoughts in the earlier sonnets. As the sonnet proceeds, we find he has reversed the situation that he set up in LXXVI and LXXVII, though it is still his thoughts which are the visitants. In those sonnets, his thoughts behaved wantonly, or at least expressed a desire to behave in an untoward way, whilst he was full of propriety. Here, he expresses the wish that his thoughts will behave properly (assuming 'goe' is in the imperative mood, which seems likely since 'fill', 'speake', 'behold' and 'blesse' are). He doubts, however, that he is capable of the same propriety as his thoughts:

> But pure affections bred in spotlesse brest,
>   and modest thoughts breathd from wel tempred sprites,
>   goe visit her in her chast bowre of rest,
>   accompanyde with angelick delightes.
> There fill your selfe with those most ioyous sights,
>   the which my self could never yet attayne:
>   but speake no word to her of these sad plights,
>   which her too constant stiffenesse doth constrayn.

He is determined to do the right thing by his mistress and to behave in a way that is fitting for her 'rare perfection', but, as Kostic points out, 'One feels that Spenser is at the same time half regretful that his mistress does not approve of the pleasures of the other sort as well'.[24]

Towards the end of the sonnet, he begins to concentrate more on his own feelings, and his self-pity and regret for this situation are hinted at. His reference to her 'too constant stiffenesse' has a faint note of censure, or complaint. Although 'stiffenesse' has the more neutral sense of 'strength' in the sixteenth century (a quality which the lover celebrates in LIX) the phrase, in this sonnet, has a strong echo of an earlier criticism which was directed at the mistress – her 'too portly pride'. This suggests there may be a play on the sense of obstinacy or haughtiness here, which would confirm the idea that there is a note of criticism in the lover's description. Whilst the lover recognizes the value of his mistress's 'too constant stiffenesse', and would not have her behave in any other way, it is still something with which he has to come to terms.

In these sonnets the lover struggles with feelings about what is right and proper, and what is unworthy, but when he forgets the struggle, as he does for a moment in LXIIII, and simply expresses his rapturous response to the moment when he kissed his mistress's lips, the feelings he describes are those he would wholeheartedly approve, if he were to stand aside and make a moral judgement about them:

> Comming to kisse her lyps (such grace I found),
> me seemd I smelt a gardin of sweet flowres:
> that dainty odours from them threw around
> for damzels fit to decke their lover's bowres.
> Her lips did smell lyke unto Gillyflowers,
> her ruddy cheeks lyke vnto Roses red:
> her snowy browes lyke budded Bellamoures,
> her lovely eyes lyke Pincks but newly spred,
> Her goodly bosome lyke a Strawberry bed,
> her neck lyke to a bounch of Cullambynes:
> her brest lyke lillyes, ere theyr leaves be shed,
> her nipples lyke yong blossomd Iessemynes:
> Such fragrant flowres doe give most odorous smell,
> but her sweet odour did them all excell.[25]

He recalls the moment of the kiss with enthusiastic extravagance. There is a blurring between present elation and past pleasure, in that he is recalling his feelings of rapturous response in the past, whilst reliving them in the present. The present participle 'Comming' with which the sonnet opens creates a sense of the immediacy of that moment both in the past, and as it is recollected. The parenthetical clause 'such grace I found' creates the impression that more than one sensation is vying for the lover's attention at the time of the kiss. The mistress's grace is referred to in an aside, as though it were one of a number of qualities which the lover wishes to mention and not the only, or necessarily the most important part, of the sensation he experiences.

The term 'grace' is open to a number of different, but compatible interpretations, including the lover's sudden good fortune; the mistress's bestowing of favour and mercy; her charm, ease and beauty; and possibly even the pleasant flavour of the kiss.[26] Since grace is something which is, notoriously, withheld by sonnet mistresses, the use of the word to describe the mistress's behaviour adds further significance to the moment as one of complex and overwhelming emotion in itself, but also as having importance in the narrative development of the sequence, since it indicates a change of direction in the mistress's granting of favour.

As Baroway has argued, the Song of Songs is an obvious source for comparison in this sonnet.[27] The Song of Songs is frequently alluded to in Spenser's poetry, and it is quite likely that he produced a translation of it.[28] The poet of The Song of Songs is wooing his hesitant bride and speaks of the beloved as an enclosed garden full of fruits and spices, which he looks forward to enjoying:

> 12. A garden inclosed is my sister, my spouse: a
>   spring shut up, a fountaine sealed.
> 13. Thy plants are an orchard of pomegranates, with
>   pleasant fruits, Camphire with Spikenard,
> 14. Spikenard and Saffron, Calamus and
>   Cynamoun, with all trees of Frankincense, Mirrhe
>   and Aloes with all the chief spices.
> 15. A fountaine of gardens, a well of living waters,
>   and streames from Lebanon.
> 16. Awake, O North winde, and come thou South, blow
>   upon my garden, that the spices thereof may flow
>   out: let my beloved come into his garden, and
>   eate his pleasant fruits.
>
> (Solomon's Song, 4:12–16,
> Authorized Version)

In Spenser's poem the fragrances of the flowers and fruits function as metaphors for the effect the mistress has on the lover during the kiss. The richness of the experience is suggested by the wealth of the sensations he describes, their cumulative effect, and the variety of senses drawn upon. In addition to the sense of smell being invoked, from the pungent, clove-scented gillyflower to the delicate jasmine, there is the visual appeal of the references to red, pink and white. (In a sense, these visual comparisons tend to play down the erotic element, since they contribute more to the evocation of the flowers than to that of the mistress.) There are also tactile sensations suggested by the comparison of the mistress's neck and breasts to columbines and lilies, which have soft, smooth textures. A combination of sensations is drawn upon by the comparison of her bosom with the strawberry bed – richly coloured, lush, fragrant fruit, nestling in a bed of leaves.

It is true, as Baroway argues, that both Spenser and the poet of the Song of Songs show a lack of concern for the visually incongruous effects of some of their images.[29] But Spenser establishes, at an early stage, that the comparisons in his catalogue of descriptions are to be made primarily in terms of fragrance. The 'did smell' of line 5 is not repeated, but is elliptical in each succeeding line. The omission of 'did smell' from each line does encourage other kinds of comparison, including the pictorially incongruous. ('Her goodly bosome like a strawberry bed' is difficult to think about in visual terms, for example.) In providing a basis for the comparison in terms of fragrance, Spenser is directing the reader away from the visual incongruity in a way that the poet of the Song of Songs is not.

The final compliment of Spenser's poem, offered in the couplet, is that her 'sweet odour', or the essence of her, excels the individual excellence of her parts, whether considered singly or in combination. His tribute is that he finds in her an individuality which cannot be reproduced, or matched, and which, in the end, defies analysis. This compliment is offered by the lover in a mood of joy, awe and appreciation at being blessed with the gift of his mistress. Spenser's art is such that the apparent spontaneity of the compliment, and the reverence and admiration which inform it, serve to sanctify the moment of sexual experience, represented by the kiss. This is quite different from the effect of the passage in the Song of Songs, in which the emphasis is on the poet's ardent expectation of consummation with his bride.

The sensuality of Spenser's sonnet, then, is not specifically sexual though the sexual element is implied, in that it is a kiss which occasions these feelings, and in that it is the beauty of his mistress's body – particularly her face and bosom – which stirs his response. The whole of the third quatrain is given over to thinking about the effect on the lover of the mistress's breast ('bosome', 'neck', 'brest', 'nipples') a part of her which, it can be assumed, arouses amorous feelings. Yet the sexual part of his response does not obtrude and is made a part of the more generalized sensuality he is describing. He is achieving his own moral ideal unconsciously, and setting up a standard against which his other responses can be measured.

This ideal is also achieved in the *Epithalamion*, in which the lover's sensual pleasure in the beauty of his bride is a part of his absolute worship of her. Milton was to express a similar ideal of guiltless sexual pleasure in his descriptions of the prelapsarian love-making of Adam and Eve in book IV of *Paradise Lost*. The ambivalence of Spenser's attitude towards sexual love is everywhere apparent in his poetry. He is often uneasy and puritanical about sexual feelings; but he is also capable of celebrating them with delight and with delicately evocative language which suggests an acute awareness of sensuous and sexual pleasure. His poems express the belief that sexual passion can be sanctified, even transformed, in the love relation between a man and a woman in holy matrimony. The lover persona's struggle to achieve this goal of union with his mistress is one of the major, as well as one of the more distinctive themes, of the *Amoretti*.

Another form of conflict or tension in the *Amoretti*, and one which further helps to define the character of the lover persona, is the mingling of the lover's religious ideals and his amorous devotion for his mistress. Petrarch provides the model for the presentation of conflict between spiritual and amorous devotion in the *Canzoniere* (e.g., sonnets CCLXVI, CCCLXV). There are, however, relatively few Elizabethan sonnet sequences in which conflict of this kind plays a significant part. Shakespeare's persona expresses some concern for the consequences in the after life of his behaviour (e.g. sonnets CXXIX, CXLIIII), and Astrophil announces his resolution of the conflict between love and serving 'The inward light' early in the sequence:

> True, that on earth we are but pilgrims made,
> And should in soule up to our countrey move:
> True, and yet true that I must *Stella* love.
>
> (V)

Spenser, in the *Amoretti*, gives this kind of conflict more significance than it has in either of these sequences.

In the earlier part of the sequence, before the union of lover and mistress is confirmed, the lover feels his love ought to be honourable, even sacred, in order for it to be worthy of presentation to his mistress. After their union is assured, he seeks to celebrate and sanctify their love by seeing it as an acceptable and worthy expression of Christian love. However, the kind of worship the lover wishes to bestow upon his mistress is not necessarily compatible with absolute devotion to Christ. The lover shows himself aware of this danger in a number of sonnets, and he even acknowledges that there are times when he chooses the 'hevens blisse' his mistress offers rather than the higher path (LXXII). There is, however, little doubt that the lover wants his feelings for his beloved to be in accord with, and not in opposition to, his religious ideals.

It was not unusual in secular and sacred love poetry written prior to the Renaissance for a common vocabulary to be used to describe the mistress or the beloved, as well as the object of spiritual worship. In the medieval period, for example, sacred poetry adopted the secular vocabulary more entirely than it has done in any period since. The relationship between man and God is frequently described as though it were a relationship of lover and beloved, even using Petrarchan commonplaces to describe the lover's attitude:

> Now wax I pale and wan
> For luve of my lemman.

In medieval religious poems, Christ is referred to as 'my dere and my drewry', and 'my luve, my sweting'. He is addressed as a sweet lover – 'Jesu Christ, my lemmon swete'.[30]

Conversely, of course, religious terminology is often appropriated in secular poetry for the description of various aspects of earthly love. In Chaucer's *The Knight's Tale*, for example, Arcite envies his cousin's 'paradys' (l. 1237) of being able to see Emily from the window of his prison.[31] Arcite regards his banishment from her as 'helle' (l. 1226), instead of the 'purgatorie' (l. 1226) he suffered in prison when he could see her, but not be with her. Terms of this kind occur in other of Chaucer's tales.[32] In medieval poetry, the word 'bliss' is applied to both spiritual and earthly joy. Arcite experiences 'blisse' (l. 1230) when he sees his beloved Emily. In medieval religious verse, the word is very frequently employed as a term for heavenly joy, as in the anonymous poem in praise of the Virgin, 'Nou Skrnketh Rose ant Lylie Flour':

> Whose wol fleysh lust forgon
> Ant hevene blis abyde,
> On Ihesu be is thoght anon
> That therled was ys side.

In the hymn, 'Biheld Hire Sone o Rode', 'bliss' refers to the joy Christ brought to mankind ('Neu blisse he us broute').[33]

Spenser, too, often employs religious language to describe earthly experiences in most of his work. In *An Hymne in Honour of Love*, for example, 'blisse' (l. 279), 'Paradize' (l. 280) and 'Purgatorie' (l. 278) refer to the pleasures and agonies of love. Rosalind, of *Colin Clouts Come Home Againe*, in some ways a forerunner of the mistress of the *Amoretti*, is described in hyperbolical terms as being from a higher plane:

> For she is not like as the other crew
> Of shepheards daughters which emongst you bee,
> But of divine regard and heavenly hew,
> Excelling all that ever ye did see.
>
> (II. 931–4)

The terms 'divine' and 'heavenly' were in general use as early as the late fifteenth century, to describe superior qualities, but they are used here also to imply Rosalind's spiritual perfection and excellence.

In the *Amoretti*, in the very first sonnet, the mistress is described as an 'Angel' whose 'blessed looke' has the power of life and death over her lover. She is his 'soules long-lacked foode', and his 'heavens blis'. Later in the sequence (sonnet LXIII), the lover hails the resolution of his suffering with the thought that 'All sorrowes [are] short that gaine eternall blisse'. In its context in the poem, 'eternall blisse' refers to the 'ioyous safety' (line 10) of his mistress's acceptance of him, which the lover anticipates shall be his in the near future. In such instances, language appropriate to religious experience is being used in a metaphorical way to describe experiences of secular love. There are times, however, when Spenser's lover uses religious language with a sharper edge than usual, times when he challenges the proprieties and appears to be moving outside the acceptable bounds of the interchange of vocabularies.

The first occasion of this is sonnet XXII, the Lenten sonnet:

> This holy season fit to fast and pray,
>> Men to devotion ought to be inclynd:
>> therefore, I lykewise on so holy day,
>> for my sweet Saynt some service fit will find.
> Her temple fayre is built within my mind,
>> in which her glorious ymage placed is,

on which my thoughts doo day and night attend
lyke sacred priests that never thinke amisse.
There I to her as th'author of my blisse,
will builde an altar to appease her yre:
and on the same my hart will sacrifise,
burning in flames of pure and chast desyre:
The which vouchsafe O goddesse to accept,
amongst thy deerest relicks to be kept.

Spenser's sonnet bears some relation to Desportes' sonnet 'Solitaire et pensif' from his sequence *Diane*, though not that of 'a close paraphrase', as Kastner misleadingly says it does:[34]

Solitaire et pensif, dans un bois ecarté,
Bien loin du populaire et de la tourbe espesse,
Je veux bastir un temple à ma fiere déesse,
Pour apprendre mes vœux à sa divinité.

Là, de jour et de nuit, par moy sera chanté
Le pouvoir de ses yeux, sa gloire et sa hautesse;
Et devot, son beau nom j'invoqueray sans cesse,
Quand je seray pressé de quelque adversité.
Mon œil sera la lampe ardant continuelle,
Devant l'image saint d'une dame si belle;
Mon corps sera l'autel, et mes soupirs les vœux.

Par mille et mille vers je chanteray l'office,
Puis, espanchant mes pleurs et coupant mes cheveux,
J'y feray tous les jours de mon cœur sacrifice.

Lonely and thoughtful, in a remote wood,
Far away from humanity and the pressing throng,
I will build a temple to my proud goddess,
To offer my vows to her divinity.

There, day and night, will I sing of
The power of her eyes, her glory and her nobility;
And devoutly and without ceasing I will invoke
her beautiful name
When I am burdened by misfortunes.

My eye will be a constantly burning lamp
Before the holy image of one so beautiful;
My body will be the altar, and my sighs the vows.

> Through thousands and thousands of verses I shall
> sing the service,
> Then, shedding my tears and cutting my hair,
> There, every day, I will make a sacrifice of my heart.
>
> (My translation)

The lover of Desportes' poem imagines building a temple in a peaceful, secluded wood, where he can offer vows to his mistress: '*sa divinité*'. His actions are described in terms of the actions of a religious person towards his God – chanting and singing by day and by night, offering vows and devotion, asking for help in adversity, daily making the sacrifice of his heart. The person to whom he offers these services is, however, his mistress, his Diana.

In Spenser's poem the lover imagines a similar sacrifice and ritual of worship (though the details of his imagined worship are different). The opening reference to Lent (which Lever interprets as a declamation against Desportes' 'secret, half-pagan cult', and evidence of Spenser's 'purely Christian sentiment'[35]) ought to lead the lover to the most holy and spiritual of thoughts as appropriate for such a season, but instead inspires him to find ways to offer 'service' to his mistress. The 'devotion' of line 2 has only its religious sense in that line, but as the quatrain proceeds, it becomes clear that the kind of devotion the lover is going to engage in is not of this kind, but is, instead, secular 'devotion' to his 'saynt'. Similarly, the 'fit service' he wishes to offer refers to his desire to act as the servant of Love, and of his lady (a meaning of 'service' now obsolete), and does not refer to the religious sense of the phrase, though that sense is being played with. The lover wants to offer his mistress 'service' which is comparable to that which a priest offers God, yet in desiring to do so the lover is allowing his mistress to occupy the place that would ordinarily be occupied by his Lord. Lever chooses to see the lover's 'service' simply as part of the 'universal act of Christian worship', a reading which creates the awkward problem of having to explain the use of 'goddesse' in line 13 as 'careless' and as 'striking a false note'.[36] The use of 'goddesse' is, in fact, quite consistent with the pagan element in the lover's account of the worship which he wishes to present to his mistress.

The images of pagan ritual and worship which are evoked in the poem, such as the building of an altar to appease the divinity's wrath and the offering of the heart as a sacrifice and a relic, sit uneasily with the temporal location of the poem in the holiest season in the

Christian faith, Lent. The choice of the word 'saynt' to describe the object of his devotion draws attention to the pagan element of worship (it sounds distinctly heretical to have chosen a secular figure as a saint for Lenten worship), just as the reference to the mistress as 'th' author of my blisse' underlines her usurpation of God's position in the lover's thoughts. 'Author' is a word traditionally used to describe God's role in the making of mankind. In the Authorised Version, the word occurs three times in the New Testament (1 Corinthians 14:33, Hebrews 5:9 and Hebrews 12:2).[37] In the two examples from Hebrews, the abstract phrases which follow the word author ('of eternal salvation'; 'finisher of our faith') suggest something of fundamental importance in the creation and salvation of all mankind. The lover, in contrast, is celebrating his own personal 'blisse', and he wishes to honour his mistress for being its 'author'. This is far removed from the spiritually desirable conduct of the Christian, especially during the Lenten season which is traditionally a season of abstinence.

Thus the way in which these religious terms are used, as well as the way the sonnet echoes its model, draws attention to the sacrilegious element in the lover's behaviour. It is not suggested in the poem that love of the mistress and love of God are necessarily incompatible; but Spenser is hinting that the lover has not yet reconciled his devotion for both. The Easter sonnet (LXVIII) exhibits a similar, though less blatant, play with language and ideas. The sonnet purports to be simply a celebration of the risen Lord, with an exhortation from the lover, to himself and his mistress, to follow Christ's commandments:

> Most glorious Lord of lyfe that on this day,
>   Didst make thy triumph over death and sin:
>   and having harrowd hell didst bring away
>   captivity thence captive us to win;
> This ioyous day, deare Lord, with ioy begin,
>   and grant that we for whom thou diddest dye
>   being with thy deare blood clene washt from sin,
>   may live for ever in felicity.
> And that thy love we weighing worthily,
>   may likewise love thee for the same againe:
>   and for thy sake that all lyke deare didst buy,
>   with love may one another entertayne.
> So let us love, deare luve, lyke as we ought,
>   love is the lesson which the Lord us taught.

The religious language and biblical references which continue throughout the poem, along with a syntactical organisation, particularly in the first two quatrains, which is reminiscent of that used in the collects in The Book of Common Prayer,[38] confirm that the spiritual significance of Easter is an important theme in the sonnet. As the poem proceeds, however, there is a shift from a concentration on the lover's celebration of Christ, to a concentration on his celebration of the love which he and his mistress enjoy.

The transition begins quite early in the sonnet. The pronouns 'us' (line 4) and 'we' (line 6, and elliptical in line 8) could refer to all for whom Christ died, but there is a strong implication, borne out by the couplet, that the lover is thinking particularly of himself and his mistress. The ambiguity carries over into other words – 'ioyous', 'felicity' – which are appropriate in a purely Christian context, but which apply equally well to the earthly happiness of the lovers.

The third quatrain moves away from a general account of Christ's death to an analysis of how it affects the lovers. The word 'love' is used three times in this quatrain. Christ's love and his act of salvation become the measure for the actions of the lover and his mistress. They will love him in return for the love he showed them and all mankind, and will love 'one another' for his sake. The use of 'love' in the last line of this quatrain has an ambiguity that the earlier instances do not have. The kind of love Christ commanded when he asked that 'ye love one another as I have loved you' (John 15:12) is a brotherly love for all men. The lover persona may, in fact, be professing obedience to this commandment – he does claim, for example, that they will love one another 'for thy sake that all lyke deare didst buy'. But at the same time the exclusiveness of the pronouns the lover uses ('we', line 9; 'one another', line 12), contrasting with the 'all' (line 11) which Christ's action embraces, confines the action of loving to the lover and his mistress. The word 'love' in such a context must refer primarily to the love of a man and a woman for each other. That they are to 'entertayne' each other with love (i.e. mutually sustain, perhaps even cherish[39]) again puts the emphasis on the interaction between them, rather than on a love which is to be shown to all mankind.

The degree of irreverence in the lover's failure to dedicate himself single-mindedly to the meaning of Christ's death in sonnet LXVIII can be indicated by comparison with a passage from *An Hymne of Heavenly Love* in which Spenser deals with the theme of the need for absolute devotion to Christ:

With all thy hart, with all thy soule and mind,
Thou must him love, and his beheasts embrace:
All other loves, with which the world doth blind
Weake fancies, and stirre up affections base,
Thou must renounce, and utterly displace,
And give thy selfe unto him full and free
That full and freely gave himselfe to thee.

(ll. 260–66)

The theme of the *Hymne* is that it is Christ who gives us life and we must first love him and then our brethren, for in loving them 'We give to him by whom we all do live' (l. 210). These lines share the Neo-Platonic zeal for spiritual exclusiveness, though it is not that devotion to other things eventually leads to devotion to something higher, as the Neo-Platonic ladder would suggest,[40] but that love of Christ leads to love of others:

> . . . that loving Lord
> Commaunded us to love them for his sake
>
> (ll. 204–5)

The *Hymne* tells the reader what must be done for Christ ('thou must' (l. 261); 'thou must renounce' (l. 264). 'and give' (l. 265)). But in the sonnet the lover treats Christ's commandment to love one another as though it provided a sanction for the behaviour he is already engaged in; and as though 'one another' ('with love may one another entertayne') referred primarily to himself and his mistress.

The lover's address to his 'deare love' in the couplet is a final, more obvious act of impiety since it echoes the earlier use of the term in relation to Christ – his 'deare Lord' (line 5), and Christ's 'deare blood' (line 7 – 'deare' meaning at high cost, as well as worthy and beloved). The lover is interpreting the lesson of the Lord in a particular way, one which provides justification for continued love between himself and his mistress. Hardison's and Kaske's point that in this sonnet the sexual and the spiritual are reconciled for the first time in the sequence overlooks the nature of that reconciliation.[41] The lover persona does attempt to subsume the sexual in the sacred, but he is only able to do this by interpreting his religion in a way which makes it possible to accommodate his secular love, and not rob his love of any of the importance he wants to assign to it. His love for his mistress is dominant at the end of the poem, and this

suggests the spiritual danger which the manner of his reconciliation
has involved.

It is not until LXXII that the lover fully acknowledges that there
are dangers in the path he has chosen to follow.[42] He describes times
when his spirit chooses the 'hevens blisse' that his mistress offers on
earth as his goal, and ignores the call of heaven. In that the mistress
resembles heaven, or represents heaven's qualities to him,[43] his
concentration on her is partially legitimate; but in that he is prepared
to make her his sole source of delight, bliss and ease, his worship of
her has its sacrilegious elements. From a Christian point of view the
final couplet of the poem is distinctly aberrant:

> Hart need not wish none other happinesse,
> but here on earth to have such hevens blisse.

The suggestion is that in substituting one kind of love for another,
the lover is on the verge of behaving in a blasphemous way and
allowing his devotion for his mistress to usurp the place of his
devotion to his Lord.

On the whole, the lover keeps fairly close to a conventional
Christian outlook throughout the sequence, but at times his feelings
for his mistress threaten to deflect him from the higher path.[44] His
capacity to be 'drawne with sweet pleasures bayt' (LXXII) and to
indulge in erotic fantasies (LXXVI, LXXVII) provides some insight
into the strength of the emotions that drive him and gives a glimpse
of a humorous spirit which recognizes his own human frailty.
Spenser is not providing his lover with religious philosophy, so
much as presenting his attempts to reconcile the two loves that have
importance in his life.

The overall picture of the persona which emerges from this study
is of a man of conflicting impulses, attitudes and ideals. He is both
harshly condemnatory and highly appreciative of his mistress's
qualities. He attempts to control the emotional problems of love by
intellectual means. He has high ideals of moral conduct, but at the
same time is often subject to the temptations of fleshly desire, in
ways which conflict with these ideals. He has a strong commitment
to religious values. But in some sonnets, to an almost blasphemous
extent, his amorous devotion to the mistress threatens to replace his
devotion to his Lord.

The ways in which these conflicts are presented in the _Amoretti_ clearly differentiate Spenser's persona from other sonnet lovers. Spenser's lover persona is a unique creation in the sonnet tradition and deserves recognition, along with Astrophil, and the lover persona of the dark lady sonnets, as a character of complex and distinctive qualities.

NOTES: Chapter Four

1. For a discussion of sonnets which reveal a knowledge of Christian doctrine, see above pp. 124–30, and for those which deal with Platonic doctrine, see below pp. 152–60.
2. See above pp. 71–3 and 84–6.
3. Shakespeare's persona blames and accuses his mistress in particularly virulent and nasty ways, and frequently threatens her with retribution. The more tormented he feels, the more culpable he makes his mistress. See, for example, sonnets CXXXVII, CXLII, CXLIIII and CLII.
4. There is a similar listing of tactics which the lover plans to use against the mistress in Delia, XI:

   > Yet will I weepe, vowe, pray to cruell Shee;
   > Flint, Frost, Disdaine, weares, melts, and yeelds we see.

   However, there is no strong indication in the sonnet that the lover is able to produce these emotions to order. (See Daniel, Delia, op. cit.)
5. Spenser was indebted to Tasso's Rime as a source of several of his sonnets including LIIII. Brand comments: 'Tasso's contrast of the lady's constant severity with the variety of costumes worn by the poet is worked out by Spenser in close visual detail – the theatre, the spectator, the comedy, the tragedy, the spectator's mockery'. C.P. Brand, Torquato Tasso: A Study of the Poet and his Contribution to English Literature, Cambridge University Press, Cambridge, 1965, p. 294. This suggests 'pageants' means scenes acted on the stage. It has another level of meaning as well – a part played in the drama of life. (O.E.D., sense 16.) This latter sense of 'pageants' is close to Spenser's use of the term in The Faerie Queene, III.V.i.1–3:

   > Wonder it is to see, in diverse minds,
   > How diversly love doth his pageants play,
   > And shewes his powre in variable kinds

   A further possible sense of 'pageants' in LIIII, a sense which is now obsolete, is parts acted to deceive or trick. (O.E.D., sense 1c.)
6. The subjects of the octave include the origin of the mistress's perfection, her relationship to her Maker, the way Cupid operates

through her eyes, and the ways in which 'base affections' are made 'chaste'.

7. 'Will' is the most frequently used pun in these sonnets. It refers to purpose, desire, lustful desire, the penis, the vagina, and those who are named Will – Shakespeare himself, and possibly the lover, the friend and the wife's husband. 'Will' occurs 13 times in sonnet CXXXV (and 'wilt' once in line 5), and seven times in sonnet CXXXVI. The sestet of sonnet CXXXV provides an example of spurious argument. In this sonnet the persona argues that the sea can increase in quantity when rain is added to it (rain having sexual connotations similar to those implied in the refrain of Feste's song at the end of *Twelfth Night*: 'For the rain it raineth every day'). There is, of course, no real correspondence between the sea's capacity to receive rain, and the mistress's capacity to receive lovers. The apparent validity of the argument depends on the sexual innuendo of 'rain', and the play on 'will' (line 11). For a comment on the sexual connotations of 'rain', see E. Partridge, *Shakespeare's Bawdy: A Literary and Psychological Essay and a Comprehensive Glossary,* revised edn. 1947; rpt. Routledge, Kegan Paul, London, 1968, p. 171.

8. In the sonnets in which the lover deals with the doubting of his senses (e.g. CXXXVII, CXLI, CXLVIII, CL), he becomes entangled in extraordinarily complicated reasoning processes. The frequency of words such as 'if', 'or', 'who' and 'why' indicates that the lover is caught in hypothetical possibilities, alternative explanations and endless questioning.

9. The herb moly has a white flower with a black root. Spenser is drawing upon the opposition between the white flower which is 'sweet', and the black root, which he claims is 'ill', or evil. The *O.E.D.* quotes John Lyly's use of the term in *Euphues*, (11.19) (1580, *O.E.D.,* sense 1), which draws upon a similar opposition: 'But as ye hearb Moly hath a floure as white as snow, and a roote as black as incke: so age hath a white head, showing pietie, but a black hart swelling with mischief.' Spenser does not imply any reference to the magical powers of the root, which are described in Homer's *Odyssey*. See E.H. Blakeney (ed.), *A Smaller Classical Dictionary,* 5th edn., 1910; rpt. J.M.Dent and Sons Ltd., London, 1928, p. 152.

10. These notions about the necessity and value of pain were familiar from Renaissance emblems, as well as other sources. Augustine lent authority to these ideas in his work *De doctrina Christiana* (see, for example, Augustine, *On Christian Doctrine,* trans. D.W. Robertson, Liberal Arts Press, New York, 1958, p. vii.) The Prologue to the fifteenth century Scottish poet, Robert Henryson's *Fables* includes the common metaphor 'The nuttis schell, thocht it be hard and teuch, / Haldis the kirnell, sueit and delectabill'; (R. Henryson, *The Poems of*

Robert Henryson, ed. Denton Fox, Clarendon Press, Oxford, 1981, p. 3)
Another aphoristic rendering of notions contained in sonnet XXVI
occurs in the emblem 'Post amara dulcit': 'So after paines, our pleasures
make vs glad, / But without sower, the sweete is hardlie had.' (G.
Whitney, *A Choice of Emblemes,* 1586, ed. J. Horden, Scolar Press, 1969,
p. 165.)

11. Ovid, *Metamorphoses,* trans. Mary M. Innes, Penguin Books,
Harmondsworth, Middlesex, England, 1955, book X, p. 232. In this
sonnet, Spenser may have been influenced by the examples of Petrarch
and Samuel Daniel, who make explicit use of the Pygmalion legend in
reference to the hard-hearted mistress in their sonnet sequences. See
'Behold what happe *Pigmaleon* had to frame' from Daniel's *Delia* (XIIII)
and Petrarch's sonnet LXXVIII which concludes with the lines:

> Pigmalion, quanto lodar ti dei
> de l'imagine tua, se mille volte
> n'avesti quel ch'i'sol una vorrei!

Pygmalion, how glad you should be of your statue, since you received a
thousand times what I yearn to have just once!

12. *O.E.D.,* 'bend' vb. sense 1: 'to bind, to constrain, to make fast', 1036,
now obsolete; sense 11: 'to cause (a person, the temper, spirit, mind or
will) to bow, stoop, incline or relent'.

13. This is not all the persona of the *Hymne* has to say about love, and of
course this *Hymne* must be seen in relation to the other *Hymnes.*
Spenser's retraction of the first two *Hymnes* offered in the dedication,
makes it foolish to equate Spenser's own view with the view of the
lover in the first *Hymne.* Nevertheless, the ideal view of love
represented here plays its part in the *Hymnes* as a group, as it does in the
lover's thoughts about love in the *Amoretti.*

14. The *O.E.D.* gives 'pleasure, delight' as a meaning for 'lust' until 1607.
Similarly, 'lustful', in the sense 'delightful, pleasurable', and 'vigorous'
(*O.E.D.,* 2; 3), and 'lusty', in the sense of 'joyful, merry, jocund,
cheerful, lively' (*O.E.D.,* sense l), were meanings current in Spenser's
time. An example of the use of 'lustful' with this meaning can be found
in the description of Clarion in Spenser's mythological poem
Muiopotmos:

> The fresh yong flie, in whom the kindly fire
> Of lustfull yougth began to kindle fast,
> Did much disdaine to subiect his desire
> To loathsome sloth, or houres in ease to wast;
> (ll. 33–36)

or in Colin Clout's account of his languishing for Rosalind, in which
he, like the season, is without energy or vigour. He describes his

'lustfull leafe' as 'drye and sere'. See *The Shepheardes Calendar*, January, line 37.

15. This use of the term 'lust' is defined in the *O.E.D.*, sense 4: 'Sexual appetite or desire. Chiefly and now exclusively implying intense moral reprobation: libidinous desire, degrading animal passion. (The chief current use.)' One of the examples given to illustrate this use stresses the connection of the term 'lust' with animal passion:

> Eighty two cats . . . in the time of their lust
> (commonly called catwralling) . . . are wilde and
> fierce, especially the males.
> Topsell's Four Footed Beastes (1658)

16. See *O.E.D.*, 'molest', vb., sense 1.
17. C.P. Brand, op. cit., p. 291. The Tasso poem, which is the model for both sonnets is quoted by Lever (J.W. Lever, *The Elizabethan Love Sonnet*, 2nd edn, 1966; rpt., Methuen, London, 1974, p. 110.):

> Non son si belli i fiori onde nature
>   Nel dolce april de' vaghi anni sereno
>   Sparge un bel volto, come in real seno
>   E bel quel ch'a l'autunno Amor matura.
> Maraviglioso grembo, orto e cultura
>   D'Amore e paradiso mio terreno!
>   Il mio audace pensier chi tiene a freno
>   Se quello onde si nutre a te sol fura?
> Quel che i passi fugaci d'Atalanta
>   Volser dal corso, o che guardo il dragone,
>   Son vili a mio desir ch'in te si pasce:
> Ne coglie Amor da peregrina pianta
>   Pomo ch'in pregio di belta ti done
>   Che nel tuo sen sol di te degno ei nasce.

> The flowers in the sweet April
> with which nature adorns a beautiful face,
> serene for its young years, are not as beautiful
> as what in Autumn Love ripens in a real bosom.
>   Wonderful haven, garden and nursery
>   of Love, my earthly paradise!
>   How can I hold back my audacious thought
>   if it steals only from you what it feeds on?
> Whatever changed the fast pace of Atalanta
> from her course, or (whatever) kept the dragon watchful,
> are as worthless to my desire which feeds only on you:
>   Nor can Love pick from a rare plant

a fruit that adds to your beauty
for it grows in your bosom, only worthy of you.

(trans. Luigi Buono)

18. Lever, op. cit., p. 112.
19. E. Welsford, *Spenser. Four Hymnes. Epithalamion: A Study of Edmund Spenser's Doctrine of Love*, Basil Blackwell, Oxford, 1967, p. 41.
20. Spenser uses an image similar to that used in line 2 of sonnet LXXVII to describe Belphoebe in *The Faerie Queene* (II. III. xxiv. 1–3):

> Her ivorie forhead, full of bountie brave,
> Like a broad table did it selfe dispred,
> For Love his loftie triumphes to engrave.

21. Keats, who was much influenced by Spenser, has these lines at the end of *Ode to a Nightingale:*

> Was it a vision or a waking dream?
> Fled is that music: Do I wake or sleep?

In both poems the experience that is being recalled has not receded, though it has passed.

22. The allusions are to the golden apples which Hercules took from the garden of the Hesperides after slaying the dragon at its entrance, and to the golden apples used to tempt Atalanta to pause in the race she was running against Hippomenes. See Blakeney, *A Smaller Classical Dictionary*, op. cit., p. 255 and p. 84.

23. The *O.E.D.* finds the first occurrence of 'to feed one's eyes' in *The Faerie Queene* (1590), II.VII.iv. 7–9:

> And in his lap a masse of coyne he told,
> And turned upsidowne, to feede his eye
> And covetous desire with his huge threasury.

24. Kostic makes this point in comparing this sonnet with its model in Tasso. He sees its difference lying in the fact that in the Tasso poem there is a clear distinction between two types of love – carnal and spiritual. V. Kostic, *Spenser's Sources in Italian Poetry: A Study in Comparative Literature*, Faculté de Philologie de l'Université de Belgrade, Monographie Belgrade, 1969, p. 64.

25. It is worth noting the echoes of this sonnet in Thomas Campion's song, 'There is a garden in her face' (1601), *The Oxford Book of Sixteenth Century Verse* ed. E.K. Chambers, Oxford University Press, Oxford, 1966, pp. 842–3. The 'sweet odour' of the last line may be a reminiscence of Leviticus 26:31: 'I will not smell the savour of your sweet odours'.

26. The occasional usage of 'grace' in the 16th and 17th centuries to mean 'pleasantness of flavour' is recorded in the *O.E.D.*, sense 1.

27. Israel Baroway, 'The Imagery of Spenser and the *Song of Songs'*, rpt. 1934, in *Edmund Spenser: Epithalamion*, ed. Robert Beum (The Charles E. Merrill Literary Casebook Series), Columbia, Ohio, 1968, p. 83.
28. Ponsonbie's 'The Printer to the *Gentle Reader*,' which precedes Spenser's *Complaints Containing Sundrie Small Poemes of the Worlds Vanite*, explains 'that he [Spenser] besides wrote sundrie others, namelie *Ecclesiastes*, and *Canticum cantorum* translated . . .' *Works* vol. VIII, p. 33.
29. Baroway, op. cit., p. 84.
30. See Richard Rolle, 'A Song of Love for Jesus', *Medieval English Lyrics: A Critical Anthology*, ed. R.T. Davies, Faber and Faber, London, 1963, p. 108 and 117; and M.S. Luria and R.L. Hoffman (eds.) *Middle English Lyrics*, W.W. Norton and Company, Inc., New York, 1974, pp. 105, 107.
31. The edition used is F.N. Robinson (ed.) *The Works of Geoffrey Chaucer*, 2nd edn. 1933; rpt. The Riverside Press, Cambridge, Massachusetts, 1957.
32. The Merchant, for example, prays to God that he might be a wedded man and refers to such a state as 'paradys' (1. 1265) and 'paradys terrestre' (1. 1332). The aged January's young wife, May, is described in *The Merchant's Tale* as 'His fresshe May, his paradys, his make' (1. 1822) and the narrator wryly comments on their bedtime activities:

> How that he wroghte, I dar not you telle;
> Or whether hire thoughte it paradys or helle
> (11. 1963–64)

The Wife of Bath claims to have been 'purgatorie' on earth for her fourth husband (Wife of Bath's Prologue, l. 489.)
33. Theodore Silverstein (ed.), *Medieval English Lyrics*, Edward Arnold, London, 1971, p. 47 and p. 17.
34. L.E. Kastner, 'Spenser's *Amoretti* and Desportes', *Modern Language Review*, vol. IV, 1908–9, p. 67.
The version of the sonnet which Kastner uses, and which is quoted in the text, is one which Lever says derives indirectly from 'a Rouen edition of 1611'. (Lever, op. cit., p. 105.) Lever quotes a version of Desportes' poem which appeared in editions of his sonnet sequence *Diane* from 1573 to 1581:

> Solitaire et pensif, dans un bois écarté
> Bien loin du populaire et de la tourbe espesse,
> Je veux bastir un temple à ma seule déesse,
> Pour appendre mes vœux à sa divinité.
> Là, de jour et de nuit, par moy sera chanté
> Le pouvoir de ses yeux, sa gloire et sa hautesse;

Et devôt, son beau nom j'invoqueray sans cesse,
Quand je seray pressé de quelque adversité
Mon oeil sera la lampe et la flamme immortelle.
Qui me va consumant, servira de chandelle:
Mon corps sera l'autel, et mes souspirs les vœux,
Par mille et mille vers je chanteray l'office,
Puis, espanchant mes pleurs et coupant mes chevaux,
J'y feray tous les jours de mon cœur sacrifice.

The changes in the versions do not markedly alter the sense of
Desportes' poem, but the use of '*à ma seule déesse*' (instead of the '*à ma
fière déesse*' of the Rouen edition) emphasizes the non-Christian nature
of worship. Spenser's choice of the word 'Saynt' echoes the 'saint' of
'*Devant l'image saint d'une dar:e si belle*' of the Rouen version, but has no
parallel in the earlier version.

35. Lever, ibid., p. 107.
36. Ibid.
37. 'For God is not the author of confusion, but of peace, as in all Churches
of the Saint' (1 Corinthians 14:33); 'And being made perfect, he became
the author of eternal salvation unto all them that obey him' (Hebrews
5:9); 'Looking unto Jesus the Author and finisher of our faith, who for
the joy that was set before him, endured the cross.' (Hebrews 12:2).
Authorized Version, op. cit., vol. 5.
38. 'That the Easter sonnet, "Most glorious Lord of life that on this day"
(68), echoes the style of the collects in the Book of Common Prayer has
been recognized ever since Noble's review in 1880'. Carol V. Kaske,
'Another Liturgical Dimension of *Amoretti* 68', *Notes and Queries*, vol.
222, 1977, p. 518.
39. See *O.E.D.*, 'entertain' vb., senses 1 and 14c.
40. Neo-Platonic ideas of the ladder of perfection derive from passages in
Plato's writings such as the following in *The Symposium* which enjoins
the individual to 'begin with examples of beauty in this world, and
using them as steps to ascend continually with that absolute beauty as
one's aim, from one instance of physical beauty to moral beauty, and
from moral beauty to the beauty of knowledge, until from knowledge
of various kinds one arrives at the supreme knowledge whose sole
object is that absolute beauty, and knows at last what absolute beauty
is'. Plato, *The Symposium*, trans. W. Hamilton, Penguin, Harmondsworth, Middlesex, England, 1951, p. 94.
41. Kaske notes that 'as O.B. Hardison maintains, this sonnet represents
the very first moment in the volume when the sexual is reconciled with
the spiritual' (O.B. Hardison, '*Amoretti* and the *Dolce Stil Novo*', *English
Literary Renaissance*, 11, 1972, pp. 213–14). See Carol V. Kaske,
'Another Liturgical Dimension of *Amoretti* 68', op. cit., p. 519.

42. The Neo-Platonic implications of this sonnet are discussed below pp. 164–5. Sonnet LXXII is printed below. See p. 164.

43. Brand notes that LXXII is a free version of Tasso's 'L'alma vaga di luce e di bellezza', and that Spenser adds two lines (5–6) to the original stressing that he is drawn back to earth because the lady resembles 'heaven's glory'. Brand, op. cit., p. 291.

44. The view that the persona is engaged in a Neo-Platonic quest in which he grows progressively more chaste under the mistress's influence is considerably undermined by this sonnet, which occurs late in the sequence. For a discussion of Casady's defence of this view, see below p. 162.

5. Neo-Platonism in the 'Amoretti'

The relation of ideas in Spenser's poetry to Neo-Platonic thought has been the subject of much commentary. To a large extent, such commentary has tended to be focussed on questions relating to the extent of Neo-Platonic influence and the origin of Neo-Platonic ideas within the poetry, rather than on the ways in which Spenser treats Neo-Platonic themes. It is often assumed that Spenser presents Platonic ideas as part of a body of doctrine which he endorses. Yet, as has been suggested in the case of Petrarchan and Christian ideas, it is not Spenser's habit to deal with ideas in this way in his imaginative writing. Spenser's poetic treatment in the *Amoretti* of ideas derived from, or closely related to, Platonic traditions deserves fuller exploration.

The philosophical tradition of Neo-Platonism had its beginnings in the writings of Plotinus in the third century A.D. Neo-Platonism is a nineteenth-century term used to distinguish the thought of Plotinus and his followers from that of the Platonic school itself. Plotinus (205–270) sought to expand and develop ideas which he interpreted as central to the philosophical teachings of Plato as they were recorded in the *Dialogues* or passed on through oral tradition. The complicated traditions of Platonism, together with the contribution which characterized Plotinus' development of Platonic ideas as presented in his *Enneads*, became the basis of further development in Neo-Platonic philosophy, such as the Christian Platonism of Augustine (354–430) and the pagan Neo-Platonism of the fifth and sixth centuries in Greece.

A major revival of interest in Neo-Platonic ideas was inspired by the Florentine Academy of Neo-Platonism, founded in 1462 and led by Marsilio Ficino (1433–1499) under the patronage of Cosimo di Medici. Ficino devoted 20 years to the translation of the works of Plato and Plotinus and so made these works available to the Latin West. The philosophy of Ficino and the work of his disciples, such as Pico della Mirandola and Leone Ebreo, had a considerable influence on the development of philosophical thought in Renaissance Europe.

There were many ways in which an English writer of the late sixteenth century could have gained familiarity with the teachings of Plato.[1] A few writers of the period, including Spenser himself, may have read some of the works of Plato in the original Greek. But there were several other means by which Platonic notions were given currency.

Continental influences were of paramount importance in the dissemination of Platonic ideas in England.[2] The fifteenth-century Neo-Platonic translations inspired by Ficino and his work with the Florentine Academy, revived interest in Plato's writings all over Europe. The Neo-Platonic commentaries on the texts were, themselves, a source of Platonic ideas, as were the reinterpretations of poets such as Petrarch, Tebaldeo and Tasso undertaken by the Florentine school. As evidence that these commentaries were read attentively in England, Quitslund points to the title of one of Henry Constable's sonnets (Part I, set iii, IV): 'To his Mistresse upon occasion of a Petrarch he gave her, shewing her the reason why the Italian Commenters dissent so much in the exposition thereof.'[3] Another important channel for the spreading of the influence of Platonic ideas in England was contact with French poets and philosophers, who had responded enthusiastically to the wave of interest inspired by the *trattati d'amore*. Particularly influential in this regard were Desportes and the poets of the Pléiade, although not all of these poets retained their enthusiasm for Platonism.[4]

Spenser was heir to many of these influences. He probably had some first-hand knowledge of Plato, and it is generally accepted that he was familiar with the commentaries on and translations of Plato inspired by Ficino. Renwick notes that Ficino's Latin version of Plato and Ficino's commentary on the *Symposium*, Benevieni's *Asolani,* and the third book of Castiglione's *Il Cortegiano* translated by Hoby, were all readily available to Spenser. Mulcaster, Spenser's headmaster at the Merchant Taylor's School, London, is known to have held educational views and linguistic theories which were identified with the Pléiade, and Spenser's knowledge of the Pléiade poets is evident in his frequent indebtedness to them. He also shows knowledge of Petrarch, Dante, Tasso and others whose work contained Platonic elements, or at least was considered to do so, after reinterpretation by the Neo-Platonists.[5]

Spenser's attitude to love and beauty was clearly influenced by Platonic thought, and more immediately by Neo-Platonic treatises. Many of the characteristic marks of Spenser's poetry – his passion for beauty, the desire to repudiate lust, his faith in the power of love, and his high spiritual ideals suggest a mind receptive to Platonic notions. The *Amoretti* contains a number of ideas which are almost certainly Platonic in origin. But as the radical disagreement amongst critics about the sources of ideas in Spenser's works indicates,[6] it is never easy to establish precisely their derivation.

The extent of Platonic influence in the sonnets is a subject of some debate. It has been fairly commonplace to find the sequence 'full of the influence of Plato', and to assume that Spenser uses the sequence to express his own Platonic mode of thinking. Winstanley measures its success in terms of its Platonic content: 'It helps to make amends for what otherwise might be a want of interest'. This kind of argument assumes that there are many examples of ideas in the sequence which can be considered unambiguously Platonic, that Spenser's values are the same as his lover's, and that the lover's attitude towards Platonic ideas is one of reverence and acceptance. There are others, however, who consider that Spenser's reliance on Platonic ideas has been exaggerated. Kostic, for example, sees Platonic ideas in the *Amoretti* as an excrescence, a 'non-functional ornament': 'Platonic ideas in the *Amoretti* sonnets look mostly like patches, like a superstructure, and do not contribute much to the total effect of the poem'. Dees adopts a more radical position and argues that in the *Amoretti* (particularly the Easter sonnet) a negative, or at best ambivalent, attitude is displayed towards Platonic ideas.[7]

The issue as to whether Spenser was influenced by the Florentine school at the outset of his poetic career, or at a later stage, is another point of contention. Ellrodt considers that Spenser's interest in the technicalities of Neo-Platonism came late in his career.[8] Quitslund, however, argues that Spenser 'was early in his career, significantly influenced by the revival of learned interest in Plato and the Platonic tradition which was initiated by Marsilio Ficino and his circle'. He compares sonnet VIII, considered to be one of the earliest composed sonnets, with sonnet CLIIII of Petrarch's *Canzoniere*, as evidence of this. Spenser's departures from his model and the similarity of these to the doctrines of Gesualdo, a frequenter of the Academy of Naples, lead Quitslund to believe that Spenser probably used Giovanni Andrea Gesualdo's commentary on the *Canzoniere* first published in 1533, and printed again in 1541, twice in 1553, in 1574 and in 1581. But Quitslund is not able, finally, to establish that Spenser was influenced by Gesualdo's commentary. He speculates about the similarity between Gesualdo's and Spenser's ideas, but he cannot exclude other possible sources for these ideas, or the possibility that the Platonic content of sonnet VIII is attributable more generally to a Platonic way of thinking, or habit of mind.[9]

There are many factors which make it difficult to assert that an idea or attitude which is found in Spenser's poetry is Neo-Platonic in origin. The philosophy of Neo-Platonism may appear distinctive when considered as a whole, but many characteristic ideas are paralleled in other philosophical, mythological and literary traditions. Similarly, the vocabulary used to describe attitudes to love and beauty in Platonic thought is not always distinguishable from the language and imagery of other love poems.

One of the main tenets of Neo-Platonism is that sensual love is an inferior form of love which must be transcended in man's progress towards spiritual perfection. Sexual love was treated by Plato as a lower form of love, though, in the *Symposium,* Diotima describes procreation as a divine thing in which mortal nature seeks to be everlasting. Plotinus, an important source for Ficino and other Neo-Platonists, echoes Plato's notion of the purpose of procreative love, and also asserts that such love is inferior to that in which carnal desire has no part:

> Those that love beauty of person without carnal desire love for beauty's sake, those that have – for women, of course – the copulative love, have the further purpose of self-perpetuation: as long as they are held by these motives, both are on the right path, though the first have taken the nobler way.

Ficino, in his commentary on the *Symposium*, describes sensual love in severe terms as a 'mad lasciviousness' which 'drags a man down to intemperance and disharmony and hence seems to attract him to ugliness, whereas love attracts to beauty'. He adds that 'love and the desire for physical union are not only not identical impulses, but are proved to be opposite ones'.[10] Most of the Neo-Platonists shared Ficino's disapproval of sensual love, though some went further than he in their condemnation of it. Equicola, for example, speaks of the filth of coitus; Bembo claims that when the 'material senses' are involved, 'dirty things' are desired, and that all ills spring from desire 'as trees do from their roots', whilst Bruno thought Petrarchan love 'vulgar and bestial'.[11]

Only Castiglione, among the Neo-Platonists, thought it advisable to discuss the earlier stages of physical attraction in any detail, or to allow that sensual desire might be acceptable in circumstances not related to the purpose of procreation, though even he considered sensual love to be a deceit. His account of the purpose of the kiss in the courtier's life is unusual and is perhaps included in *Il Cortegiano* because of the nature of that work: it is not a *trattato d'amore* in the traditional sense, but a socially orientated work concerned with the best ways to behave in courtly society. Even so, Castiglione feels bound to cite Plato and The Songs of Songs as justification for his defence of the kiss. He recognizes the risk that the sensual lover may incline more to the body than the soul in the experience of the kiss, but is confident that the rational lover will make it a rarefied spiritual experience. It is to be undertaken not to arouse 'any unseemly desire' but so that each can 'pour themselves into the other's body in turn and so mingle that each of them possesses two souls, and it is as if a single spirit composed of the two governs their two bodies'.[12]

Disapproval of sensual desire has a long history and played a part in attitudes that were influential in the Renaissance period. The Catholic Church regarded virginity as a superior moral state and insisted on a celibate priesthood; and whilst the churches of the Reformation eventually discontinued the requirement of celibacy for the clergy, this reform met with opposition, including that of Elizabeth I, who 'never overcame her repugnance to the marriage of the clergy', and who, of course, was known as the 'Virgin Queen'.[13] Christianity had always opposed lust and sensuality. Paul's attitude was that:

> It is good for a man not to touch a woman. Nevertheless to avoid fornication, let every man have his own wife and let every woman have her own husband . . . for it is better to marry than to burn.
>
> (1 Corinthians 7: 1–3, 7:9)

The tradition of courtly love, begun by the eleventh-century troubadour poets, and continued to some extent by Petrarch and his imitators, viewed the sublimation of passion as a virtue. To the courtly lover, love was an art with rules to follow – to love the wife of another of higher status than himself, to keep the affair secret, to undergo hardships to please the beloved and to keep the relation unconsummated, sublimating passion in the services of the lady. Chastity and the restraining of carnal desire were 'reckoned among the virtues' and their opposites, lust and sexual indulgence 'reckoned among the vices'.[14] Petrarch, himself, was troubled by his physical desire and earthly longing for Laura, and frequently saw them as a hindrance to his spiritual progress. In the *Secretum*, a dialogue he composed between himself and St Augustine, Petrarch has Augustine accuse him of loving Laura in the wrong way, and in the *Canzoniere* he is never really satisfied that he has achieved a love worthy of Laura's divine perfection or purified enough for his own salvation. Petrarch could not fully accept, as Dante did, that his love for his mistress and his love for God were entirely complementary.[15]

The second stage of the Neo-Platonic notion about the baseness of sensual love is that, once this love has been overcome, there can be progression up the ladder to love towards divine perfection. This also has its parallels in other systems of thought. The medieval notion of the universal hierarchy that leads to God grew out of the Neo-Platonic philosophy of the third century, particularly from the thinking of Plotinus. He saw the necessity of properties of the absolute overflowing into 'the Other' and so creating an order, or scale of being.[16] Augustine and the sixth-century Greek philosopher Pseudo-Dionysius took over this complex of thought and reformulated it into the system which had currency through the Middle Ages and down to the late eighteenth century.

The account Dante gives of his journey towards God in *La Vita Nuova,* and *La Divina Commedia* also has points of similarity with Neo-Platonism. Dante's concentration on the nature of Beatrice's excellence, which in itself is not unlike the Neo-Platonic concentration on the abstract quality of beauty, has the result of freeing him from physical desire and opening the path to a higher spiritual perfection. In life, and in death, Beatrice is Dante's spiritual guide. She eventually leads him to that vision of God which is the crown of his experience, and which he describes in book 3 of *La Divina Commedia.*

Dante's vision of God is not unlike the stage of the Neo-Platonic ladder where the soul 'aflame with the sacred fire of true divine love . . . flies to unite itself with the angelic nature'.[17] The Neo-Platonist discards each previous step as he progresses up the ladder, ultimately discarding sense and reason in order to unite himself with the One. Dante, on the other hand, comes to a higher perfection through loving Beatrice. At every stage his love for her is the guiding force and it is she who leads him, through ascending spheres of bliss, to God. The stages through which Dante and the Neo-Platonist move are similar, though their philosophies are antithetical, and their methods different.

Spenser's poetry often draws upon images and motifs which could be Neo-Platonic in origin, but which are also familiar from other sources. He frequently uses images of light to suggest the spiritual nature of the mistress of the *Amoretti*. In sonnet VIII, for example, she is described as 'More then most faire, full of the living fire / Kindled above unto the maker neere', and in XVI, her 'fayre eyes' are referred to as 'my love's immortal light'. The strain of idealism in Spenser's sequence, of which the imagery of light is a part, is not necessarily derived from, or expressive of, the Neo-Platonic belief in the immaterial origin of physical beauty.

A splendidly ornate expression of this Neo-Platonic belief is provided by Bembo, the chief character in Castiglione's *Il Cortegiano*. Beauty is described as

> an influx of divine goodness which, like the light of the sun, is shed over all created things but especially displays itself in all its beauty when it discovers and informs a countenance which is well proportioned and composed of a certain joyous harmony of various colours enhanced by light and shadow and by symmetry and clear definition.[18]

This description has similarites with Petrarch's way of describing beauty in the *Canzoniere*. Petrarch employs ideas which have affinities with Platonic concepts but do not rest upon a substructure of specifically Platonic ideas. He sees the beauty of Laura's face, and the divine lights ('divina belezza') of her eyes as proof of her heavenly power (CLIX), and refers to her appearance radiating beams of divine beauty.[19]

In *La Divina Commedia*, it is the power of Beatrice's brilliant and loving glance that guides Dante to his vision of divinity:

> A lady summoned me – so blest, so rare,
> I begged her to command my diligence.
>
> Her eyes outshone the firmament by far
> As she began, in her own gracious tongue,
> Gentle and low, as tongues of angels are.[20]
>
> (book 1, canto XI, ll. 53–8)

Ronsard often sees a link between the light of his mistress's beauty and her inner spiritual power, though his vision of that power is perhaps more worldly than either Petrarch's or Dante's view of it:

> If your eyes knew their own divine puissance,
> or as I see them could themselves admire,
> they'd understand why mortals in their presence
> burn and are ravaged by immortal fire.[21]

Sidney describes Stella's beauty in similar terms. He refers to Stella's 'heav'nly face', which sends forth beams, and to the 'sacred lights' her eyes:

> For though I never see them, but straight wayes
> My life forgets to nourish lauguisht sprites;
> Yet still on me, ô eyes, dart downe your rayes:
> And if from Majestie of sacred lights,
> Oppressing mortall sense, my death proceed,
> Wrackes Triumphs be, which *Love* (high set) doth breed.
>
> (XLII)

There were, then, a host of possible sources for Spenser's imagery of light, and he may have drawn on any, or all, of those mentioned here.

The view that love is a cause of bodily languishing, is another motif which gives rise to a set of images which could suggest Neo-Platonic attitudes, particularly when coupled with the expression of a desire to transcend passion. Spenser frequently suggests that love causes physical symptoms,[22] many of which are similar to those of diseases, as do many of the Neo-Platonic treatises. Ficino and Ebreo, both physicians, included medical references in their accounts of love, and Bembo describes the symptoms of the lover who fails to transcend his physical passion as 'paleness and dejection, continuous sighings and weepings, mournfulness and lamentations, silences and desire for death'.[23]

The idea of love as a physical disorder goes back to Sappho[24] and Ovid,[25] who treats the idea somewhat ironically, and also occurs in Plato.[26] Dante[27] says his first sight of Beatrice vexed and impeded the natural functions of his body, leaving him weak and reduced, and Petrarch is renowned for his dramatization of the processes of his bodily languishing, as a result of love in the *Canzoniere*. Troilus in Chaucer's *Troilus and Criseyde* likewise suffers this 'wondre maladie'.[28] Medieval and Elizabethan poets continued the convention. Those who were love-struck suffered from 'weeping, sighing, pallor, sleeplessness, alternative seizures of hot and cold, desires for solitude, and loss of appetite'. Most lovers in sonnets, including Spenser's, suffer from some, or all of these symptoms.[29]

The notion of love entering and wounding the heart through the eye occurs in the *Amoretti*, as it does in most Elizabethan sonnet sequences. The Neo-Platonic treatises accorded the faculty of sight a role of this kind:

> Love, through whom high truth I do discern.
> thou openest the black diamon doors;
> Through the eyes enters my deity, and through seeing
> Is born, lives, is nourished, and has eternal reign;
> Shows forth what heaven holds, earth and hell:
> Makes present true images of the absent;
> Gains strength: and drawing with straight aim,
> Wounds, lays bare and frets the inmost heart.[30]

This notion is not, however, exclusively Neo-Platonic and occurs in many other sources which were available to Spenser. The classical idea of Cupid's firing his darts into the eye of the beholder and so inflaming the heart was common in ancient poetry and has continued through Petrarch to the Renaissance.[31] The troubadour love poets also made use of the notion. Chrétien de Troyes describes the process in *Cligés*:

> Then tell me, if the dart passed through the eye, how is it that the eye itself is not injured or put out. If the dart entered through the eye, why does the heart in the breast complain, when the eye which received the first effect, makes no complaint of it at all? I can readily account for that: the eye is not concerned with the understanding, nor has it any part in it; but it is the mirror of the heart, and through this mirror passes, without doing harm or injury, the flame which sets the heart on fire.[32]

Sordello, writing in the thirteenth century, makes use of a similar image:

> By noble nature she knew how to rob me of my faithful heart the first time that I saw her, with a sweet amorous look that her thieving eyes threw me. With such a look and on such a day love penetrated through my eyes to my heart in such a form that it pulled my heart away and placed it at her command, so that it is with her wherever I go or stay.[33]

There is, then, a need for caution in developing hypotheses about the sources of Platonic ideas, and about the extent of their influence or presence in Spenser's poetry. However, Spenser's interest in, and sympathy towards, Platonic ideas cannot be disputed, and in at least a few sonnets (III, XXXV, XLV, LXXII, LXXVII and LXXXVII), he seems deliberately to evoke ideas which appear to be Platonic in origin, or, at least, to be constant with, if not exclusive to, Platonism.

On the whole, the attitude which Spenser has his persona adopt towards the Platonic notions employed in these sonnets is not the reverent one that would be expected of a disciple of that philosophy. Platonism is not rejected out of hand by the lover, for certain of its characteristic ideas are of interest to him, but he is never used simply as an instrument for the exposition, or celebration, of Platonic ideas.

A light-hearted, overtly comical approach is taken to Platonic notions and their effects in sonnet III, an approach which alerts the reader, at an early stage of the sequence, to the possibility that Platonic notions are not necessarily going to be treated with the gravity that might have been anticipated. The sonnet is one of praise of the mistress's 'soverayne beauty':

> The soverayne beauty which I doo admyre,
>   witnesse the world how worthy to be prayzed:
> the light wherof hath kindled heavenly fyre,
>   in my fraile spirit by her from basenesse raysed.
> That being now with her huge brightnesse dazed,
>   base thing I can no more endure to view:
> but looking still on her I stand amazed,
>   at wondrous sight of so celestiall hew,
> So when my toung would speak her praises dew,
>   it stopped is with thoughts astonishment:
> and when my pen would write her titles true,

it ravisht is with fancies wonderment:
Yet in my hart I then both speake and write
the wonder that my wit cannot endite.

The opening lines of the poem lead the reader to expect a formal sonnet of praise in which the mistress's excellence is described by her suitor. One reason for this expectation is that in the two previous sonnets both lover and mistress have been given conventional roles. In the first, dedicatory, sonnet, the mistress is a figure of great beauty and semisanctity, and her lover an abjectly humble suitor (though there is rather more conviction that her grace will be forthcoming than is usual in a dedicatory sonnet). In the second sonnet, the mistress is his 'fayrest proud', cruel and disdainful of his unquiet thoughts.

Spenser gives a comic twist to the roles of lover and mistress in the third sonnet by parodying the postures already established, as well as by exaggerating the traditional notion of the suitor's being struck dumb by his mistress's beauty. The mistress's beauty and radiance (her spiritual qualities) are so bright that they daze the lover, and his admiration for his mistress is so overwhelming, that he is incapacitated by it. This reading of the poem does not detract from the lover's earnest celebration of his mistress's beauty, but it does add a dimension that is overlooked if the poem is treated simply as a sonnet of praise.

One of the notions being played with is that of the inner worth of the beloved revealing itself in light or divine radiance akin to the light of God. In Ellrodt's view, the imagery of light and fire in this sonnet has its origin in Petrarch and is not related to the Platonist's Heavenly Beauty.[34] Spenser may well have drawn the idea from Petrarch or other sources, though it needs to be acknowledged that radiance of such apparently transforming kind has strong affinities with Neo-Platonic accounts of beauty, and it is this element of the idea which is deployed in sonnet III.

Another idea which is present in this sonnet is that of love's having the power to raise the basest human being to a higher spiritual plane. Again, this notion is related to the system of thought expressed by the symbol of the Platonic ladder, though it is also familiar in other traditions of thought.[35] The lover's belief that his mistress is his spiritual superior, and that loving her is a transforming and improving experience is a frequent motif in the sequence; but it is usually dealt with in a witty way. In XIII, for example, the lover plays with ideas of degree (lowliness and loftiness) so that he can point to the paradoxes in his mistress's behaviour towards him, and persuade her to favour him with more of her attention. He uses arguments about the spiritual dimensions of these notions simply to persuade her to give up her hardhearted, proud behaviour. The ambiguity of the couplet of sonnet XIII allows two possible readings – that her humility or 'lowlinesse' in deigning to look upon him shall lead her to greater worthiness, or that his 'lowlinesse' shall increase her loftiness:

> Yet lowly still vouchsafe to looke on me,
> such lowlinesse shall make you lofty be.

In either instance it is her increased worthiness which is looked forward to; not his. In a Platonic or Neo-Platonic world, love of the mistress would be a source of spiritual elevation for him, but in the world evoked by the lover he becomes the potential agent of his mistress's advancement. Again, in LXVI, the lover argues that it is his darkness which makes her light appear the brighter, and concludes that:

> Yet since your light hath once enlumind me
> with my reflex yours shall encreased be.

In both these examples, the lover draws on ideas that might be considered Platonic, but uses them to define a relation of mutual dependence and interaction with his mistress that is inconsistent with the spirit and implications of Platonism.

In sonnet III, the mistress inflames the lover's heart, raises him from baseness and dazzles him. It is as if the light from the mistress accomplishes these things simultaneously. The divine radiance of the mistress (her 'huge brightnesse')[36] is positively numbing and blinding in its power. The lover is transfixed in an attitude of worship – struck dumb, as it were. The play on 'still' (meaning that he is gazing on her continuously, as well as without moving) emphasizes his comically bemused state. He is a figure in whom love has indeed worked wonders, but of a strange and incapacitating kind.

In the third quatrain, the dumbstruck behaviour of the lover is more fully conveyed. When he tries to express his admiration, he is pulled up short and can express nothing. The syntactic and rhythmic patterns reflect this notion of his attempts at action being suddenly halted. The inversion of auxiliary and participle in the first half of lines 10 and 12 causes the first stress in each of these two lines to fall on the stem of the verb, and the second on the auxiliary (ĭt stóppĕd iś / ĭt rávisĥ't ĭs), so that attention is drawn to the verb describing the hindrance of action. The caesura in these lines adds to the sense of the action coming to a sudden halt by interrupting the flow of the rhythm in a way that does not occur in lines 9 and 11. This pattern of the quatrain echoes the notion that the lover's will to act is being interfered with in an abruptly comical way.

The lover's personification of tongue and pen, as beings with a will of their own, adds to the humour of this quatrain. They become surrogates of the lover, attempting to present his praises to the mistress, but finding themselves impotent. They are silenced by intangible forces – the tongue by 'thoughts astonishment', the pen by 'fancies wonderment'. There is a further indignity for the pen – it fails to do any ravishing, and it is itself ravished. Thus, indirectly, the lover is made a figure of fun, unable to act at all.

In spite of being tongue-tied by the sight of his mistress's beauty, the lover still offers her his praises silently in his heart. His claim in the couplet that he cannot put the wonder he feels into words is, of course, amusingly contradicted by the existence of the sonnet. 'Endite', which means both 'put into words', and 'give literary form to', sharpens the contradiction and focuses on the lover's dual role as poet and foolish admirer. There is the possibility of further wordplay, involving sexual overtones, in the terms 'pen' and 'endite'. Partridge[37] notes that 'pen', from the late sixteenth century was slang for the male member, and that the expression 'to have no more ink in one's pen' meant 'to be temporarily impotent'. Evans[38] points out Sidney's double entendre with the word 'endite' in the fourth song of *Astrophil and Stella*:

> Youre faire mother is abed,
> Candles out, and curtaines spread:
> She thinks you do letters write
> Write, but first let me endite:
> Take me to thee, and thee to me
> No, no, no, no, my Deare, let be.

In investing the lady with heavenly radiance, Spenser may have been

chiefly concerned, as Ellrodt suggests, to 'outdo the hyperboles of
his predecessors'[39]; but it is important to recognize that Spenser
outdoes them, not simply by taking the familiar pattern of complaint
one stage further, but by providing a different, subversively comic
view of it. He explores the comic possibilities that lie in thinking of
the lover's plight as a *victim* of his mistress's radiance. The result is a
witty sonnet, eminently presentable to the mistress as a conventional, idealizing, compliment, but, at the same time, including
playful, anti-Platonic innuendo.

In sonnet, XLV, Platonic notions are drawn upon in a different
way, and for a different end. In sonnet III, the lover presents himself
as someone who is relatively unaware of the relationship of his
experience to larger ideas, but, in sonnet XLV, he is a far more
knowing and manipulative figure. Ellrodt's view that the way in
which Spenser uses Platonic notions in XLV suggests either that he
did not care for philosophical accuracy, or that he had not as yet
grasped the theory of abstraction or idealization,[40] is difficult to
support, since the detailed implications of Platonic notions are a part
of the lover's reasoning processes. Spenser does not use Platonic
ideas to express a Platonic frame of mind, but rather as part of his
rhetorical strategy to persuade his mistress to incline towards him.

At the point where this sonnet appears in the sequence, the lover's
attitude towards his mistress is a mixture of irritation that her cruelty
persists (her mirror-gazing is the cause of further irritation, pro-
ducing the slightly critical note of the opening line of XLV), and
determination to make her change her ways towards him. The
sonnet, a variation on the classical and Renaissance poetic topos of
persuasion, is designed to oblige the mistress to give up her cruelty:

> Leave lady in your glasse of christall clene,
>   Your goodly selfe for evermore to vew:
>   and in my selfe, my inward selfe I meane,
>   most lively lyke behold your semblant trew.
> Within my hart, though hardly it can shew
>   thing so divine to vew of earthly eye:
>   the fayre Idea of your celestiall hew,
>   and every part remaines immortally: \
> And were it not that through your cruelty,
>   with sorrow dimmed and deformed it were:
>   the goodly ymage of your visnomy,
>   clearer then christall would therein appere.

But if your selfe in me ye playne will see,
remove the cause by which your fayre beames darkned be.

The first quatrain, with its reference to the mirror, and the inward
self, evokes the Platonic notion that the heart is like a mirror,[41]
though it is not until the second quatrain, with the reference to 'Idea',
that the Platonic content of the terms is confirmed. Ficino had
outlined the procedures that were consequent upon gazing into the
mirror of the heart in his *Commentary* as follows:

> There is also the fact that the lover engraves the figure of the beloved on
> his own soul. And so the soul of the lover becomes a mirror in which the
> image of the beloved is reflected. For that reason, when the beloved
> recognizes himself in the lover, he is forced to love him.[42]

That the beloved of Spenser's sonnet will be compelled to return
love once she gazes into the lover's heart or soul, is, presumably, one
of the lover's motives in persuading her to look there, instead of in
her mirror.

Ellrodt argues that 'Idea' must mean 'image' in the second
quatrain, or else the conceit of the second quatrain would be
absurd.[43] Yet it is possible to read 'Idea' as the Platonic Idea which
informs the soul, if it is recognized that the lover is making use of this
notion for a purpose of his own and that Spenser is using the notion
in a witty way, rather than a predominantly doctrinal one.

The lover, according to Platonic doctrine, at approximately the
third stage of the ladder, trains himself to rely on the image or 'Idea'
of beauty which he gains by concentrating on the image of the
mistress when in her presence. The 'Idea' of beauty in his soul is
more beautiful than the actual physical source, since the physical
body is an imperfect representation of the ideal. The Platonic idea is
also of divine origin and so everlasting. The lover transfers his desire
from the beloved to the Idea of her in his soul in order to liberate
himself from dependence on physical beauty.[44]

Spenser's lover takes this notion of the image's gaining perfection
in the heart ('Within my heart . . . ') and uses it, somewhat
irreverently, as a way to encourage his mistress to turn towards him,
and not as a way of decreasing his own dependence on his mistress.
He offers her the inducement of the picture of her true self ('the fayre
Idea of her celestiall hew') as an alternative to the picture she finds in

her mirror. He is attempting to bribe her away from her mirror –
gazing by offering her a morally perfect vision of herself.

The second stage of the lover's argument, that if his mistress
ceases to be cruel her image will appear 'clearer then christall',
depends on the idea that the beams from her eyes transmit the image
of her to his heart through his eyes.[45] It is unclear whether her image
is clouded because of his sorrow (in the form of tears or grief) caused
by her continued cruelty, or because her cruelty in turning away
from him causes the transmission of the image to his heart to
be affected. In either case, however, it is only a change in her
expression towards him that can restore the image of her to its divine
perfection.

In the couplet, the lover brings moral pressure to bear upon his
mistress to cease the cruelty which has such ill effects. He implies
that the blame will rest with her if her immortal image remains
dimmed and distorted, and that the cure lies in her hands. The lover
freely makes use of Platonic notions as a means of inclining the
mistress towards the course he wants her to follow, and not in order
to encourage her to follow a Platonic path. Neither his, nor her,
spiritual edification has been his goal.

In sonnet XXXV,[46] Spenser develops the idea that a Platonic
course of action may give the lover some consolation, but does not
ultimately provide him with a fully satisfying way of dealing with
his plight. One of the basic tenets of Platonism is that the visible
universe is composed of inferior simulacra of the forms of reality. In
the last line of this sonnet, the lover's words imply that the
opposition between manifestation and form is dissolved in the
particular case of the mistress:

> My hungry eyes through greedy covetize,
>   still to behold the obiect of their paine:
>   with no contentment can themselves suffize,
>   but having pine and having not complaine.
> For lacking if they cannot lyfe sustayne,
>   and having it they gaze on it the more:
>   in their amazement lyke *Narcissus* vaine
>   whose eyes him starv'd: so plenty makes me poore.
> Yet are mine eyes so filled with the store
>   of that faire sight, that nothing else they brooke,
>   but lothe the things which they did like before,
>   and can no more endure on them to looke.

All this worlds glory seemeth vayne to me,
and all their showes but shadowes saving she.

The idea in the sestet has connections with Plato's account of how the philosophers who are to rule in his ideal republic[41] progress from illusion to a greater understanding of truth. The analogy Plato chooses is that of bound prisoners in a cave partly lit by fire, who cannot see themselves or each other, but only the shadows cast on the wall in front of them. These prisoners are deluded into thinking that what they see is reality, but if one of them were to be freed and taken into the daylight, he would eventually perceive the reality of the world outside the cave. Once he had attained this level of understanding ('the upward progress of the mind into the intelligible realm'), he would be reluctant to return to the cave where his eyes would be 'blinded by darkness':

> And if he had to discriminate between the shadows, in competition with the other prisoners, while he was still blinded and before his eyes got used to the darkness – a process that might take some time – wouldn't he be likely to make a fool of himself? . . . Then you will perhaps also agree with me that it won't be surprising if those who get so far are unwilling to return to mundane affairs, and if their minds long to remain among higher things . . . But our argument indicates that this capacity is innate in each man's mind, and that the faculty by which he learns is like an eye which cannot be turned from darkness to light unless the whole body is turned; in the same way the mind as a whole must be turned away from the world of change until it can bear to look straight at reality, and at the brightest of all realities which is what we call the Good.[47]

In addition, Spenser's sonnet invokes the Narcissus myth, which also deals with the contrast between shadow and substance, though from a different point of view, as noted in Ficino's *Commentary on the Symposium*. According to Edwards, Ficino's allegorized version of this myth had such a pervasive influence 'that scarcely a writer who used the myth failed to show some trace of it'.[48].

Spenser may have been influenced by Ficino's commentary, as Edwards suggests. But the affinities between Ovid's version of the story and the lover's use of the myth, at least in the octave, are more readily apparent. Ovid stresses the frustrations and paradoxes involved in the plight of Narcissus and the insolubility of his problem:

I am on fire with love for my own self. It is I who kindle the flames which I must endure. What should I do? Woo or be wooed? But what then shall I seek by my wooing? What I desire, I have. My very plenty makes me poor.[49]

In Spenser's sonnet, Narcissus is invoked not as 'soul', as he is in Ficino's version, but as a figure, like Ovid's Narcissus, who loved an object he could not attain and so was doomed to endless torment. When the lover in Spenser's sonnet denies his eyes the sight of his mistress, they are unfed, and 'cannot lyfe sustayne', yet the more the lover feeds his eyes on the sight of her, the more his hunger increases: 'so plenty makes me poore'.[50]

The lover stresses the similarities of Narcissus's plight with his own, presumably to encourage sympathy for what he perceives as the seriousness of his situation, but there are obvious differences. Narcissus was worshipping an image of himself, whereas the lover admires someone different from himself; and Narcissus starves to death as a consequence of his behaviour, whereas the lover is unlikely to come to such an end, because his starving is of a different kind. The knowledge of these differences tends to undermine the degree of seriousness with which the reader is encouraged to view the lover's use of the Narcissus myth to dramatize his situation.

Those who wish to offer a Platonic interpretation of the sonnet consider that it is more concerned with the spiritual value of the contemplation of the mistress, than with the pain of loving: they see the sestet as offering a Platonic solution to the problems posed by the lover in the octave. Rogers, for example, interpreting the 'Yet' of line 9 as a denial that the lover is really a Narcissus figure, reads the sestet as a positive affirmation of the value of the contemplation of beauty. Rogers argues that at this point in the sonnet, the lover is on a rung of the Platonic ladder of love, for the lover has learned the lesson Narcissus failed to learn, and rests content with the value of being wooed away from dwelling on transitory physical things: 'In the octave the poet [lover persona] suffers the pangs of unrequited love; in the sestet he realized and asserts the genuine reward of his service'.[51]

There is another way of reading the sestet which does not involve assuming the lover is content with the contemplation of his mistress, an assumption which, in my view, runs counter to the tone and implications of the sestet. In this reading, Spenser's lover values the 'store' he has of his mistresss (line 9), but it is not fully satisfying to him. To have his eyes filled with the store of his mistress so that they can 'brooke' nothing else ('endure', in the sense of 'stomach', or possibly 'digest mentally')[52] is fulfilling and nourishing at the spiritual level, but not at other levels.

The words 'filled', 'store' and 'brooke' of line 9 are part of the food/nourishment imagery ('hungry', 'greedy', 'contentment', 'suffize', 'having', 'having not', 'lacking', 'not sustayne', 'starv'd', 'plenty', 'poore', 'filled', 'store', 'brooke') which runs right through the sonnet, and which is inextricably linked with the references to sight ('behold', 'gaze', 'sight', 'looke', 'showes', 'shadows'). The conceit that eyes need to be nourished by the things they look at, which is the basis of the sonnet, provides a context in which it is evident that to be filled with the store of the sight of the mistress is spiritually fulfilling but leaves the lover without the 'nourishment' he needs. His eyes remain 'hungry' even whilst filled with her 'store'.

The 'Yet' of line 9 marks a change in the tone of the sonnet (and possibly a rejection of the idea of the lover's similarity with Narcissus suggested by Rogers), but it does not mark a recognition of the solution to the lover's problems. In the octave, he has presented his complaint in the wryly exaggerated, almost comical, way that is familiar from other sonnets (e.g. XX, XXX and XXXI); but in the sestet he moves to more serious contemplation of the 'store' he has of his mistress. The satisfaction this brings him is mixed with frustration, for the 'store' still does not suffice: his world without her presence remains meaningless and painful.

Edwards argues that the problem at this point is 'that the lady has left him dissatisfied with the shadow world without satisfying the hunger she has aroused for a higher reality'. Edwards uses Ficino's commentary to explain the lover's psychology:

> The speaker's dilemma is that he becomes conscious of the divine splendour only through the lady, but can attain that splendour only if he goes beyond the lady.[53]

It is true that the lady has left him dissatisfied with his shadow world, but there is no evidence in the sonnet that what he seeks is 'a higher reality', or that he wants to go 'beyond the lady'.

The transformation of the lover's world into 'showes' and 'shadowes', which the sight of the mistress has brought about for him, in fact, brings further pain. There are unfortunate consequences, whether he looks at her, or does not look at her, and, in addition, the rest of the world has become loathsome to him. The Neo-Platonist would have the lover rejoice in this stage of his journey towards the contemplation of the divine. He should close his eyes to his mistress, and look beyond her, so that the eyes of his soul may be opened – but there is no indication that the lover recognizes any error in his ways (as Narcissus eventually does, though too late for it to save him), or that he plans to move beyond his need of his mistress. His priorities are different from the Platonist's – his inward knowledge of the mistress reveals to him the illusory nature of the real world, but this brings with it a stronger desire for his mistress's presence, as she is the only thing that has any reality for him. Semblance and reality coalesce in the mistress, creating a philo-sophical paradox in which Platonic shadow (the lady's physical presence perceived by the 'hungry eyes') and the ideal forms which the lover's eyes reflect are one and the same.

There is a similar reference to 'starving' for the want of the mistress in LXXXVIII, a sonnet of complaint about the mistress's absence:

> Since I have lackt the comfort of that light,
>> The which was wont to lead my thoughts astray:
>> I wander as in darknesse of the night,
>> affrayed of every dangers least dismay.
> Ne ought I see, though in the clearest day,
>> when others gaze upon theyr shadowes vayne:
>> but th'onely image of that heavenly ray,
>> whereof some glance doth in mine eie remayne.
> Of which beholding the Idaea playne,
>> through contemplation of my purest part:
>> with light thereof I doe my selfe sustayne,
>> and thereon feed my love-affamisht hart.
> But with such brightnesse whylest I fill my mind,
>> I starve my body and mine eyes doe blynd.

The reference to 'light' in line 1 suggests that the mistress's presence transforms the world for her lover, bringing the comfort and security that he seeks. The lover sees his mistress, not as an emanation of the divine who can bring him close to that source, which is the way the Platonist would see her, but as the source of everything that makes his world perfect. In presenting her as the source of light, rather than as its agent, and in longing for her physical presence, he challenges the values of Platonism. In the second quatrain, the association of light with comfort, and darkness with despair is superseded by new associations. Spenser has the lover move temporarily into a Platonic world. Others may gaze upon their 'shadowes vayne' (shadows without value or significance), but he is unable to see anything without her light. Consequently, he looks into his own self where he knows he will find some trace of his mistress, and is rewarded by 'th'onely image of that heavenly ray', some remnant of which remains in his eye. The account of Bembo's speech in *Il Cortegiano* of the way an adherent of Platonic philosophy attempts to overcome the grief of absence contains a similar image of the need for introspection:

> The soul turns to contemplate its own substance, and as if awakened from deepest sleep it opens the eyes which all men possess but few use and perceives in itself a ray of that light which is the true image of the angelic beauty that has been transmitted to it, and of which in turn it transmits a faint impression to the body.

The Platonist is encouraged to make the image 'lovely and clear to his soul' so that he can 'enjoy it there always day and night, and in every time and place, without fear of ever losing it'.[54] There are, however, important differences in the behaviour of Spenser's lover from the course described here. Spenser's lover does not appear to be concerned about making the transition to a contemplation of abstract beauty. He does not envisage relying indefinitely on the image within, as he plans to contemplate it only until his mistress's return. The image does not seem to be valued for its Platonic worth, but as a means of providing contact with his mistress. Further, the fear the lover feels without her (line 4) does not seem to be fully dispelled by the 'ray' within. Nevertheless, the ray within does offer Spenser's lover some comfort, and he finds the contemplation of the image of his mistress within himself preferable to a world without her, though not preferable to her presence.

The Platonic notion of the 'Idea', introduced in the third quatrain, is a further means of establishing the lover's hierarchy of preferences. 'Idea', as Ellrodt points out in his refutation of Fletcher's and Renwick's interpretation of the term as being equivalent to 'image' in a non-Platonic sense, is used by Spenser with its Platonic implications, as 'the idea informing the individual soul'.[55] By contemplating his own soul, the lover is able to contemplate the abstract Idea of his beloved (assuming that 'of' in line 10 does not mean 'with'). Yet, it seems again that he wants to do this, not for a Platonic end, to 'turn away from the body to beauty alone',[56] but in order to have some illusion of contact with his mistress; some light in his spiritual darkness. The 'Idea' he contemplates sustains him but it does not fully satisfy him, as her presence does.

In the couplet, the inadequacy of the Platonic 'light' of line 11 (in contrast to the 'light' of line 1) is made more explicit. The lover fills his mind with the brilliance of the idea of his mistress, but whilst this brings him sustenance, it does not fully satisfy his needs. His body is still starving, and his eyes are blinded, either by the brightness of the light in his mind, or by tears. The final line of the poem finds the lover in darkness ('mine eyes doe blynd'), as he was at the beginning of the poem. His inward contemplation has provided some relief, but it has also made him more conscious of the deprivation he experiences without his mistress's presence.

In LXXVIII, another sonnet about absence, Platonic ideas are introduced in a different way from that found in the sonnets just discussed, but the poetic function of the ideas is similar. The Platonic resonances of certain expressions in the sonnet act as a ghostly counter argument to the one the lover is advancing. The subject of the sonnet is, again, the grief and feelings of loss the lover experiences at his mistress's absence:

> Lackyng my love I go from place to place,
>   lyke a young fawne that late hath lost the hynd:
>   and seeke each where, where last I sawe her face,
>   whose ymage yet I carry fresh in mynd.
> I seeke the fields with her late footing synd
>   I seeke her bowre with her late presence deckt,
>   yet nor in field nor bowre I her can fynd:
>   yet field and bowre are full of her aspect.
> But when myne eyes I thereunto direct,
>   they ydly back returne to me agayne,
>   and when I hope to see theyr trew object.
>   I fynd my selfe but fed with fancies vayne.
> Ceasse then myne eyes, to seeke her selfe to see,
>   and let my thought behold her selfe in mee.

The relation of the imagery of this sonnet to that of LXVII underlines the theme of the lover's urgent need for the mistress's presence. In LXVII, the mistress is the elusive deer who finally submits herself to captivity; in this sonnet the lover sees himself as the fawn seeking its mate, but being unable to find her. At this stage of the sequence, when a shared relationship, however transitory, has been experienced, separation brings a different kind of loneliness from that of earlier frustrated unhappiness – a loneliness that is powerfully transmitted by the image of the solitary fawn.

In the first 12 lines of the sonnet, the language which could be considered Platonic – 'ymage', 'trew object', fancies vayne' – is not used in a specifically Platonic way. 'The 'ymage' is one in his mind, not his heart, and is closer to being the equivalent of his memory of his mistress rather than the 'Idea' of her. The 'trew object' he seeks refers to the object he is looking for (i.e. his mistress), and 'fancies vayne' to his foolish imaginings. In the couplet, 'her selfe in mee' does seem more closely tied to its Platonic sense, though it could refer to the memory of her.

In the octave, we learn that the 'ymage' of the mistress does not relieve his pain. She is fresh in his mind, just as the fields and bowers are full of her aspect, but this reminder of her presence does not make her absence any easier to bear. The knowledge that the image or 'Idea' brings comfort to the Platonist and makes absence less painful is brought to mind by the reference of 'ymage' in this context. This idea creates a sense of paradox that would not otherwise be there. In a Platonic situation the image provides comfort and lessens despair; but in the lover's case it adds to his loneliness. The Platonic associations are drawn into the argument to hint at this paradox and to add further to the lover's feelings of bewilderment and pain.

Spenser reminds the reader of the Platonic associations of 'trew object' (line 11) by referring to the lover's eyes which 'return to mee agayne', in the immediately preceding line. (The Platonist seeks within himself for the image of beauty which his reason trains him to see; a beauty with more truth than the image of the beloved.) At the same time, the parallel structuring of lines 9 and 11 ('But when . . . I'/'and when I') counters this Platonic notion by setting up a different meaning. The link between the lines suggests the lover is still seeking his mistress 'thereunto' (i.e. in field and bower) and that when he hopes to see his mistress, he directs his eyes outwards. His exhortation to himself in the couplet to cease trying to find her outside of himself supports this reading.

The 'trew object' that he seeks in line 11, then, refers both to his mistress's presence ('trew' in the sense of real, 'object' meaning something material) and to the 'Idea' of her in his heart. When the lover fails to find the 'trew object' that he seeks and finds 'fancies vayne' (line 12), the Platonic connotations that have been hinted at appear to add to the complexity and insolubility of the lover's dilemma. He seeks what is true, but only finds what is valueless; he seeks an object, only to find an illusion.

In the couplet, he decides to give up looking for his mistress in the outward world, and turn his thoughts inward where he knows he can find her. He has known all along that, in the Platonic sense, he has her 'selfe' within himself (line 4), but he so wanted her presence ('selfe', line 13) that he would settle for nothing less. A hierarchy has again been established in which the 'trew object' of his sight is superior to his 'fancies vayne'. Thus, by the end of the poem, he has decided that since he cannot have her presence he would rather contemplate her within himself, than seek her where she cannot be found.

In both these absence sonnets (LXXVIII and LXXXVIII), the Platonic way of dealing with the grief of absence is thought of as being of temporary consolation, rather than of permanent value. Consolation is one of the beneficial effects of following a Platonic path, but Spenser's lover is seeking this benefit without indicating that he is following that path for its own sake. The Platonic path allows a certain degree of dependence on the image of the beloved within the self in the early stages of love, but it is to be risen above, and not indulged in as it is in Spenser's lover's case. If there were any suggestion that Spenser's lover was progressing up the Platonic ladder, such a degree of dependence on the inward image would be a thing of the past, at this point in the sequence.

Casady, in his discussion of the Neo-Platonic ladder in Spenser's *Ameretti*, claims there is 'no obstacle to prevent interpreting the sequence as a study of the lover's attempts to climb the Neo-Platonic ladder', and proceeds to relate the stages outlined in Castiglione's *Il Cortegiano* to the stages the lover moves through in the *Amoretti*. He argues that the mistress grants her favours only as the lover progresses up the ladder. Thus she lets the lover 'kisse her lyps' because he has 'aroused his reason . . . and shut the way to sense and appetite'.[57] If this were true, then it would be expected that the lady would refuse her favours when the lover slips back down the ladder, as Casady claims he does in LXXII and LXXIII, and again in

LXXVI. Her doubts about their union are referred to in sonnet LXV but these do not appear to have anything to do with the lover's behaviour, but more with a maidenly reluctance to commit herself to 'bands'. There is no evidence that once she has submitted to him she withdraws her favours or acceptance. Although, in sonnet LXXXVI, the lover records a breach in their peace, it is caused by some outside force, and presumably is not permanent, since in the very next sonnet the lover waits for the return of his 'love' with confidence that her presence will restore the contentment he has lost. Her absence in this and in the next two sonnets is not explained, but it does not seem due to punishment or withdrawal of favour on the mistress's part.

There is, then, no real similarity between the lover's behaviour and a Neo-Platonist's expected behaviour pattern. Spenser's lover makes no consistent progress, his ups and downs have no recognizable pattern (he even omits certain steps in his progress backwards and forwards), the full range of the ladder is not used, and at the end of the sequence he is still entirely dependent on the mistress's physical presence. In the sequence as a whole, there is no indication that the lover is using his love for his mistress as a stage in his progress towards the divine. In fact, his relationship with his mistress has an importance for him that could be considered equal to the importance of his 'glorious Lord of lyfe'. In his most spiritual moments, he sees the two relations as part of each other, but at other times there are hints that his personal relationship has assumed more importance than it ought.

The central importance of the mistress to the lover is stressed in sonnet LXXII. The reference to the soul's being transported on wings in line 1 brings to mind the Platonic idea of the soul ascending on wings:

> When it [the soul] is perfect and winged it moves on high and governs all creation, but the soul that has shed its wings falls until it encounters solid matter . . .
> The function of a wing is to take what is heavy and raise it up into the regions above, where the gods dwell.[58]

In Spenser's sonnet LXXII, the lover does not attempt to purge his soul of material darkness by allowing it to ascend on 'bolder wings', as he would do if he were attempting to follow a Platonic path, but rather exults in the happiness he finds in steeping his fancy in the bliss of his mistress's presence:

Oft when my spirit doth spred her bolder winges,
In mind to mount up to the purest sky:
it down is weighd with thoght of earthly things
and clogd with burden of mortality,
Where with that soverayne beauty it doth spy,
resembling heavens glory in her light:
drawne with sweet pleasures bayt, it back doth fly,
and unto heaven forgets her former flight.
There my fraile fancy fed with full delight,
doth bath in blisse and mantleth most at ease:
ne thinks of other heaven, but how it might
her harts desire with most contentment please.
Hart need not wish none other happinesse,
but here on earth to have such hevens blisse.

It is not that the lover is unaware of higher things – his spirit does attempt to 'mount up to the purest sky' on occasion, but he finds it easily distracted and in the end he rejects the higher heaven for 'hevens blisse' on earth, deciding that no other happiness could surpass his earthly bliss, for it is heaven's bliss to him. This is more than an inability to purge his fancy; it is a conviction that he does not need the higher happiness since his mistress brings him 'hevens blisse'.

Casady argues that in this sonnet the lover is hovering near the fifth rung of the ladder, in a stage 'very noble and such as few attain'. In order to explain the lover's choice to return to 'that soverayne beauty,' he refers to the idea expressed through the character of Bembo in *Il Cortegiano* that although the imagination, at this stage of the ladder, considers universal beauty in the abstract and intrinsically, it does not discern that beauty clearly or without ambiguity, because of the likeness which phantoms bear to substance. Yet Spenser's lover makes a choice that involves him in avoiding abstract beauty and in being readily seduced by particular beauty.

It is not because the lover is one of those who 'dare not go far from their nest or trust themselves to the winds and open sky' that he fails to reach a higher state, as Casady, quoting Castiglione, asserts that it is, but because his spirit settles for the more immediately attractive earthly pleasures. Once the lover is drawn back by the sight of his mistress, he forgets the spiritual heaven and decides not to continue on a path which would deprive him of her.

Casady notes, in support of his argument that Spenser's sonnet deals with a stage of the Neo-Platonic ladder, that the sonnet on which Spenser's was modelled, Tasso's 'L'alma vaga di luce e di bellezza', was annotated by Tasso to show its Neo-Platonic significance. This, in itself, does not establish that Spenser's attitude to Neo-Platonic content was the same as Tasso's, and, furthermore, there is considerable disagreement amongst critics as to the extent to which Neo-Platonic thought is present in Tasso's sonnet, and also as to the degree to which Spenser has modelled his sonnet on the Tasso poem.[59]

At the other end of the spectrum, Kostic argues that in this sonnet Spenser's Platonism is not part of the structure, but is simply 'an ornament which he neatly drives home in the last couplet to round off the sonnet and to pay a compliment to his lady'.[60] This clearly under-estimates the way in which Platonism is used in the poem. It is invoked in the first line, with the reference to wings, and is subsequently present in the poem as an ideal which the lover systematically subverts by reversing the procedures that Platonic processes normally follow. Instead of love acting as an ennobling force that raises him to greater spiritual heights, his love encourages him to abandon flight for descent, as it were, so he can be with his mistress.

Throughout the sequence the lover uses Platonic and Neo-Platonic notions to define the mistress's qualities of beauty and perfection and the attraction she has for him, to explore his grief and pain, and to dissuade her from her cruelty. However he does not see his love for her as something that follows, or ought to follow, a strictly Platonic course. It is not that the lover wishes to deny either his mistress's heavenly beauty or the value of her image in his heart, or to belittle the worth of their spiritual union in any way. But he has a different goal from the Platonist – he wants a physical, emotional and spiritual union with his mistress, and for him this is an end in itself, not a stage to a higher spiritual state.

There are many ways in which the sonnets in Spenser's *Amoretti* counter the principles of Neo-Platonic idealization of the love relation. In several sonnets, the mistress is accused of being treacherous and careless of life; there is clear acknowledgement of the lover's sensual feelings; and, most importantly, the sequence as a whole indicates the conclusion of the courtship in marital union. Such a union is not entirely out of keeping with Neo-Platonic doctrine; but in the *Amoretti* the emphasis is on the lover's union with the mistress as the supreme culmination of desire rather than as a stage of love to be transcended by other forms of the realization of human desires. On the occasions in the sequence when the lover invokes Platonic notions, he often finds them wanting. They cause him inconvenience and hardship and fail to bring the satisfaction that he desires. The mistress's celestial beauty dazzles him and robs him of his faculties; absence proves unsatisfactory with few of the promised compensations; the 'Idea' or image in the heart is not as uplifting as it ought to be. At best it offers consolation, whilst at the worst it increases his sense of loss.

It is clear from this discussion that Platonic ideas have neither a merely ornamental, nor a centrally unifying role in the sequence. They are rather to be seen as instruments in the rhetorical strategies of the lover persona. Whilst the lover may appear to endorse Platonism at a particular moment in a sonnet, he usually does so as part of his strategy or argument to incline his mistress towards him. He is not an exponent of Platonic philosophy, but is cast in the role of one who sometimes draws on the ideas of Platonism to fashion the arguments of praise, persuasion or complaint.

Spenser's treatment of Platonism takes its place amongst the other methods he uses in the sequence to provide a perspective on the lover's attitude to his mistress and their gradually developing relationship. He is more concerned with exploring the pains, pleasures and strategies of love than with developing a coherent philosophy about it. Insofar as there is a body of philosophical thought in Spenser's *Amoretti*, its use is eclectic rather than dogmatic, rhetorical rather than doctrinaire. The lover alternately criticizes, condemns or turns to such notions as consolation, but his view of his relationship with his mistress is not confined by the bounds of Platonism. Spenser does not endorse Neo-Platonism as a philosophy in the *Amoretti*, but uses it in a witty and complicated way, as part of the framework of ideas.

NOTES: Chapter Five

1. Satterthwaite states that Spenser studied Plato in the original at Cambridge. (Alfred W. Satterthwaite, *Spenser, Ronsard and Du Bellay*, Kennikat Press, Port Washington, New York, London 1960, p. 21.)

This seems likely in view of the popularity of Plato at Cambridge around the time of Spenser's attendance. Ascham, in a letter written in 1542, commenting on the establishment of the Regius Professorships, one of which was a chair in Greek, remarked that Aristotle and Plato were being read even by 'the boys'. (James Bass Mullinger, *The University of Cambridge from the Royal Injunctions of 1535 to the Accession of Charles the First*, Cambridge University Press, Cambridge, 1884. p. 52.) The result of the new interest in Greek was that Plato's writings were prescribed as part of the curriculum in the statutes of Edward VI. (James Jackson Higginson, *Spenser's Shepherd's Calender*, Columbia University Press, New York, 1912, p. 263.)

It is often difficult to establish whether Renaissance writers had read Plato in the original Greek, even though it may be possible to establish that Greek was studied at the school or university which was attended. Sidney, for example, who attended Shrewsbury under Ashton, and then Oxford, studied Latin and some Greek (*The Poems of Sir Philip Sidney*, ed. William A. Ringler, Jr, Clarendon Press, Oxford, 1962, p. XVII and p. XVIII), but it is uncertain whether he read Plato in Greek.

See also Satterthwaite's discussion of the problem in relation to Ronsard and Du Bellay. Satterthwaite, op. cit. p. 174 and p. 187.

2. In England, Ficino's Latin *Plato* was referred to in the 1589 Catalogue of Corpus Christi College, Oxford. It was apparently less popular than the copy of the Latin translation in 1578 of *Opera Platonis*, by the French humanist, Serranus, which was held in the same library. See Sears Jayne, 'Ficino and the Platonism of the English Renaissance', *Comparative Literature*, vol. IV, 1952, p. 220.

3. Quitslund is referring to the Constable sonnet as it is printed in *The Poems of Henry Constable*, ed. Joan Grundy, Liverpool University Press, Liverpool, 1960, p. 133. Jon A. Quitslund, 'Spenser's *Amoretti VIII* and Platonic Commentaries on Petrarch', *Journal of the Warburg and Courtauld Institutes*, 36, 1973, p. 261.

4. Bhattacherje points out that the interest of Ronsard, Du Bellay and Pontus de Thyard in Platonism was short-lived, and that some other members were positively hostile to the philosophy. See Mohinimohan Bhattacherje, *Platonic Ideas in Spenser*, Greenwood Press, Connecticut, 1935, p. 181.

5. W. L. Renwick, *Daphnaïda and Others Poems*, The Scholartis Press, London, 1929, p. 209. It is usually assumed that the fourth book of *Il Cortegiano* was also available. For information about Mulcaster, see Satterthwaite, op. cit., p. 20.

6. One of the reasons for this is the difficulty, aptly commented on by Enid Welsford, that Neo-Platonic treatises 'repeat one another incess-

antly because of their conviction that the most important truths about the nature of things are already known'. Enid Welsford, *Spenser: A Study of Edmund Spenser's Doctrine of Love*, Basil Blackwell, Oxford, 1967, p. 4.

7. Lilian Winstanley (ed.) *Fowre Hymnes*, Cambridge University Press, Cambridge, 1907, p. xxv. Not all consider the sequence as 'full of the influence of Plato' as Winstanley does. Siegel, for example, finds only 'the pale golden glow of Neo-Platonic idealism'. (Paul N. Siegel, 'The Petrarchan Sonneteers and Neo-Platonic Love', *Studies in Philology*, XLII, 1945, p. 179.)

For the views of those who consider that Spenser's reliance on Platonic ideas has been exaggerated see, Veselin Kostic, *Spenser's Sources in Italian Poetry: A Study in Comparative Literature*, Faculté de Philologie de l'Université de Belgrade Monographies, Belgrade, 1969, p. 70; Robert Ellrodt, *Neoplatonism in the Poetry of Spenser*, Librairie E. Droz, Geneva, 1960; rpt. Folcroft Library Editions, 1978, p. 40 and Jerome Dees, 'Spenser's Anti-NeoPlatonism' *A Special Session of the Thirteenth Conference on Medieval Studies at Kalamazoo*, May 1977.

8. Ellrodt op. cit., p. 40.

9. Quitslund op. cit., pp. 257, 261, 265. Quitslund sees a parallel between what he calls 'the religious character of Spenser's devotion' in sonnet VIII and Gesualdo's exposition of the love of true beauty that inspires love of the celestial, an idea not contained in the Petrarch poem. There is some doubt that Spenser's lover is thinking of 'the celestial life' in the sense that Gesualdo speaks of it. There is, in fact, an equation of the mistress with the light of the divine, and the heavenly beauty he aspires to includes, rather than excludes, the mistress. Nor is there anything peculiarly distinctive about Gesualdo's account of the Neo-Platonic view. As Quitslund points out himself, the metaphors Spenser chooses do not come from Gesualdo's text, but are his own. op. cit., p. 263. For further discussion of sonnet VIII, see above, pp. 101–2.

10. Diotima's description of procreation is given in Plato, *The Symposium*, trans. W. Hamilton, Penguin, Harmondsworth, Middlesex, 1951, pp. 86–87. For Plotinus' view of procreative love see Plotinus, *Psychic and Physical Treatises*, trans. Stephen MacKenna, Phillip Lee Warner, London 1921, vol. 2, p. 55. Ficino's comments are recorded in Marsilio Ficino, *Commentary on Plato's Symposium on Love*, trans. and ed. Sears Jayne, Spring Press, Dallas, 1985, p. 41.

11. See John Charles Nelson, *Renaissance Theory of Love: The Context of Giordano Bruno's 'Eroici Furori'*, Columbia University Press, New York, 1963, pp. 70, 107, 173 and *Pietro Bembo's 'Gli Asolani'*, trans. Rudolf B. Gottfried, Indiana University Press, Bloomington, 1954, p. 309.

12. Baldesar Castiglione, *The Book of The Courtier*, trans. George Bull, 2nd

edn. 1967; rpt. Penguin, Harmondsworth, Middlesex, England, 1976, pp. 327, 336.
13. The first and second Lateran Councils (1123 and 1139) had declared that those entering the priestly orders should be celibate, and the tradition has continued to the present day, though with some opposition in recent times. The Documents of Vatican II include the statement that 'With respect to the priestly life, the Church has always held in especially high regard perfect and perpetual continence, on behalf of the kingdom of heaven'. From *Documents of Vatican II*, ed. Walter M. Abbot, S.J., Herder and Herder, New York, 1966, p. 565.

Elizabeth I's remark is quoted in Henry C. Lea, *An Historical Sketch of Sacerdotal Celibacy in the Christian Church*, Mifflin and Co., New York, 1884, p. 491. The history of the opposition to reform is outlined on pp. 461–512.
14. Andreas Capellanus, *The Art of Courtly Love*, trans. John Jay Parry, F. Ungar Publishing Co., New York, 1959, p. 192.
15. F. Petrarch, *Petrarch's Secrets*, trans. William H. Draper, Chatto and Windus, London, 1911, pp. 114–126. See, for example, Petrarch's *Canzoniere*, CCLXIV.
16. Elements of this view of the universe can be traced back further to Plato (*Timaeus*, for example) and Aristotle, but it was not coherently formulated until the Neo-Platonists of the third century. See, also Arthur O. Lovejoy, *The Great Chain of Being*, Harvard University Press, Cambridge, Massachusetts, 1961, pp. 62–3.
17. Castiglione, op. cit., p. 340.
18. Castiglione, ibid., pp. 325–6.
19. See David Thomson (ed.), *An Anthology of Petrarch*, Harper and Row, New York, 1971, Preface to the *Secretum*, p. 43:
'a beautiful lady shining with an indescribable light about her eyes, like the sun, seemed to send forth rays of such light that they made me lower mine own before her'.
20. Dante Alighieri, *The Divine Comedy*, trans. Dorothy L. Sayers, Penguin Books, Harmondsworth, Middlesex, England, 1949.
21. Pierre Ronsard, *Sonnets for Helen*, trans. Humbert Wolfe, Unwin Books, London, 1972, sonnet XVI, book 2. See also sonnets XXXII, book 1; and XIV, book 2.
22. See below pp. 98–9.
23. Nelson provides an account of Ficino's and Ebreo's view of love as illness. He notes, for example, that Ficino described vulgar love as a *male d'occhio* carried by spirit from the blood of one person to the eye of another. (Nelson, op. cit. p., 74 and p. 79). Bembo's account of the symptoms of love are given in Castiglione, op. cit., p. 327.
24.   My tongue sticks to my dry mouth
         Thin fire spreads beneath my skin

My eyes cannot see and my aching ears
Roar in their labyrinths

Chill sweat slides down my body
I shake, I turn greener than grass
I am neither living nor dead and cry
From the narrow between

But endure, even this grief of love.

Sappho, *Poems and Fragments*, trans. Guy Davenport, The University of Michigan Press, Ann Arbor, Michigan, 1965, p. 20.

25. Ovid, *The Art of Love and Other Poems*, trans. J.M. Mozley, William Heinemann Ltd., London, 1942, p. 63 and p. 185.
26. Plato, *Symposium*, op. cit.., pp. 54–5.
27. Dante Alighieri, *La Vita Nuova*, trans. D.G. Rossetti, George G. Harrap and Co., Cheylesmore Press, Coventry (undated), p. 15.
28. *Troilus and Criseyde*, book 1, 11. pp. 484–504, *The Works of Geoffrey Chaucer*, ed. F.N. Robinson, 2nd edn. 1933; rpt. The Riverside Press, Cambridge, Massachusetts, 1957, p. 394.
29. Mark Rose, *Heroic Love: Studies in Sidney and Spenser*, Harvard University Press, Cambridge, Massachusetts, 1969, p. 10. In the sixteenth century, Burton continues this tradition by treating love as a kind of melancholy which affects the liver. He describes the symptoms as paleness, leanness, dryness, no appetite, breathing difficulties, etc. See Robert Burton, *The Anatomy of Melancholy*, Everyman, J. M. Dent and Sons, London, 1961, vol. III, p. 133.

   Examples of sonnet personae who suffer physical disturbances as a result of love can be found in Shakepeare's sonnet 30; Griffin's *Fidessa*, sonnets XIX and XXXII; and *Astrophil and Stella*, sonnets 87 and 93.
30. Giordano Bruno, *The Heroic Enthusiasts*, Part the First, trans. L. Williams, George Redway, London, 1887, p. 50.
31. The notion of Cupid's inflaming the heart through the eye is discussed in M.B. Ogle, 'The Classical Origin and Tradition of Literary Conceits', *American Journal of Philology*, vol. 34, February, 1913, pp. 144–6.
32. Chrétien de Troyes, *Arthurian Romances*, trans. W. W. Comfort, Everyman's Library, Dent, London, 1963, *Cligès*, p. 100.
33. Sordello's poem is printed in Bernard O'Donoghue, *The Courtly Love Tradition*, Manchester University Press, Manchester, 1982, pp. 148–9.
34. Ellrodt, op. cit., p. 40. Bhattacherje expresses a different view. He argues that the vision of beauty, causing amazement and dazing the senses of the lover in sonnet III appears to have been suggested by *Phaedrus*, though Tasso is also referred to as a possible source. Bhattacherje, op. cit., p. 195.
35. The similarity between the Platonic ladder and other systems of thought is discussed above. See pp. 142–8.

The idea of the uplifting effect of love is part of the Platonic code. Bembo, for example, describes how the lover can ascend to an angelic state by following certain procedures (Castiglione, op. cit., pp. 337–41), but this idea is not confined to Platonism. The courtly love tradition embraces the notion. See, for example, the Provençal poet Arnaut Daniel's poem translated by O'Donoghue, op. cit., p. 141; 'Every day I become better and purified, because I serve and honour the most noble in the world'.
Chaucer also uses the idea in *Troilus and Criseyde* book 1, 11. 1076–85, when Troilus is transformed by love;
> For he bicom the frendlieste wight,
> The gentilest, and ek the mooste fre,
> The thriftiest and oon the beste knyght,
> That in his tyme was or myghte be.
> Dede were his japes and his cruelte,
> His heighe port and his manere estraunge,
> And ecch of tho gan for a vertu chaunge.

36. 'Huge' in the sixteenth century could be more easily related to immaterial things, and here means something close to 'immensely powerful'. It is a serious statement about the power of the mistress's beauty; yet it has comic overtones, which find expression in the hyperbolic language of the sonnet.

37. Partridge notes that 'pen' was slang for the male member from the late sixteenth century, and that the expression 'to have no more ink in the pen' meant to be temporarily impotent; also from the late sixteenth century. Eric Partridge, *A Dictionary of Slang and Unconventional English*, Routledge and Kegan Paul Ltd., London, 5th edn., 1961, vol.1.

38. Maurice Evans (ed.), *Elizabeth Sonnets*, J.M. Dent and Sons Ltd., London, 1977, p. 194. Elizabeth Bieman's account of the wordplay of Spenser's sonnet III supports such readings. She refers to the way in which the linguistic detail of lines 8–10 'proclaims the potency of sexual fantasy'. Her comments deal with Spenser's use of 'ravisht' and 'fancies'. See Elizabeth Bieman, '"Sometimes I . . . mask in myrth lyke to a Comedy": Spenser's *Amoretti*', Spenser Studies: A Renaissance Poetry Annual, A.M.S. Press, Inc., New York, IV, 1984, p. 135.

39. Ellrodt, op. cit., p. 40).

40). Ibid, p. 42.

41. There are close parallels between some of the ideas in this sonnet and those in Daniel's sonnet XXIX. The tone of irritation is similar, and Daniel's lover uses the idea of himself as a mirror to further his persuasion of his mistress (assuming the 'mirror' of line 10 refers both to the glass and to himself), though the case is argued much less forcibly:

O why doth *Delia* credite so her glasse,
Gazing her beautie deign'd her by the skyes:
And dooth not rather look on him (alas)
Whose state best shewes the force of murthering eyes.
The broken toppes of loftie trees declare,
The fury of a mercy wanting storme:
And of what force your wounding graces are,
Upon my selfe you best may finde the forme.
Then leave your glasse, and gaze your selfe on mee,
That Mirrour shewes what powre is in your face:
To viewe your forme too much, may daunger bee,
Narcissus chaung'd t'a flowre in such a case.
And you are chaung'd, but not t'a Hiacint;
I feare your eye hath turn'd your hart to flint.

Samuel Daniel, *Delia With the Complaint of Rosamund* (1592), Scolar Press, 1969.

The idea of the heart's being like a mirror is not confined to Platonism. Renwick points out that Petrarch has a mirror sonnet, and other examples of the idea are provided by Serafino da Aquila, Tebaldeo, Clément Marot, Maurice Scève, Desportes and Passerat. Renwick, op. cit., p. 200.

42. Ficino, *Commentary*, op. cit., p. 57.
43. Ellrodt, op. cit., p. 42.
44. This stage of the ladder is described by Casady with reference to Pico della Mirandola and 'Castiglione; Casady, op. cit., p. 94. See also Castiglione, op. cit. p. 338.
45. Ficino writes of the beams from the eyes of the object of love mingling with those of the beholder and so uniting their spirits. op. cit., pp. 221–2.
46. Sonnet XXXV is repeated, with very few alterations, as LXXXIII. For a discussion of the repeated sonnet, see above p. 17.
47. Plato, *The Republic*, trans. H.D.P. Lee, Penguin Books, Harmondsworth, Middlesex, England, 1960, pp. 281–3.
48. Ficino's version runs:
   A certain young man, Narcissus, that is the soul of bold and inexperienced man, does not see his own countenance, he never notices his own substance and virtue, but pursues its reflection in the water, and tries to embrace it; that is, the soul admires the beauty in the weak body, an image in the flowing water, which is but the reflection of itself. It deserts its own beauty and never catches its shadow, since the soul neglects itself in worshipping the body, and is never satisfied by enjoyment of the body. For it does not really seek the body itself, but only its own beauty, [and is] seduced by

bodily beauty, which is the image of its own beauty. In this way Narcissus desires, and since he pays no heed to that [true beauty] while he desires and pursues something else, he cannot satisfy his desire. Therefore he is destroyed, melted into tears; that is, the soul, so placed outside itself, and having fallen into the body, is racked by terrible disturbances, or infected by the diseases of the body, and dies, so to speak, since it already seems to be more body than soul. So that Socrates might avoid this death, Diotima led him from Body to Soul, from that to the Angelic Mind, and from that back to God.

Reprinted from *Marsilio Ficino's Commentary on Plato's Symposium*, trans. Sears Jayne, The University of Missouri Studies, vol. XIX, 1944, p. 212, by permission of Missouri Press and the author. Copyright 1944 by Sears Jayne. See also Calvin R. Edwards, 'The Narcissus Myth in Spenser's Poetry', *Studies in Philology*, vol. 74, 1977, p. 69.

49. Ovid, *Metamorphoses*, trans. Mary M. Innes, Penguin Books, Harmondsworth, Middlesex, England, 1955, p. 87.

50. 'Plenty makes me poor' is a translation of Ovid's words '*Inopem me copia fecit*', but in Renaissance times the words had the status of a proverb, so Spenser may not have taken them from Ovid. The Variorum edition notes the proverb was a favourite with Spenser, and cites *The Shepheardes Calendar*. September, l. 261, and *The Faerie Queene*, I.IV. xxix.4, as other instances of its use. See *Works*. vol. 8, p. 432.

51. William Elford Rogers, 'Narcissus in *Amoretti* XXXV', *American Notes and Queries*, vol. XV, no. 2, October, 1976, pp. 19, 20.

52. The relevant senses of 'brook' in the *O.E.D.* are
1. To enjoy the use of, make use of, profit by; to use, enjoy, possess, hold.
2. To make use of (food), in later usage, to digest, retain, or bear on the stomach.
2c. To digest mentally.
3. To put up with, bear with, endure, tolerate (in figurative sense 'to stomach').

53. Edwards, op. cit., pp. 72, 74.

54. Castiglione, op. cit., pp. 338–9.

55. Ellrodt, op. cit., p. 44, quotes Ficino's description of the term.

56. Castiglione, op. cit., p. 338.

57. Casady, op. cit., pp. 103, 98.

58. Plato, *Phaedrus*, Penguin Books, Harmondsworth, Middlesex, England, 1973, p. 51.

59. The reference to Casady's views are from Casady, op. cit., pp. 101, 102.

Janet Scott states that sonnet LXXII is one of three complete sonnets which are translations from the Italian. Janet Scott, 'The Sources of Spenser's *Amoretti*', *Modern Language Review*, 1927, vol. XXII, 191; whilst Renwick claims that only the first five lines are imitation and the rest are Spenser's own ideas (Renwick, op. cit., p. 202). Brand argues that lines 5 and 6 are Spenser's addition to what otherwise would be a free translation of Tasso's 'L'alma vaga di luce e di bellezza'. (C.P. Brand, *Torquato Tasso, A Study of the Poet and his Contribution to English Literature*, Cambridge University Press, Cambridge, 1965, p. 291.)

60.   Kostic, op. cit., p. 61.

Conclusion

This study demonstrates that critical intelligence, imagination and wit pervade every aspect of Spenser's poetic achievement in the sonnet sequence, *Amoretti*. The subjects Spenser invokes as part of the intellectual framework in the sequence include Christian doctrine, Platonic and Neo-Platonic ideas, conventional attitudes towards love as they are defined by Petrarchan and Renaissance models, as well as traditional motifs of medieval and Renaissance religious and secular poetry. It has been shown that the behaviour and feelings of the lover persona are frequently at odds with the ideals which are embodied in these systems of thought and belief. Platonic notions of love, for instance, are sometimes evoked in the sequence, but the lover does not behave in conformity with Platonic ideals. Christian belief, and the goals and attitude of one who would follow that faith, provide a context which enables the reader to make judgements about the lover's attempts to reconcile his fleshly desires and more exalted spiritual goals. Conventional expressions of praise and complaint, traditional attitudes to love and the mistress, as well as Renaissance attitudes and beliefs in general, are often used as models against which the lover's address to his mistress is to be seen. Familiar conventions and idealistic attitudes to love are treated in a critical, thoughtful and often amusing manner.

Spenser's characterization of lover and mistress is another area which demonstrates his skill and artistry. The examination of the mistress figure shows that, although she is in some ways similar to conventional sonnet mistresses, she is also presented as a figure of independent qualities. Her shrewd perceptiveness and quick-witted

175

responses to her lover suggest liveliness of mind, and, whilst her
character is not as fully developed as some commentators have
suggested, the lover's own description of her as being possessed of
'deep wit' (XLIII) is well borne out in her presentation in the
sequence as a whole.

In its complexity and extent of development, the portrait of the
lover persona in the *Amoretti* is comparable with those of the lover
figures in the sequences of Sidney and Shakespeare. Spenser's
treatment of his lover's emotional and intellectual responses to the
problems of love, and of his moral and spiritual dilemmas, creates a
richly varied psychological portrait. In general, Spenser's lover uses
a less bitter register than Shakespeare's, and a less energetic and
flamboyant one than Sidney's Astrophil; but his range of tones,
which includes violent anger, as well as exuberance and joy, is varied
and lively.

The lightness of touch with which Spenser achieves his effects of
irony is another characteristic mark of his style. He displays a
remarkable inventiveness, skill and range of method in the achievement of this end. One of Spenser's favourite methods in this regard is
the witty and frequent use of wordplay, within the individual sonnet
and across the sequence as a whole. Other techniques include
manipulation of detail within the arguments of sonnets, verbal and
syntactical ambiguities, and games with rhetorical strategies, as well
as the use of hyperbole, to create comic perspectives in the
presentation of the lover figure. Spenser's treatment of these devices
provides a consistent undercurrent of playfulness throughout the
sequence.

Spenser's irony does not have the bite or range of Chaucer's, nor
the breadth of perspective offered by Sidney or Shakespeare. But the
nature of Spenser's irony in the *Amoretti* is refined and elegant. It
encourages amusement at the lover's antics and lovesickness, and
allows recognition of his foolishness; at the same time, it does not
diminish his stature, an important factor in the overall development
of the sequence. The lover is presented by Spenser as one who deals
with love's problems in idiosyncratic and often comical ways. When
he reaches his goal of a mature and loving relationship, he is no
longer a target of irony. The forms of irony employed in the earlier
part of the sequence invite sympathetic humour, rather than ridicule
or condemnation, and this allows the persona to emerge finally in a
favourable and attractive light, as one worthy of the mistress.

Spenser's reputation as one of the finest poets of the English Renaissance has in the past rested largely on his achievement in *The Shepheardes Calendar* and *The Faerie Queene*. The *Amoretti*, whilst obviously a minor work in relation to these, should, nevertheless, be given recognition as a sequence remarkable both for its technical mastery and its humane and witty exploration of the problems of love.

Bibliography

The asterisked texts indicate the editions of sonnet sequences which are used for quotation throughout the book.

Primary sources

Alighieri, Dante. *The Divine Comedy*, trans. Dorothy L. Sayers, Penguin Books, Harmondsworth, Middlesex, England, 1949.

Alighieri, Dante. *La Vita Nuova*, trans. D.G. Rossetti, George G. Harrap and Co., Cheylesmore Press, Coventry (undated).

Aristotle. *Historia Animalium*, trans. A.L. Peck, 3 vols., Loeb Classical Library, Harvard University Press, Cambridge, Massachusetts, 1970.

Augustine, St. *On Christian Doctrine*, trans. D.W. Robertson, Liberal Arts Press, New York, 1958.

*Barnes, Barnabe. *Parthenophil and Parthenophe* (1593), ed. Victor A. Doyno, Southern Illinois University Press, London, 1971.

Bembo, Pietro. *Pietro Bembo's 'Gli Asolani'*, trans. R.B. Gottfried, Indiana University Press, Bloomington, 1954.

Brook, George Leslie (ed.). *The Harley Lyrics*, Manchester University Press, Manchester, 3rd edn, 1964.

Brooke, Fulke Greville. *Selected Writings of Fulke Greville*, ed. Joan Rees, Athlone Press, London, 1973.

Bruno, Giordano. *The Heroic Enthusiasts*, Part the First, trans. L. Williams, George Redway, York Street, London, 1887.

Burton, Robert. *The Anatomy of Melacholy*, 3 vols., Everyman, J.M. Dent and Sons, London, 1961.

Capellanus, Andreas. *The Art of Courtly Love*, trans. John Jay Parry, F. Ungar Publishing Co., New York, 1959.

Castiglione, Baldesar. *The Book of The Courtier*, trans. George Bull, 2nd edn, 1967; rpt. Penguin Books Ltd., Harmondsworth, Middlesex, England, 1976.

*Chaucer, Geoffrey. *The Works of Geoffrey Chaucer*, ed. F.N. Robinson, 2nd edn, 1933; rpt. The Riverside Press, Cambridge, Massachusetts, 1957.

Chrétien de Troyes. *Arthurian Romances*, trans. W.W. Comfort, Everyman's Library, Dent, London, 1963.

Constable, Henry. *Diana* (1594), A Scolar Press Facsimile, Scolar Press, 1973.

*Constable, Henry. *The Poems of Henry Constable* (1592 and 1594), ed. Joan Grundy, Liverpool University Press, Liverpool, 1960.

*Daniel, Samuel. *Delia, With The Complaint of Rosamond* (1592), Scolar Press, 1969.

Davies, R.T. (ed.). *Medieval English Lyrics: A Critical Anthology*, Faber and Faber, London, 1963.

Desportes, Philippe. *Les amours de Diane*, eds. F. de Malherbe and V.E. Graham, Genève, Librairie E. Droz, 1959.

*Drayton, Michael. *Idea, Poems by Michael Draiton, Esquire* (1605), The Spenser Society, Burt Franklin, New York, Part II, 1967.

Elyot, Sir Thomas. *The Book Named the Governor* (1531), Scolar Press, 1970.

Evans, Maurice (ed.). *Elizabethan Sonnets*, J.M. Dent and Sons Ltd., London, 1977.

Ficino, Marsilio. *The Philebus Commentary*, trans. and ed. Michael J.B. Allen, University of California Press, Berkeley, 1975.

Ficino, Marsilio. *Commentary on Plato's Symposium*, trans. Sears Jayne, University of Missouri Studies vol. XIX, 1944.

Ficino, Marsilio. *Commentary on Plato's Symposium on Love*, Spring Press, Dallas, 1985.

*Fletcher, Giles. *Licia, or Poems of Love in Honour of the Admirable and Singular Virtues of his Lady*, in *Elizabethan Sonnets*, 2 vols., ed. Sidney Lee, Archibald Constable and Co. Ltd., Westminster, 1904, vol. II.

*Fowler, William. *The Tarantula of Love* (c.1590), in *The Works of William Fowler*, 3 vols., ed. Henry W. Meikle, William Blackwood and Sons, Edinburgh, 1914, vol.I.

Googe, Barnabe. *Eclogs, epytaphes and sonettes* (1563), Scholar's Facsimiles and Reprints, Gainesville, Florida, 1968.

*Griffin, Bartholomew. *Fidessa – more chaste than kind* (1596), in *Elizabethan Sonnets*, 2 vols., ed. Sidney Lee, Archibald Constable and Co. Ltd., Westminster, 1904, vol. II.

Heninger, S.K., Jr (ed.). *Selections from the Poetical Works of Edmund Spenser*, Houghton Mifflin Co., Boston, 1970.

Henryson, Robert. *The Poems of Robert Henryson*, ed. Denton Fox, Clarendon Press, Oxford, 1981.

Jonson, Ben. *Discoveries* (1641) *Conversations with William Drummond of Hawthornden* (1619), The Bodley Head Ltd., London, 1923.

*L[inche], R[ichard]. *Diella. Certain Sonnets, adjoined to the amorous poem of Dom Diego and Gyneura* (1596), in *Elizabethan Sonnets*, 2 vols., ed. Sidney Lee, Archibald Constable and Co. Ltd., Westminster, 1904, vol. II.

*Lodge, Thomas. *Phillis. Honoured with Pastorall, Sonnets, Elegies and Amorous Delights* (1593), in *The Complete Works of Thomas Lodge*, 3 vols., printed for the Hunterian Club, Glasgow, 1883, vol. 2.

Luria, M.S. and Hoffman, R.L. (eds.). *Middle English Lyrics*, W. W. Norton and Company, Inc., New York, 1974.

Lyly, John. *Euphues: The Anatomy of Wit* (1579), A. Murray and Son, London, 1868.

Meres, Francis. *Palladis Tamia: Wits Treasury*, ed. Arthur Freeman, Garland Publishing, Inc., New York, 1973.

Ovid. *The Art of Love and Other Poems*, trans. J. H. Mozley, William Heinemann Ltd., London, 1942.

Ovid. *Heroides and Amores*, trans. G. Showerman, Loeb Classical Library, Harvard University Press, London, 1977.

Ovid. *Metamorphoses*, trans. Mary M. Innes, Penguin Books, Harmondsworth, Middlesex, 1955.

*Percy, William. *Sonnets to the Fairest Coelia* (1594), in *Elizabethan Sonnets*, 2 vols., ed. Sidney Lee, Archibald Constable and Co. Ltd., Westminster, 1904, vol. II.

Petrarch, Francesco. *An Anthology of Petrarch*, ed. David Thompson, Harper and Row, New York, 1971.

*Petrarch, Francesco. *Petrarch's Lyric Poems, The 'Rime Sparse' and Other Lyrics*, trans. and ed. Robert M. Durling, 2nd edn, 1976; rpt. Harvard University Press, Cambridge, Massachusetts, 1981.

Petrarch, Francesco. *Petrarch's Secret*, trans. William H. Draper, Chatto and Windus, London, 1911.

Petrarch, Francesco. *Selected Sonnets, Odes and Letters*, ed. Thomas G. Bergin, Meredith Publishing Co., New York, 1966.

Petrarch, Francesco. *Sonnets and Songs*, trans. Anna Maria Armi, Pantheon, New York, 1978.

Plato. *Phaedrus*, Penguin Books, Harmondsworth, Middlesex, 1973.

Plato. *The Republic*, trans. H.D.P. Lee, Penguin Books, Harmondsworth, Middlesex, 1960.

Plato. *The Symposium*, trans. W. Hamilton, Penguin Books, Harmondsworth, Middlesex, 1951.

Plato. *Timaeus*, trans. H.D.P. Lee, Penguin Books, Harmondsworth, Middlesex, 1965.

Pliny. *Natural History*, 10 vols., trans. H. Rackham, eds. T.E. Page, E. Capps, W.H.D. Rouse, L.A. Post and E.H. Warmington, Loeb Classical Library, Harvard University Press, Cambridge, Massachusetts, 1967.

Plotinus. *Psychic and Physical Treatises*, 2 vols., trans. Stephen Mackenna, Philip Lee Warner, publisher to the Medici Society, The Library of Philosophical Translations, London, 1921.

Puttenham, George. *The Arte of English Poesie* (1589), eds. A. Walker and G.D. Willcock, 1936; rpt. Cambridge University Press, London, 1970.

Renwick, W.L. *Daphnaïda and Other Poems*, Scolar Press, 1929.

Robbins, Rossell Hope (ed.). *Secular Lyrics of the Fourteenth and Fifteenth Centuries*, Oxford University Press, London, 1964.

Ronsard, Pierre. *Sonnets for Helen*, trans. Humbert Wolfe, Unwin Books, London, 1972.

Sappho. *Poems and Fragments*, trans. Guy Davenport, The University of Michigan Press, Ann Arbor, 1965.

*Shakespeare, William. *Shakespeare's Sonnets*, ed. Stephen Booth, Yale University Press, New Haven, 1977.

Shakespeare, William. *Shakespeare's Sonnets*, ed. Martin Seymour-Smith, Heinemann, London, 1967.

Shakespeare, William. *The Poems*, ed. F.T. Prince, 1960; rpt. Methuen, London, 1982.

Shakespeare, William. *The Sonnets*, Signet Classics, New American Library, Inc., New York, 1964.

Sidney, Sir Philip. *The Countess of Pembroke's Arcadia*, ed. M. Evans, Penguin Books, Harmondsworth, Middlesex, 1977.

Sidney, Sir Philip. *Miscellaneous Prose of Sir Philip Sidney*, eds. Katherine Duncan-Jones and Jan van Dorsten, Clarendon Press, Oxford, 1973.

Sidney, Sir Philip. *Sidney's Apologie for Poetrie*, ed. J. Churton Collins, Clarendon Press, Oxford, 1907.

Sidney, Sir Philip. *Sir Philip Sidney: Selected Poems*, ed. Katherine Duncan-Jones, Clarendon Press, Oxford, 1973.

*Sidney, Sir Philip. *The Poems of Sir Philip Sidney*, ed. William A. Ringler, Jr, Clarendon Press, Oxford, 1962.

Silverstein, Theodore (ed.). *Medieval English Lyrics*, Edward Arnold, London, 1971.

*Smith, William. *Chloris or The Complaint of the passionate despised Shepherd* (1596), in *Elizabethan Sonnets*, 2 vols., ed. Sidney Lee, Archibald Constable and Co. Ltd., Westminster, 1904, vol. II.

Spenser, Edmund. *Amoretti and Epithalamion* (1595), A Facsimile reprint, Scolar Press, 1968.

Spenser, Edmund. *Edmund Spenser's Poetry*, ed. Hugh Maclean, 2nd edn, 1968; rpt. W.W. Norton and Co., New York, 1982.

Spenser, Edmund. *Poems of Spenser*, selected and with an introduction by W.B. Yeats, T.C. and E.C. Jack, Edinburgh (undated).

Spenser, Edmund. *Spenser: Poetical Works*, ed. J.C. Smith and E. de Selincourt, 1912; rpt. Oxford University Press, London, 1975.

*Spenser, Edmund. *The Works of Edmund Spenser*, 9 vols., eds. E. Greenlaw, C.G. Osgood, F.M. Padelford and R. Heffner, 1947; rpt. The Johns Hopkins Press, Baltimore, 1966. The *Amoretti* is printed in *The Minor Poems*: Part 2, vol. 8.

Surrey, Henry Howard, Earl of. *The Poems of Henry Howard, Earl of Surrey*, W. Pickering, London, 1831.

*Tofte, Robert. *Laura, The Toys of a Traveller or The Feast of Fancy*(1597) in *Elizabethan Sonnets*, 2 vols., ed. Sidney Lee, Archibald Constable and Co. Ltd., Westminster, 1904, vol. II.

Tottel, Richard. *Songs and Sonnets*, (Tottel's Miscellany, 1557), Scolar Press, 1970.

Watson, Thomas. *The Hecatompathia or Passionate Centurie of Love* (1582), introd. S.K. Heninger, Jr, Scholars' Facsimiles and Reprints, Gainesville, Florida, 1964.

Whitney, G. *A Choice of Emblemes, and other Devises* Leyden, 1586; Scolar Press, 1990.

*Wyatt, Sir Thomas. *Collected Poems*, ed. Joost Daalder, Oxford University Press, London, 1975.

Zepheria (1594). Anonymous, Burt Franklin Research and Source Works, Series 150, New York, 1967.

Secondary sources

Bibliographical collections, concordances and general reference works.

Birmingham Shakespeare Library. *A Shakespeare Bibliography*, The catalogue of the Birmingham Shakespeare Library, Birmingham Public Libraries, Mansell, London, 1971.

Blakeney, E.H. (ed.). *A Smaller Classical Dictionary*, 5th edn 1910; rpt. J.M. Dent and Sons Ltd., London, 1928.

Brewer, Ebenezer Cobham. *Brewer's Dictionary of Phrase and Fable*, ed. Ivor H. Evans, 1970; rpt. Cassell, London, 1981.

Carpenter, F.I. *A Reference Guide to Edmund Spenser*, The University of Chicago Press, Chicago, 1923.

Consiglio Nazionale delle Ricerche. *Concordanze del Canzoniere di Francesco Petrarca*, 2 vols., Accademia Della Crusca, Firenze, 1971.

Donow, Herbert S. *A Concordance to the Sonnet Sequences of Daniel, Drayton, Shakespeare, Sidney and Spenser*, Southern Illinois University Press, Carbondale, 1969.

Hornsby, Sam and Bennett, James R. *The Sonnet: An Annotated Bibliography from 1940 to the Present*, in *Style*, vol. 13, Spring 1979.

Jobes, G. *Dictionary of Mythology, Folklore and Symbols*, Scarecrow Press, Inc., New York, 1961.

McNeir, Waldo and Provost, Foster. *Edmund Spenser: An Annotated Bibliography, 1937–72*, Duquesne University Press, Pittsburgh, 2nd edn, 1975.

Osgood, Charles Grosvenor. *A Concordance to the Poems of Edmund Spenser*, Peter Smith, Gloucester, Massachusetts, 1963.

Partridge, Eric. *A Dictionary of Slang and Unconventional English*, 2 vols., Routledge and Kegan Paul Ltd., London, 5th edn, 1961.

Preston, Michael J. (ed.). *A Concordance to the Middle English Shorter Poem*, Parts 1 and 2, W.S. Maney and Son Ltd., Leeds, 1975.

Tatlock, John S. and Kennedy, Arthur G. *A Concordance to the Complete Works of Geoffrey Chaucer*, Peter Smith, Gloucester, Massachusetts, 1963.

Washington, Mary A. *Sir Philip Sidney: An Annotated Bibliography of Modern Criticism, 1941–1970*, University of Missouri Press, Columbia, 1972.

Watson, George. *The English Petrarchans: A Critical Bibliography of the 'Canzoniere'*, Warburg Institute, London, 1967.

Withycombe, E.G. *The Oxford Dictionary of English Christian Names*,

2nd edn, 1945; rpt. Clarendon Press, Oxford, 1977.
Wright, William Aldis. *The Authorised Version of the English Bible*
(1611), 5 vols., Cambridge University Press, Cambridge, 1909.
Wurtsbaugh, Jewel. *Two Centuries of Spenserian Scholarship: 1609–
1805*, The Johns Hopkins Press, Baltimore, 1936.

Critical Works

Abbot, W.M., S.J., (ed.). *Documents of Vatican II*, Herder and
Herder, New York, 1966.
Ackerman, Bert. W. *Backgrounds to Medieval English Literature*,
Random House, Inc., New York, 1966.
Alpers, A. *Dolphins*. Pauls Book Arcade, Auckland and Hamilton,
1963.
Alpers, Paul J. *Elizabethan Poetry*, Oxford University Press,
London, 1967.
Alpers, Paul J. *The Poetry of 'The Faerie Queene'*, Princeton
University Press, New Jersey, 1967.
Ault, Norman. *Elizabethan Lyrics*. Longman's, London, 1966.
Baine, Harris R. (ed.). *The Significance of Neo-Platonism*, Inter-
national Society for Neo-Platonic Studies, Old Dominion
University, Norfolk, Virginia, 1976.
Barkan, Leonard. *Nature's Work of Art*. Yale University Press, New
Haven, 1975.
Baroway, Israel. 'The Imagery of Spenser and the *Song of Songs*',
1934; rpt. in *Edmund Spenser: Epithalamion*, ed. Robert Beum,
Charles E. Merrill Publishing Co., Ohio, 1968.
Barthel, Carol. '*Amoretti*: A Comic Monodrama?', *Spenser at
Kalamazoo, Proceedings from a Special Session at the Thirteenth
Conference on Medieval Studies in Kalamazoo*, Michigan, 5–6 May,
1978, Cleveland State University.
Bayley, Peter. *Edmund Spenser: Prince of Poets*, Hutchinson Univer-
sity Library, London, 1971.
Berger, Harry, Jr. (ed.). *Spenser: A Collection of Critical Essays*,
Prentice-Hall, Inc., Englewood Cliffs, New Jersey, 1968.
Bernardo, Aldo S. *Petrarch, Laura and the Triumphs*, State University
of New York Press, Albany, 1974.
Bhattacherje, Mohinimohan. *Platonic Ideas in Spenser*, 2nd edn, 1935;
rpt. Greenwood Press, Connecticut, 1970.
Bieman, Elizabeth. '"Sometimes I . . . mask in myrth lyke to a

Comedy": Spenser's Amoretti', in Spenser Studies: A Renaissance Poetry Annual, A.M.S. Press, Inc., New York, 1984, vol. 4.

Bradbrook, Muriel C. Shakespeare and Elizabethan Poetry: A Study of his Earlier Work in Relation to the Poetry of his Time, Chatto and Windus, London, 1951.

Brand, C.P. Torquato Tasso: A Study of the Poet and his Contribution to English Literature, Cambridge University Press, Cambridge, 1965.

Brown, James Neil. 'The Critics' Poet: Spenser in the 'Seventies', AUMLA, 43, 1975.

Brown, James Neil. '"Lyke Phoebe", Lunar, Numerical and Calendrical Patterns in Spenser's Amoretti', in The Gypsy Scholar, 1, University of Massachusetts, Amherst, 1973.

Bullen, A.H. (ed.). Anacreon, trans. Thomas Stanley Lawrence and A.H. Bullen, London, 1893.

Bush, Douglas. Mythology and the Renaissance Tradition in English Poetry, W.W. Norton and Co., Inc., New York, 1963.

Buxton, John. Elizabethan Taste, Macmillan, London, 1963.

Carpenter, F.I. 'G.W. Senior and G.W.I' Modern Philology, vol. 22, 1924.

Carrol, W.M. Animal Conventions in the English Renaissance Non-Religious Prose 1550–1600, Bookman Associates, New York, 1954.

Casady, Edwin. 'The Neo-Platonic Ladder in Spenser's Amoretti', in Renaissance Studies in Honor of Hardin Craig, eds. Baldwin Maxwell, W.D. Briggs, Francis R. Johnson and E.N.S. Thompson, Stanford University, California, 1941.

Cassirer, Ernst. The Platonic Renaissance in England, trans. James P. Pettegrove, 1953; rpt. Gordian Press, New York, 1970.

Cheney, Donald. 'Spenser's Fortieth Birthday and Related Fictions', Spenser Studies: A Renaissance Poetry Annual, A.M.S. Press, Inc., New York, 1984, vol. IV.

Church, R.W. Spenser, Macmillan and Co., London, 1883.

Clark, Anne. Beasts and Bawdy, J.M. Dent and Sons Ltd., London, 1975.

Cooper, Sherod M., Jr. 'The Sonnets of Astrophil and Stella: A Stylistic Study', Studies in English Literature, vol. XLI, 1968.

Copleston, F.C. Medieval Philosophy, Methuen and Co. Ltd., London, 1952.

Cory, Herbert E. The Critics of Edmund Spenser, Haskell House, New York, 1964.

Cotter, James Finn. 'The "Baiser" Group in Sidney's *Astrophil and Stella'*, *Texas Studies in Literature and Language*, vol. 12, March, 1970.

Craig, Hardin. 'Recent Scholarship of the English Renaissance', *Studies in Philology*, vol.XLII, 1945.

Cruttwell, P. *The English Sonnet*, published for the British Council and the National Book League by Longman, London, 1966.

Cruttwell, P. 'The Love Poetry of John Donne: "Pedantique Weedes or Fresh Invention?"' *Metaphysical Poetry*, eds. Malcolm Bradbury and David Palmer, Indiana University Press, London, 1970.

Cruttwell, P. *The Shakespearean Moment and its Place in the Poetry of the Seventeenth Century*, Random House, Inc., New York, 1960.

Cummings, L. 'Spenser's *Amoretti VIII*: New Manuscript Versions', *Studies in English Literature*, IV, 1964.

Cummings, Peter. 'Spenser's *Amoretti* as an Allegory of Love', *Texas Studies in Literature and Language*, 12, Summer 1970.

Cummings, R.M. (ed.). *Spenser: The Critical Heritage*, Routledge and Kegan Paul, London, 1971.

Daly, Peter M. *Literature in the Light of the Emblem*, The University of Toronto Press, Toronto, 1979.

Danby, John Francis. *Poets on Fortune's Hill: Studies in Sidney, Shakespeare, Beaumont and Fletcher*, Kennikat Press, Port Washington, 1966.

Davis, Stevie (ed.). *Renaissance Views of Man*, Manchester University Press, Manchester, 1978.

Davis, B.E.C. *Edmund Spenser: A Critical Study*, Russell and Russell, Inc., New York, 1962.

Dees, Jerome. 'Spenser's Anti-Neoplatonism', *A Special Session of the Thirteenth Conference on Medieval Studies at Kalamazoo*, May 1977, Cleveland University Press, Cleveland.

Dronke, Peter. *Medieval Latin and the Rise of the European Love Lyric*, 2 vols., Oxford University Press, London, 1965.

Dunlop, Alexander. 'Calendar Symbolism in the *Amoretti*', *Notes and Queries*, January 1969.

Dunlop, Alexander. 'The Drama of the *Amoretti*',*Proceedings of a Special Session at the Thirteenth Conference on Medieval Studies in Kalamazoo, Michigan, May, 1978*, Cleveland State University, Cleveland, 1978.

Dunlop, Alexander. 'The Drama of *Amoretti*', *Spenser Studies. A Renaissance Poetry Annual*, eds. P. Cullen and T.P. Roche, Jr,

A.M.S. Press, Inc., New York, 1978, vol. 1.

Dunlop, Alexander. 'The Unity of Spenser's *Amoretti'*, in *Silent Poetry: Essays in Numerological Analysis*, ed. Alastair Fowler, Barnes and Noble, New York, 1970.

Edmonds, J.M. (ed.). *Elegy and Iambus with the Anacreontea*, 2 vols., Harvard University Press, Cambridge, Massachusetts, 1979.

Edwards, Calvin R. 'The Narcissus Myth in Spenser's Poetry', *Studies in Philology*, vol. 74, 1977.

Eliot, T.S. *Selected Prose of T.S. Eliot*, Faber and Faber, London, 1975.

Elliot, John R., Jr (ed.). *The Prince of Poets: Essays on Edmund Spenser*, New York University Press, New York, 1968.

Ellrodt, Robert. *Neoplatonism in the Poetry of Spenser*, Librairie E. Droz, Geneva, 1960; rpt. Folcroft Library Editions, 1978.

Erskine, John. *The Elizabethan Lyric*, Columbia University Press, New York, 1931.

Evans, Maurice. *English Poetry in the Sixteenth Century*, Hutchinson University Library, London, 1967.

Fish, Stanley Eugene. *Self-Consuming Artifacts: The Experience of Seventeenth-Century Literature*, University of California Press, Berkeley, 1972.

Fletcher, J.B. 'Benevieni's *Ode of Love* and Spenser's *Fowre Hymnes'*, *Modern Philology*, April 1911.

Forster, Leonard. *The Icy Fire*. Cambridge University Press, London, 1969.

Fowler, Alastair. *Edmund Spenser*, Writers and their Work, ed. Ian Scott-Kilvert, Longmans, Green and Co. London, 1977.

Fowler, Alastair (ed.). *Silent Poetry*, Routledge and Kegan Paul, London, 1970.

Fowler, Alastair. *Truimphal Forms: Structural Patterns in Elizabethan Poetry*, Cambridge University Press, Cambridge, 1970.

Freeman, Rosemary. *Edmund Spenser*, Writers and their Work, 1957; rpt. Longmans, Green and Co., London, 1962.

Freeman, Rosemary. *English Emblem Books*, Chatto and Windus, London, 1948.

Fuller, John. *The Sonnet*, Methuen and Co. Ltd., London, 1972.

Gilson, Etienne. *History of Christian Philosophy in the Middle Ages*, Random House, Inc., New York, 1955.

Gottfried, R. 'The "G.W. Senior" and "G.W.I." of Spenser's

Amoretti', in *Modern Language Quarterly*, vol. 3, December, 1942, no. 4.

Goulston, Wendy. 'The "Figuring Forth" of Astrophil: Sidney's Use of Language', *Southern Review*, November 1978, vol. 11.

Grundy, Joan. 'Shakespeare's Sonnets and the Elizabethan Sonneteers', *Shakespeare Survey*, vol. 15, Cambridge University Press, Cambridge, 1962.

Gurr, Andrew. 'Shakespeare's First Poem: Sonnet 145', *Essays in Criticism*, 21, 1971.

Hamilton, A.C. 'Our New Poet: Spenser, "Well of English Undefyld"', *Essential Articles: For the Study of Edmund Spenser*, ed. A.C. Hamilton, Archon Books, Hamden, Connecticut, 1972.

Hamilton, A.C. 'Sidney's *Astrophil and Stella* as a sonnet sequence', *English Literary History*, vol. 36, 1969.

Hankins, John Erskine. *Source and Meaning in Spenser's Allegory: A Study of 'The Faerie Queene'*, Clarendon Press, Oxford, 1971.

Hardison, O.B., Jr. *'Amoretti* and the *Dolce Stil Novo'*, in *English Literary Renaissance*, vol. 2, Spring 1972, no.2.

Hardison, O.B., Jr. *The Enduring Monument*, University of North Carolina Press, Chapel Hill, 1962.

Harris, Victor and Husain, Itrat. (eds.). *English Prose 1600–1660*, Holt, Rinehart and Winston, New York, 1965.

Harrison, John S. *Platonism in English Poetry of the Sixteenth and Seventeenth Centuries*, Columbia University Press, London, 1903.

Hieatt, A. Kent. 'A Numerical Key to Spenser's *Amoretti* and Guyon in the House of Mammon', *Yearbook of English Studies*, 3, 1973.

Hieatt, A. Kent. *Short Time's Endless Monument*, Columbia University Press, New York, 1960.

Higginson, James Jackson. *Spenser's Shepherd's Calender*, Columbia University Press, New York, 1912.

Hopper, Vincent Foster. *Medieval Number Symbolism*, Cooper Square Publishers, Inc., New York, 1969.

Howe, Ann Romayne. *'Astrophil and Stella*: Why and How', *Studies in Philology*, LXI, 1964.

Hunter, G.K. 'The Dramatic Technique of Shakespeare's Sonnets', *Essays in Criticism*, 3, 1953.

Hunter, G.K. 'Spenser's *Amoretti* and the English Sonnet Tradition', *A Theatre for Spenserians*, eds. Judith M. Kennedy and James A. Reither, University of Toronto Press, Toronto, Buffalo, 1973.

Ing, Catherine Mills. *Elizabethan Lyrics: A study in the development of*

English metres and their relation to poetic effect, Chatto and Windus, London, 1951.

Jayne, Sears Reynolds. 'Ficino and the Platonism of the English Renaissance', *Comparative Literature*, vol. 4, 1952.

John, Lisle Cecil. *The Elizabethan Sonnet Sequences*, Russell and Russell, Inc., New York, 1964.

Johnson, William C. 'Amor and Spenser's *Amoretti*', *English Studies*, vol. 51, 1973.

Johnson, William C. 'Spenser's *Amoretti VI*', *The Explicator*, vol. 29, no. 5, 1971.

Johnson, William C. 'Spenser's *Amoretti* and the Art of Liturgy', *Studies in English Literature*, 14, Winter 1974.

Johnson, William C. 'Spenser's Sonnet Diction', *Neuphilologische Mitteilungen*, 71, 1970.

Kalil, Judith. '"Mask in Myrth Lyke to a Comedy": Spenser's Persona in the *Amoretti*', in *Thoth*, 20, Spring 1973.

Kalstone, David. *Sidney's Poetry: Contexts and Interpretations*, Harvard University Press, Cambridge, 1965.

Kalstone, David. 'Sir Philip Sidney and "poore Petrarchs long deceased woes"', *Journal of English and Germanic Philology*, 63, January 1964.

Kaske, Carol V. 'Another Liturgical Dimension of *Amoretti* 68', *Notes and Queries*, vol. 222, 1977.

Kaske, Carol V. 'Spenser's *Amoretti* and *Epithalamion* of 1595: Structure, Genre and Numerology', *English Literary Renaissance*, vol. 8, no.3, Autumn 1978.

Kastner, L.E. 'Spenser's *Amoretti* and Desportes', *Modern Language Review*, vol. IV, 1908–09.

Kellogg, Robert. 'Thought's Astonishment and the Dark Conceit of Spenser's *Amoretti*', *Prince of Poets*, ed. John J. Elliott, Jr, University of London Press Ltd., London, 1968.

Kelly, Douglas. *Medieval Imagination: Rhetoric and the Poetry of Courtly Love*, University of Wisconsin Press, Madison, 1978.

Kermode, Frank. *Shakespeare, Spenser, Donne: Renaissance Essays*, Routledge and Kegan Paul, London, 1971.

Klibanksy, R. *The Continuity of the Platonic Tradition During the Middle Ages*, The Warburg Institute, London, 1950.

Kostic, V. *Spenser's Sources in Italian Poetry: A Study in Comparative Literature*, Faculté de Philologie de l'Université de Belgrade, Monographie, Belgrade, 1969.

Krailsheimer. A.J. (ed.). *The Continental Renaissance*. Penguin Books Ltd., Harmondsworth, Middlesex, England, 1971.

Kristellar, Paul Oskar. *The Philosophy of Marsilio Ficino*, trans. Virginia Conant, Columbia University Press, New York, 1943.

Kristellar, Paul Oskar. *Renaissance Thought and its Sources*, Michael Mooney, Columbia University Press, New York, 1979.

Landry, Hilton (ed.). *New Essays on Shakespeare's Sonnets*, A.M.S. Press, Inc., New York, 1976.

Lea, Henry C. *An Historical Sketch of Sacerdotal Celibacy in the Christian Church*, Boston, Houghton Mifflin and Co., New York, 1884.

Leavis, F.R. *Revaluation: Tradition and Development in English Poetry*, 1936; rpt. Penguin Books, Harmondsworth, Middlesex, England, 1967.

Legouis, Emile. *Spenser*, J.M. Dent and Sons Ltd., New York, 1926.

Leishman, James Blair. *Themes and Variations in Shakespeare's Sonnets*, 1961; 2nd edn, Harper and Row, New York, 1966.

Levarie, Janet. 'Renaissance Anacreontics', *Comparative Literature*, vol. XXV, 1973.

Lever, J.W. *The Elizabethan Love Sonnet*, 2nd edn, 1966; rpt. Methuen, London, 1974.

Lewis, C.S. *The Allegory of Love: A Study in Medieval Tradition*, 1936; rpt. Oxford University Press, London, 1967.

Lewis, C.S. *English Literature in the Sixteenth Century Excluding Drama*, Clarendon Press, Oxford, 1954.

Lievsay, John L. 'Greene's Panther', *Renaissance Studies in Honor of Hardin Craig*, eds. Baldwin Maxwell, W.D. Briggs, Francis R. Johnson and E.N.S. Thompson, Stanford University Press, California, 1941.

Lovejoy, Arthur O. *The Great Chain of Being*, Harvard University Press, Cambridge, Massachusetts, 1976.

McCulloch, Florence, *Medieval Latin and French Bestiaries*, The University of North Carolina Press, Chapel Hill, 1962.

Martz, Louis L. 'The *Amoretti*: "Most Goodly Temperature"', *Form and Convention in the Poetry of Edmund Spenser*, ed. William Nelson, Columbia University Press, New York, 1961.

McElderry, B.R. Jr. 'Archaism and Innovation in Spenser's Poetic Diction', *PMLA*, 1932.

McNeir, Waldo. 'An Apology for Spenser's *Amoretti*', *Essential*

Articles for the Study of Edmund Spenser, ed. A.C. Hamilton, Archon Books, Hamden, Connecticut, 1972.

Minto, William. *Characteristics of English Poets*, Blackwood, Edinburgh, 1874.

Miola, Robert S. 'Spenser's Anacreontics: A Mythological Metaphor', *Studies in Philology*, 77, 1980.

Montgomery, Robert. 'Reason, Passion and Introspection in *Astrophel and Stella*', *Studies in English*, University of Texas, XXXVI, 1957.

Müeller, William R. (ed.). *Spenser's Critics: Changing Currents in Literary Taste*, Syracuse University Press, Syracuse, 1959.

Mullinger, James Bass. *The University of Cambridge From the Royal Injunctions of 1535 to the Accession of Charles the First*, Cambridge University Press, London, 1884.

Murphy, James J. *Rhetoric in the Middle Ages: A History of Rhetorical Theory from Saint Augustine to the Renaissance*, University of California Press, Berkeley, 1974.

Murrin, M. *The Veil of Allegory: Some Notes towards a Theory of Allegorical Rhetoric in the English Renaissance*, Chicago University Press, Chicago, 1969.

Neely, Carol Thomas. 'The Structure of English Renaissance Sonnet Sequences', *English Literary History*, vol. 45, 1978.

Nelson, John Charles. *Renaissance Theory of Love: The Context of Giordano Bruno's 'Eroici Furori'*, 2nd edn, 1958; rpt. Columbia University Press, New York, 1963.

O'Donoghue, Bernard. *The Courtly Love Tradition*, Manchester University Press, Barnes and Noble Books, New Jersey, 1982.

Ogle, M.B. 'The Classical Origin and Tradition of Literary Conceits', *American Journal of Philology*, vol. 34, February, 1913.

Ogle, M.B. 'The White Hand as Literary Conceit', *Sewanee Review*, vol. 20, October, 1912.

Opie, Peter and Iona. *The Classic Fairy Tales*, Oxford University Press, London, 1974.

Palgrave, Francis L. 'Essays on the Minor Poems of Spenser', *Complete Works*, ed. A. Grosart, 9 vols., The Spenser Society, London 1882–84, vol. 4.

Partridge, Eric. *Shakespeare's Bawdy: A Literary and Psychological Essay and a Comprehensive Glossary*, revised edn, 1947; rpt. Routledge and Kegan Paul, London, 1968.

Pearson, Lu Emily. *Elizabethan Love Conventions*, Barnes and Noble, New York, 1967.

Pebworth, T.L. 'A Net for the Soul: A Renaissance Conceit and the Song of Songs', *Romance Notes*, 13, 1971.

Peterson, Douglas L. *The English Lyric from Wyatt to Donne: A History of the Plain and Eloquent Styles*, Princeton University Press, New Jersey, 1967.

Phipson, Emma. *The Animal Lore of Shakespeare's Time*, Kegan Paul, Trench and Co., London, 1883.

Piper, William Bowman. 'Spenser's "Lyke As a Huntsman"', *College English*, XXII, March 1961.

Prescott, Anne Lake. 'The Thirsty Deer and the Lord of Life: Some Contexts for *Amoretti* 67–70', *Spenser Studies: A Renaissance Poetry Annual*, A.M.S. Press, Inc., New York, vol. VI, 1985.

Quitslund, Jon A. 'Spenser's *Amoretti VIII* and Platonic Commentaries on Petrarch', *Journal of the Warburg and Courtauld Institutes*, 36, 1973.

Rebholz, Ronald A. *The Life of Fulke Greville First Lord Brooke*, Clarendon Press, Oxford, 1971.

Rees, Joan. *Samuel Daniel: A Critical and Biographical Study*, Liverpool University Press, Liverpool, 1964.

Renwick, W.L. *An Essay on Renaissance Poetry*, Edward Arnold Ltd., London, 1964.

Ricks, Don. M. 'Convention and Structure in Edmund Spenser's *Amoretti*', *PUASAL*, 44, 1967.

Ricks, Don M. 'Persona and Process in Spenser's *Amoretti*', *Ariel*, 3, October, 1972.

Rix, Herbert David. 'Rhetoric in Spenser's Poetry', *The Pennsylvania State College Bulletin*, no. 7, July 1940.

Robb, Nesca Adeline. *Neoplatonism of the Italian Renaissance*, George Allen and Unwin Ltd., London, 1935.

Rogers, William Elford. 'Narcissus in *Amoretti XXXV*', *American Notes and Queries*, vol.15, no. 2, October 1976.

Rose, Mark. *Heroic Love: Studies in Sidney and Spenser*, Harvard University Press, Cambridge, Massachusetts, 1963.

Rudenstine, Neil. *Sidney's Poetic Development*, Harvard University Press, Cambridge, Massachusetts, 1967.

Ryken, Leland. 'The Drama of Choice in Sidney's *Astrophel and Stella*', *Journal of English and Germanic Philology*, vol. LXVIII, October 1969.

Ruthven, K.K. *Critical Assumptions*, Cambridge University Press, Cambridge, 1979.

St. Clare Byrne, M. (ed.). *The Elizabethan Zoo. A Book of Beasts Both Fabulous and Authentic*, Nonpareil Books, Boston, 1979.

Saintsbury, G. *A History of English Prosody From the Twelfth Century to the Present Day*, 3 vols., Macmillan and Co. Ltd., 1906, vol. 2.

Salingar, L.G. 'The Elizabethan Literary Renaissance', in *Pelican Guide to English Literature*, 7 vols., Penguin Books, Harmondsworth, Middlesex, 1968, vol. 2.

Satterthwaite, Alfred W. *Spenser, Ronsard and Du Bellay*, Kennikat Press, Port Washington, New York, London, 1960.

Scanlon, James. 'Sidney's *Astrophil and Stella*: "See what it is to Love Sensually!"' *Studies in English Literature*, 16, 1976.

Schaar, Claes. *An Elizabethan Sonnet Problem: Shakespeare's Sonnets, Daniel's 'Delia' and their literary background*, C.W.K. Gleerup, Lund, 1960.

Scott, Janet. 'The Sources of Spenser's *Amoretti*', *Modern Language Review*, vol. XXII, 1927.

Siegel, Paul N. 'The Petrarchan Sonneteers and Neoplatonic Love', *Studies in Philology*, vol. XLII, 1945.

Smith, Charles G. *Spenser's Proverb Lore With Special Reference to His Use of the 'Sententiae' of Leonard Culman and Publilius Syrus*, Harvard University Press, Cambridge, Massachusetts, 1970.

Smith, Hallett D. *Elizabethan Poetry: A Study in Conventional Meaning and Expression*, Harvard University Press, Cambridge, Massachusetts, 1952.

Sonnino, L. *A Handbook of Sixteenth-Century Rhetoric*, Routledge and Kegan Paul Ltd., London, 1968.

Spencer, T. 'The Poetry of Sir Philip Sidney', *English Literary History*, 12, 1945.

Stewart, Jack F. 'Spenser's *Amoretti*, LXXIX, 10', *The Explicator*, vol. XXVII, no. 9, May 1969.

Stewart, James T. 'Renaissance Psychology and the Ladder of Love in Castiglione and Spenser', *Journal of English and Germanic Philology*, 56, 1957.

Stillinger, Jack. 'The Biographical Problem of *Astrophil and Stella*', *Journal of English and Germanic Philology*, 59, 1960.

Tennenhouse, Leonard. *Power on Display: The Politics of Shakespeare's Genres*, Methuen, New York and London, 1986.

Theobaldi. *Physiologus*, ed. P.T. Eden, E.J. Brill, Leiden, 1972.

Tuve, Rosemond. *Elizabethan and Metaphysical Imagery: Renaissance Poetic and Twentieth-Century Critics*, The University of Chicago Press, Chicago, 1968.

Tuve, Rosemond. *Essays by Rosemond Tuve: Spenser; Herbert; Milton*, ed. Thomas P. Roche, Jr, Princeton University Press, Princeton, 1970.

Vasari, Giorgio. *Artists of the Renaissance: A Selection from 'Lives of the Artists'*, trans. George Bull, Penguin Books, London, 1965; rpt. Allen Lane, London, 1978.

Watkins, W.B.C. *Shakespeare and Spenser*, Princeton University Press, New Jersey, 1950.

Welsford, E. *Spenser: Four Hymnes and Epithalamion: A Study of Edmund Spenser's Doctrine of Love*, Basil Blackwell, Oxford, 1967.

Wilkins, Ernest Hatch. *Petrarch's Later Years*, Mediaeval Academy of America, Cambridge, Massachusetts, 1959.

Willey, Basil. *The Seventeenth-Century Background: Studies in the Thought of the Age in Relation to Poetry and Religion*, Penguin, Harmondsworth, Middlesex, England, 1967.

Wilson, Katherine M. *Shakespeare's Sugared Sonnets*, George Allen and Unwin Ltd., London, 1974.

Wilkins, Ernest Hatch. *Life of Petrarch*, University of Chicago Press, Chicago, 1963.

Winbolt, S.E. *Spenser and His Poetry*, George G. Harrap and Co. Ltd., London, 1918.

Winstanley, Lilian (ed.). *The Fowre Hymnes*, Cambridge University Press, Cambridge, 1907.

Winters, Yvor. *Forms of Discovery: Critical and Historical Essays on the Forms of the Short Poem in English*, Swallow, Denver, 1967.

Wölfflin, Heinrich. *Classic Art: An Introduction to the Italian Renaissance*, trans. P. and L. Murray, 1953; rpt. 2nd edn, Phaidon Publishers, New York, 1959.

Yates, Frances Amelia. *Giordano Bruno and the Hermetic Tradition*, University of Chicago Press, Chicago, 1964.

Doctoral Dissertations

Goldman, Lloyd Nathaniel. 'Attitudes Toward the Mistress in Five Elizabethan Sonnet Sequences', University of Illinois, 1964.

Hilton, Michael. 'The Anacreontea in England to 1683', 2 vols., Oxford, 1981.

Johnson, William C. '"Vow'd to Eternity": A Study of Spenser's *Amoretti*', The University of Iowa, 1969.

Rahm, Linda Kathryn. 'The Poet-Lover and Shakespeare's Sonnets', Cornell University, 1971.

Traister, Daniel Harris. '"Pity the Tale of Me": A Reading of Sidney's *Astrophil and Stella*,' New York University, 1973.

Index

Alciatus, Andreas 94n
Alighieri, Dante 34, 144–6, 147,
169n, 178
All's Well That Ends Well 96n
Alpers, A. 94n
Alpers, J. Paul 13, 7–8n
Amoretti, origin of title 34–5;
sonnets *see* index of first lines
Amoretti: A Comic Monodrama?
(Barthel) 57n, 88n
*Amoretti and the Dolce Stil Novo,
The* (Hardison) 30n, 88n, 137n
*Amoretti: 'Most Goodly
Temperature', The* (Martz) 9n,
30n
Anacreontics 13, 14, 15; origin of
29n
Anatomy of Melancholy (Burton)
170n
*Animal Conventions in English
Renaissance Non-Religious Prose
1550–1600* (Carroll) 96n
animal imagery in *Amoretti*: bee
41–2; bird 42; cokatrice 38; deer
25–7; dolphin 83–4, 94–6n, 106;
lamb 71; lion 26, 38, 71–2, 89n;
panther 26, 38, 85–6, 96–7nn;
spider 42, 81–2; tiger 26, 38,
73, 90n

*Animal Lore of Shakespeare's Time,
The* (Phipson) 90n
*Another Liturgical Dimension of
Amoretti 68* (Kaske) 137n
Apology for Spenser's Amoretti, An
(McNeir) 9n, 88n
Art of Courtly Love, The
(Capellanus) 169n
Art of Love, The (Ovid) 170n
Arthurian Romances (Chrétien de
Troyes) 94n, 170n
Ascham, Roger 167n
Astrophil and Stella (Sidney) 2, 39,
44–8, 58–9n, 91n, 100, 122,
146, 151–2, 170n
Augustine of Hippo 132n, 139, 144
author/lover persona relation, *see
also* lover persona
vii, viii, 61–97; accurate reporter
72, 86; analogy techniques 80–
7; comic roles 66–9, 81–7;
distinction between 61–4, 87;
fool 69–70; hyperbole 64, 66–
70, 87, 152; irony 61, 64, 65–6,
70–72, 87, 176

Barnes, Barnabe xv, 33, 72–3
Baroway, Israel 120, 121, 136n
Barthel, Carol 36, 57n, 59n;
author/lover persona 63, 88n

196

Index of first lines

Spenser's *Amoretti*

Page

Page

Index of first lines

Shakespeare's Sonnets